THE TEACHING OF CLASSICS

THE
TEACHING OF CLASSICS

ISSUED BY THE

INCORPORATED ASSOCIATION OF
ASSISTANT MASTERS IN
SECONDARY SCHOOLS

SECOND EDITION

CAMBRIDGE
AT THE UNIVERSITY PRESS

1961

PUBLISHED BY
THE SYNDICS OF THE CAMBRIDGE UNIVERSITY PRESS

Bentley House, 200 Euston Road, London, N.W. 1
American Branch: 32 East 57th Street, New York 22, N.Y.
West African Office: P.O. Box 33, Ibadan, Nigeria

THIS EDITION

©

CAMBRIDGE UNIVERSITY PRESS

1961

First printed in Great Britain at the University Press, Cambridge
Reprinted by offset-litho by the University Press, Oxford

CONTENTS

CONTENTS

FOREWORD

The Teaching of Classics, issued by The Incorporated Association of Assistant Masters in Secondary Schools, is the sixth book in the Association's post-war series on the teaching of the main subjects in the secondary school curriculum. *The Teaching of Science, The Teaching of Modern Languages, The Teaching of History, The Teaching of English* and *The Teaching of Geography* have already been warmly welcomed, and the companion volume on Mathematics* will appear in due course. In the preparation of these publications the Association has the good fortune to be able to draw upon the devotion, knowledge, and experience of many members and friends, to all of whom it would express its most grateful thanks.

The far-reaching reforms in the administration of secondary education foreshadowed in the Education Act of 1944, the development of a wide variety of types of secondary education suited to the abilities and aptitudes of all children in the secondary stage of their education, and the need for further advancement of the 'grammar-school type' of secondary education combine to make it essential that there should now be a thorough examination of the whole content of what is taught in the schools.

It is the earnest hope of the Executive Committee that this present publication will bring to that study a contribution of no mean value and that its wide circulation will exert an important influence on the theory and practice of the teaching of Classics in secondary schools of all types.

A. W. S. HUTCHINGS

Secretary, Incorporated Association of
Assistant Masters in Secondary Schools

1 *August* 1953

* Published 1957

vii

PREFACE

IT has been a privilege and an honour to be entrusted with the task of adding another volume to the list of those sponsored by the Incorporated Association of Assistant Masters, to give some assistance in the teaching of different subjects by making available to them the results of wider experience in schools of different natures than any one teacher is likely to possess.

This book, like its companions, is the work of enthusiasts, none of them knowing the whole subject, but all working to one end, and having as their only aim the attempt to be of some use to their colleagues and the well-being of classical studies.

We sincerely hope that we shall be judged to have achieved our aim in spite of the difficulties encountered. One of these was that in the teaching of Classics there is no single royal road to success. Widely different approaches may achieve equally satisfactory results, and the choice of method depends on the personal predilection of the teacher. We have, therefore, often been inclined to be encouraging and helpful rather than dogmatic. Nor should it be assumed that in this work the opinions expressed have always commanded the unanimous approval of the Committee. Such uniformity could hardly exist in any representative body of teachers.

Another difficulty in the teaching of Classics, of Latin in particular, is related to the different stages to which it is taken, and the various purposes for which it is used. We have tried to show that, at whatever stage the subject be dropped from the curriculum of any pupil, what has been done should be capable of being appreciated as an educative unit, and should not merely be something begun, abruptly ended, and consequently of little value.

We have, indeed, gone further and devoted a chapter (ch. VII) to demonstrating how widely the Classics may be used as an educative factor among those children who have not the time, ability or opportunity to learn Latin or Greek as languages, for we are confident that there is much of value in the Classics for such children, in whatever type of secondary school they happen to be.

It will be noted that we have refrained from recommending any particular text-books. Not only would such a selection be invidious, but we feel that any choice depends largely on the teacher's individual needs, having regard both to his pupils and himself. In any case we do not wish any teacher slavishly to follow any text-book; the only perfect one is that which each would write for himself. Nor do we wish anyone to attempt to follow slavishly all that is in this book. We merely hope that everyone will find something useful according to his needs.

Appended are the names of the Corresponding Members, for whose assistance, particularly in outlining the scope of the work, we offer our sincere thanks; as are also the names of the main Committee, on whom falls the ultimate responsibility, and to whom any criticisms should be addressed. It is only just, however, to point out that Mr T. W. Melluish, M.A., the Honorary Secretary, should be the recipient of nothing but praise. He has had a colossal task, and has carried it out with the thoroughness and good humour one associates with everything he does.

To many others, some outside our Association, we offer our hearty thanks for their generous assistance in giving us advice and information on particular points. Among them we would specially mention:

J. A. McC. Creighton, Royal Academy, Belfast (Visual Aids); S. Sheppard Frere, Lancing College (Archaeology); G. M. Lyne, Blackpool Grammar School (Classical Plays in Schools); H. C. Oakley, City of London School (Verse Composition); Mrs Dora Pym, Dept. of Education, Bristol University (help with some portions of ch. vii); C. A. Stott, Aldenham School, Herts (the Project Method and help with the School Library); Miss A. Woodward, Royal Holloway College, Englefield Green, and Professor L. R. Palmer, Professor of Philology at Oxford (criticisms of Appendices on Pronunciation, and valuable suggestions); Professor R. G. Austin, University College, Cardiff (reading drafts and offering valuable suggestions). To the following whom the Committee has consulted on certain points the Committee acknowledges its indebtedness: C. W. Baty, H.M.I.; H. L. O. Flecker, H.M., Christ's Hospital, Horsham; H. G. Lord, N.W. Polytechnic, N.W. 5; F. Kinchin Smith, Institute of Education, London University; Miss P. E. Winter, H.M., Birkenhead High School.

Finally, we express our gratitude for all the ungrudging help given by everyone at Headquarters, in particular to Mr C. Greenwood, and to those on the clerical staff who translated into neatly typewritten sheets many pages of very indifferent handwriting.

H. V. L.

1 *August* 1953

SECOND EDITION

In this edition the chapters on Examinations, Aids to the Teaching of Classics and the Appendices have been completely revised. We acknowledge with gratitude the valuable assistance rendered by Mr W. E. Slater of the Cambridge University Press.

T. W. M.

March 1961

MEMBERS OF THE COMMITTEE

H. V. LOSEBY, M.A., M.ED. (*Chairman*)
Belle Vue Grammar School, Bradford.

T. W. MELLUISH, M.A. (*Hon. Secretary*)
Bec School, Tooting, S.W. 17.

D. G. BENTLIFF, M.A.
Liverpool Institute High School, Mount St., Liverpool, 1.

*D. S. COLMAN, M.A.
The Schools, Shrewsbury.

J. A. JONES, B.A.
Market Drayton Co. G.S.; Nantwich G.S., Cheshire.

A. R. MUNDAY, M.A.
Priory School, Shrewsbury; The Academy, Glasgow.

C. RACE, M.A.
Wolverhampton G.S.; H.M., The City G.S., Chester.

*G. SYKES, M.A.
Peter Symonds School, Winchester.

J. G. TALBOT, M.A.
King Edward VI School, Southampton;
County Education Office, Chelmsford, Essex.

G. S. THOMPSON, M.A.
Westminster City School, S.W. 1.

J. M. WILLIAMS, M.A.
Swansea Grammar School, Wales.

R. D. WORMALD, M.A.
Royal Grammar School, Worcester.

* Resigned May 1949.

CORRESPONDING MEMBERS

(SCHOOLS, OCT. 1948)

D. A. BEACOCK, Caterham School, Surrey.

F. K. BEESE, Swansea Grammar School.

R. L. CHAMBERS, Bury Grammar School.

H. E. COUSENS, Dulwich College Preparatory School, S.E. 21.

B. V. CROWLEY, St Bede's Grammar School, Bradford.

J. D. DARBY, St Philip's Grammar School, Birmingham, 16.

R. E. DUNT, King Edward's School, Birmingham.

A. M. DURKIN, March Grammar School, Cambs.

L. HAMPSHIRE, Slough Grammar School, Bucks.

R. D. HODGES, Carlisle Grammar School.

T. HORN, Grammar School, Stockport.

A. H. JENNINGS, Chesterfield Grammar School.

E. LAWLER, St Mary's College, Crosby, Liverpool.

J. L. LINTON, 175 Chichester Road, Bognor Regis, Sussex.

H. G. LORD, N.W. Polytechnic, N.W. 5.

J. D. MORTIMER, Enfield Grammar School, Middlesex.

C. MULLEY, Hampton Grammar School, Middlesex.

H. L. O'CONNOR, St Bonaventura's School, Forest Gate, E. 7.

W. L. ROWE, King's School, Grantham, Lincs.

G. A. C. SAWTELL, Bolton School, Lancs.

T. L. STODDARD, Kelly College, Tavistock, Devon.

C. A. STOTT, Aldenham School, Elstree, Herts.

L. R. W. TAYLOR, St Clement Dane's School, W. 12.

W. B. THOMPSON, King Edward VI School, Southampton.

I

INTRODUCTION

1. WHY WE TEACH THE CLASSICS

'Latin and Greek are not dead languages; they have merely
ceased to be mortal.'   (J. W. MACKAIL)

'IN a broken world we are fortunate that we have kept our
classical inheritance.'[1] So wrote in 1945 a distinguished President
of the Classical Association, no *laudator temporis acti*, but a man
known in other realms of activity as well as in the world of
classical studies. It is in the belief that he sets forth that the present
volume has been written, to render in all due humility what aid
we can to those who endeavour to pass on to our successors that
fortunate inheritance.

'Fortunate?' comments the critic. 'Is it not unfortunate rather
that in these times, when so many new paths are being opened up
before mankind, when scientific developments hitherto beyond
the reach of man's imagination have been made possible, when
opportunities for power over the material world as yet undreamed
of have been set within man's grasp, there should still be found men
of intelligence and learning whose eyes are turned backward rather
than forward? Why now of all times turn a backward gaze on
civilizations and literature, arts and achievements past, over and
done with?'

Yet lovers of the Classics stand secure in the knowledge of their
good fortune, and are not to be argued out of their birthright quite
so easily. New paths there are and new opportunities, as none will
deny. Only a hermit or recluse would turn his back for ever on
the modern world. On the other hand even the scientist cannot
wholly cut himself off from the past, but must feel his way carefully along the roads indicated by his predecessors. So too it has
been said of the Classics, that not their least value is that they

[1] Sir Maurice Bowra, Presidential Address to the Classical Association, 1945.

supply us with a record of completed experiments. Nor were these experiments with the material world alone, but experiments with humanity itself.

The antiquity of the records cannot diminish their validity. It may indeed be argued that the very age of the story they have to tell constitutes its virtue. The experiments have been carried through to the end. We know the issue of the tale; we can view its unfolding in a true perspective. Again, as we look upon the world of Greece and Rome we behold a world in miniature. Relatively to the modern world their activities were limited and their achievements on a tiny scale. This very characteristic makes them more easy of comprehension. Their records are brief and their ways almost endearingly simple. As we examine the picture we find that the foreground is not cluttered up with distracting detail. Classical literature is indeed reputed for its objectivity, which is only matched by the objectivity with which the dispassionate reader may now study the story. Our own mental camera is not obscured by the kind of emotional prejudices which can fog the picture when we study our national history or present-day affairs. It is not suggested for a moment that only the civilizations of Greece and Rome are worthy of our study. The zealous propagation of such extravagances in an earlier generation has done much harm. Unless, however, we are to bow to the doctrine that all 'history is bunk', that human nature has radically changed, that all past experience is valueless, we must claim that the civilizations of Greece and Rome must still be studied with sympathy and understanding. 'With understanding' is a most important qualification, because such understanding is not fully possible without some knowledge of the language and literature of the two peoples. The aim of such study will be more than a mere antiquarian curiosity; among other things it will include a search for a standard with which to compare our own developing culture, wherein if in some respects the ancient civilization seems to fall short of our own we shall find cause for humble thankfulness rather than arrogant contempt.

But there is more in the study of the Classics than this. Great and important as are the lessons they have to teach us, we turn to

Greece and Rome not only for instruction but also for enjoyment. The fact is that the achievements of the Greeks and Romans in art, architecture and literature have by their intrinsic beauty moved men through the changing fashions of two thousand years to wonder, pity and delight. It will doubtless be said that such an end is attainable even without a knowledge of Greek and Latin. One may remain innocent of the declensions and still admire the massive and efficient grandeur of a Roman aqueduct, without knowing the Greek alphabet one may be charmed by the balanced grace of a Greek temple or enthralled by the exquisite but un-affected perfection of an Attic red-figure vase. Yet strangely enough this contention is true only up to a point. Appreciation based on imperfect understanding is apt to wear thin. The Greekless and Latinless soon begin to be aware, however dim their appre-hension, that something is missing, and the realization grows with their increasing mastery of these tongues that their enjoyment is keener and their appreciation truer the more they can hear and understand the language of the people who wrought these master-pieces.

Yet Greek and Latin are not studied merely to heighten the appreciation of art and architecture. Much of this part of the legacy of antiquity has suffered from the ravages of time, and in any case few of us can go to Athens or to Rome to see the shattered glory of the Parthenon or the mutilated and shabby grandeur of the Colosseum. The literatures of the two peoples must surely be conceded to be the noblest and at the same time the most durable part of our heritage. We are nearer to the past when in our own homes we look over Atticus' shoulder to read a gossipy letter from Cicero, or chuckle with Plato at Socrates poking gentle fun at Protagoras, than when we stand gazing at the silent stones of the Forum or stumble breathlessly over the Acropolis on a conducted tour.

If a real appreciation of classical art and architecture is to some extent dependent on a knowledge of Greek and Latin, the same, but without any qualification, is *a fortiori* true of classical literature. Voices will be raised on behalf of translations, a field in which it is difficult for the expert to carry conviction to the layman. Nevertheless, the truth must be told even at the risk of appearing to be dogmatic. Translations are rarely anything but a shadow of the original. They may perhaps give us the content or even some general impression of a work. But the excellence of classical literature, particularly of poetry, lies not in the story so much as the manner of its telling. The magic of Virgil's word-pictures, the subtle ellipses and elegant rapidity of Sophoclean dialogue, 'the surge and thunder of the *Odyssey*' defy translation, however skilful, and can only be transmitted in the authentic tones of Greece and Rome. Like the melodies and harmonies of the great composers, the music of classical literature is preserved in writing and in print, to be brought to life in all its majesty, grace and charm for those who can read and interpret the score. But in a world where nobody understood musical notation or the Greek and Latin languages, the voices of Bach and Mozart, of Homer and Catullus would be stilled.

Primarily we study the Classics because the works written in those languages are beautiful and good, and the contemplation of the beautiful and good is a noble exercise of the highest faculties. Has the process of learning those languages any inherent value to the learner other than what may be gained from the acquisitions themselves? Much ink and many words have been spent in discussing whether and to what extent the training acquired in one subject is transferable to some different sphere. It is generally conceded that men trained in the Classics have achieved remarkable success in conspicuously diverse fields. Those who would contest the claims put forward on behalf of the Classics attribute such success to natural gifts rather than any particular type of training. It appears to be difficult to prove or disprove such contentions either way. To those who gird at the Classics on the grounds of difficulty it may be said that modern educational psychology admits that it is as evil not to stretch the wits enough as to stretch them too far, and that the plastic mind of youth is better filled than left empty. When all is said there remains the argument summarized in the 1921 *Report on the Value of Classics* that they provide a course of training which requires the exercise of many different powers of the mind, and forms a remarkable combination of memory-training, imagination, aesthetic appreciation and scientific method, and an invaluable habit of thinking out the real meaning of words.

It is here in fact that the Classics can make a most valuable contribution to Education. The pursuit of that modern elixir in Education, 'non-verbal ability', has gone to such lengths that there is a danger of a generation growing up in our midst to whom words are becoming in an increasing degree uncomprehended and incomprehensible. It would indeed be ironic if the achievement of this century were to perfect the means of communication while inadvertently killing by neglect the meaning of communications. The learning of an inflexional language can be a useful corrective here. A study that calls for a close inspection of the written word, for careful scrutiny instead of 'the once-over'—that characteristic coinage of recent times—for disciplined thinking in place of slipshod guesswork, is a study that has its part to play in keeping the jungle back from civilization. The skills that Latin demands are sorely needed in a world where loose thought and careless speech are rife. If the study of Latin be continued for only four, three, or even two years, in this time something of a corrective dose can be administered. As a subject for study by a wide range of pupils the disciplinary value of Latin—and we stand by the phrase undaunted by bogy-words—is its greatest educational asset.

The difficulty of attempting to put the classical case in a few paragraphs is almost insuperable, but it is hoped that some inkling of it has by now been given. Perhaps the greatest weakness of the presentation of the Classics in the past has been the failure to relate them sufficiently to other subjects, and some observations on this will follow. It would be a real loss if men of classical learning ceased to exist, and it would be a sub-human world if great literature and great achievements were no longer valued for their own sake, and no longer received admiration, respect and imitation—even, on the humblest plane, the perhaps grudging imitation of the schoolboy grappling with his Latin exercise. Yet the value of the Classics is the greater as they are constantly related to present and future problems. While we urgently need our knowledge of the physical sciences, of the history of our own country and its neighbours, of the language, literature and culture of our contemporaries and of ourselves, we also need all the guidance of the past that we can squeeze into so crowded a field. To disregard the models and completed experiments of antiquity is needless folly. The problem now is how to find time to acquire and digest all the knowledge that will help us. We shall be called upon, whether we wish it or not, to prune and select ruthlessly; economic pressure may force us to give priority to subjects offering quick returns and material gains. Yet surely the difference between the civilized man and the savage is that the former takes a longer and a wider view. The greatest danger of our complex civilization lies in its forcing of the individual into the narrow lines of specialization, 'knowing more and more about less and less', until outside his own particular subject he is forced into reliance upon the expert. He is left with no standards of his own and has no faith in his own individual choice. In a word he has lost his liberty. That is why somehow or other room must be made in our Education for the teaching of the Classics in all their comprehensiveness. Moreover, all, not just a favoured few, must be encouraged to approach them. These ends must be constantly borne in mind by the teacher, and even through the early drudgery —and what subject of value can dispense with its basic technique?—and even to childish minds, some of the inspiration can be transmitted.

To sum up in one phrase, the fortunate inheritance of the Classics may seem to savour of the wildest optimism. Perhaps it may be said that they represent some episodes in man's history when he was at his best, when the individual counted for most, when in spite of limited resources he achieved the most, when the material was most subjected to the spiritual. If the aim of Education be correctly defined as being to give a knowledge of the best and noblest things done or said in the world, then Education must keep a place for the Classics or be untrue to itself. How that place may best be used the rest of this volume attempts to show.

2. Classics and the Link with other Subjects

'O that I had but followed the Arts!'　　　　　(*Twelfth Night*)

'Historically we are, to a greater extent than we ever realize, the children of Greece, in literature, in art, in thought, in ethics, in politics and notably in religion'　　　(GILBERT MURRAY)

This book exists to proclaim that the Classics are worth studying in themselves. But it is worth observing that their study makes the study of other subjects more profitable, not least by teaching that the division of the sum of knowledge into 'subjects' is in itself unsatisfactory. It might indeed be claimed that Latin and Greek, rightly interpreted, are not so much subjects in themselves as the foundation of other subjects. This is most plain of course in literature, especially in poetry, whether of England or of any Western European country, but it is just as true of other and more practical subjects. To expound this doctrine thoroughly would require a bulky volume, but what now follows may briefly indicate some of the lines of approach.

Let us begin with that subject on which some claim that the hours devoted to Classics might be more profitably spent. 'Instead of wasting time on Latin and Greek', they say, 'teach your pupils English properly. Make them practise writing good English, not bad Latin prose; encourage them to read their own poets and not those of the ancient past, who lived in a world now remote.' (The present writers would assert that the ancient world is remote only on time charts, not in its influence nor its consequences, but that is another matter.) Consider first then English.

English can of course be well spoken and written and intelligently read by people who do not consciously know a single word of Latin or Greek. But it may be affirmed that those who do possess such knowledge gain an additional awareness of their native language. You can use correctly the words 'invidious' or 'palatial' or 'synoptic' without knowing their derivation, but you do not perfectly apprehend them. And the line 'O mother Ida, many-fountained Ida' may be judged simply as a line of English verse—but it is much more than that. The line 'The Spartans on the sea-wet rock sat down and combed their hair' is in its context perfectly pointless unless Thermopylae means something to you. A passage in Milton such as:

> ...pleasing was his shape,
> And lovely, never since of serpent-kind
> Lovelier, not those that in Illyria changed
> Hermione and Cadmus; nor to which transformed
> Ammonian Jove or Capitoline was seen,
> He with Olympias, this with her who bore
> Scipio the highth of Rome.

is so much indebted to the Classics both in substance and in form as to be merely unintelligible without classical training, or some synthetic substitute for it. We may indeed be in danger of losing the power to understand our own poets.

Such passages as these, chosen almost at random, will be enough to remind us how much English literature, and especially English poetry, owes to the classical influence. It should be our aim from the beginning to make it possible for a boy to enter easily and as of right upon the whole of his heritage. And if we allow that the other literatures of Europe are part of the family heritage, then we may claim that in teaching a boy Latin (and Greek too) we are helping him to claim his share of the Romance languages as well.

How far this presentation of the Classics can be achieved must inevitably depend upon the circumstances of each school. But even if the time available is limited, something can be done at all stages of classical study, especially where there is easy co-operation between classical teachers and those responsible for the other studies with which it is suggested that the classical work should be linked.

For instance, in the Sixth Form a useful term's work can be done on oratory, involving samples of the art chosen from three or four languages, ancient and modern; or a study of a Greek tragedy can be combined with a glance at Aristotle's *Poetics* and some specimens of the French classical drama; Ovid can be made to throw light on English poetry, Plutarch upon Shakespeare. What matters is that our classical studies should not be conducted in a closed compartment and that our pupils should learn from the beginning to pass from the ancient world to the modern and back again with something of the unconscious ease with which such a transition was made by Dryden or Shelley, Burke or Dr Johnson. This is never to be achieved by the sedulous application of the pupil to handbooks or the deliberate inculcation of 'background' by a teacher of English or of History. It must be natural growth whose root is in a grasp of the ancient culture, not necessarily wide but certainly firm. To acquire a knowledge of the sources in this way is pleasanter, surer and more scholarly than to excavate them from commentaries and footnotes. And it may be doubted whether there is any other way by which a boy may come to understand something of the sweep and continuity of the cultural traditions of which our generation is the inheritor.

A second subject that is, or should be, inextricable from Classics is of course Divinity. Not for nothing have the Churches long included in the training of their ministers a knowledge of classical languages. Much of the New Testament was originally written in Greek; much of the Old transmitted to us through the Greek Septuagint version. It was in the Greco-Roman world that Jesus lived and St Paul travelled. Use the Greek Testament or the Vulgate as an occasional reader in junior classical forms—they are not difficult, and some boys at least will remember the translation—and see the result. Or in the Sixth link up with the Pauline Epistles the Greek and Roman moral codes; perhaps compare with Marcus Aurelius' writings in the next century. In tracing forward the growth of Christianity notice how often the spread of the Christian and the revival of the classical traditions went hand in hand, despite their apparent conflict. Recall that the international outlook of the Roman Catholic Church springs from the supratribal outlook of the Roman Empire at its best. Or trace back the growth of pagan and Hebrew moral codes and see their varied reactions to similar problems.

But the value of intelligent classical training and knowledge is not limited to these two most obvious examples. Its use in throwing cross-shafts of illumination, alike down the main paths or into the obscure corners, is apparent in almost every subject.

9

In some branches of learning this illumination is most valuable at the Advanced Level, at the stage where synthesis of ideas becomes as essential as, if not more essential than, mastery of facts. But this is not everywhere so. A boy does not need to be studying comparative philology, nor even to be aware that such a science exists, to derive both interest and practical use from the fact that Latin is the direct ancestor, not merely of many English words, but of five modern national languages, the so-called Romance languages ('What an odd name!', thinks the non-Latinist)— French, Spanish, Italian, Portuguese and Roumanian, as well as of Provençal, Catalan, Corsican and Swiss Romansch and Ladin. Utilitarian instances are best taken from French, as the most commonly studied of these. The debt of French literature to the Classics is even more manifest than that of English literature and need not be treated here in detail. As for vocabulary, one who knows many words in Latin finds that he knows many in any Romance tongue; his reading is simplified and accelerated. If one descends to a quite junior level one finds that at least one stumbling-block in learning French accurately, those apparently irrational genders, is more easily surmounted by the pupil who knows and applies his Latin. One wonders why the pen for instance should be *la plume*, till one connects it with the Latin *pluma*, first declension and so almost certainly feminine; or *la raison* from *ratio* (abstract noun in *-io*, feminine); or *la liberté* from *libertas* (abstract in *-tas*, feminine). Latin, in short, follows comprehensible rules, but French follows derivations. Surely, if you happen to know even elementary Latin, much labour is saved by recalling that masculine and feminine genders in French are usually (unhappily not always) the same as in Latin and that Latin neuters usually become masculine in French. Examples of this type of correlation could be indefinitely multiplied from any Romance language, and the student with a good foundation of Latin finds his learning much simplified. It is a tragic example of the modern fragmentation of knowledge that so few teachers are qualified to apply in practical detail and not merely in lip service the direct descent of modern European languages from a common ancestor.

The debt of modern languages to Greek is less obvious—at any rate in the words of common speech. But the internationally used technical terms of so many subjects, from literary criticism to biology, are predominantly of Greek derivation, as a passage dealing with science attempts to indicate elsewhere in this work.

But it is not only on the linguistic plane that Classics are valuable in other subjects. There are more reasons why the historian should know Latin and Greek than the possible need to study medieval chroniclers. Professor G. M. Trevelyan's autobiography reminds us that he owes much of his stylistic ability to much juvenile practice in the composition of Latin prose. More important are the words of Professor Toynbee, in *My View of History* (1947):

> For any would-be historian—and especially for one born in these times—a classical education is, in my belief, a priceless boon. As a training ground the history of the Greco-Roman world has its conspicuous merits. In the first place Greco-Roman history is visible to us in perspective and can be seen by us as a whole—in contrast to the history of our Western civilization, which is a still unfinished play.... In the second place the field of Greco-Roman history is not encumbered and obscured by a surfeit of information.... The surviving materials are not only manageable in quantity and select in quality; they are also well balanced in their character.... The third and perhaps greatest merit is, that its outlook is oecumenical rather than parochial.

For conciseness and depth of insight these phrases can hardly be bettered; the uninitiated may think them rhetorical, but the good teacher can transmute them. It does not need the learning of a Toynbee to grasp the fact that on the small stage of Greece almost every constitutional experiment was attempted, or that Rome had to grapple, and successfully, with one of the greatest modern problems, the harmonizing of diverse races and traditions without the imposition of a crushing uniformity. The imposition indeed of such uniformity could never have been achieved in an era when the engines of propaganda were relatively so weak. Then the influence of classical ideas on the Renaissance, on the stirring that preceded the American and French Revolutions and their consequences, on nineteenth-century liberalism likewise, both

explains and illuminates many matters. The historian acquainted
with the Classics can accumulate further instances at his leisure.

In short the study of any part of Western civilization should
never be carried out by one ignorant of its sources. This may well
be an argument for more acquaintance with scientific progress
and the Christian religion, but that does not make it any less
potent as an argument for the stimulating of interest in Greece
and Rome. Few question that the other sources have a central
place in true education; a similar position must surely be granted
to the Classics.

Akin to History, at the Sixth-Form Level, is such a subject as
Politics, or as it is often called, Civics. One would like to think
that Civics classes in higher forms should go more deeply into
the meaning of citizenship than is involved in mere discussions of
current problems or in purely factual lectures on the machinery
of modern government (valuable as a knowledge of the latter,
properly presented, can be). But if this deeper aim is to be achieved,
there obtrude themselves almost inevitably the views of thinkers
like Thucydides, Plato, and him whom Dante called 'the master
of them that know', Aristotle. The *Republic* and the *Politics* are
timeless books, though written with the problems of a particular
age in mind. One recent thinker (trained as a scientist) on the
evils of specialization has suggested as one remedy that every
undergraduate, whatever his branch of learning, should be familiar
with the *Republic*. But the political thinker should not be confined to theory; as already suggested in an earlier paragraph, let
him not forget the practical experience of ancient Greece and
Rome.

Metaphysics, moral philosophy and psychology are seldom
studied in schools, and it is doubtful whether they are really
comprehensible to the immature. Some, however, attempt them
as an introduction to the university course or with the general
aim of providing a wide background. If the attempt is made,
probably the wisest course for the novice to follow is in the steps
of the most acute novices who pioneered in these fields, in fact
in the steps of the ancient Greeks. It may be added that though
the great growth of psychology is a comparatively recent develop-

ment and though it is one of the studies which has progressed
farthest beyond Plato's first hints and questionings, its technical
terms remain an abiding memorial of the contribution of the
Classics to our vocabulary.

The critics may say: 'I grant you your points, or at least some
of them, in the "Arts" subjects, but what of the natural sciences?
There surely we have progressed so far from Aristotle and Thales,
from Empedocles and Hippocrates, that their childish speculations
can be rightly left buried in the ruins of their authors' extinct
towns.' But can they? The modern science teacher encourages
his pupils to develop their scientific interests by experiment and
speculation. It may be that a Fourth-Form boy soon grasps, or
thinks he has grasped, facts and principles which baffled the most
subtle Ionian physicists, but he must go through the same mental
processes on a simpler scale. It was the scientists, the intellectually
curious, the men most reaching out to new horizons, who welcomed the Renaissance and encouraged the rebirth of classical
study, even more perhaps than the literary and the artistic. The
scientist must go back to the pioneers for the great questions, even
if he can now supply better answers.

Last, but for the Classic certainly not least, comes Art. Here is
material for a book (indeed many have been written), not a paragraph. The paintings of antiquity have perished utterly. The wall
frescoes that survive at Pompeii are mass-production stuff, though
not without their influence on European decorative styles. The
real legacy of the Classics to the painter lies of course in the themes
which they give to the great Italians—Botticelli's *Venus Anadyomene*
is an obvious instance—and thence to their pupils and to the main
stream of European painting. But in sculpture and architecture
the Greeks have remained among the great exemplars; there would
be scope here for many chapters of the book, whether one's taste
prefers the windswept Victory of Samothrace or the contortions
of Laocoon, the legendary grace of the Parthenon or the utilitarian
solidity of Roman buildings. Ancient town-planning too deserves
study, though one must admit that the regular blocks of Piraeus
or Pergamon, with their series of blind crossroads, are scarcely
models for a motorized generation.

In short, the background of the so-called 'dead languages' and of those who used them is, whether we acknowledge it or not, the background against which the drama of modern living is played. We would not plead that every good idea was evolved in ancient times nor that every valuable lesson that experience teaches may be drawn from the generations before Christ. What we would suggest is this—few subjects that deal with the human rather than the material can fail to be enriched by him who knows and values Greece and Rome.

3. Principles and Aims in Teaching the Classics

'We love the precepts for the teacher's sake.'   (FARQUHAR)

The arguments for the general desirability of a classical training being thus set forth, we now turn to the classical master, already convinced, presumably, of the value of his studies by virtue of the career he has chosen, and anxious to translate his conviction into more practical terms. He knows that his pupils, if properly taught, will be the better for their Classics. He believes that if he can secure for Classics an adequate share of the time allowed by the curriculum the training will not only prove to be of intrinsic value but should engender an attitude towards other studies and pursuits which will be both scholarly and effective. He is aware, even if he has not been told so by others, that non-classical boys often benefit from the mere presence in their midst of classical boys. Conviction alone, however, is not enough. He must be able to confirm his beliefs in practice. Abandoning general arguments and abstract appeals to the imponderable and intangible, he will concentrate on arriving at a working creed, realizable aims, and successful results. In claiming a place in the school curriculum worthy of his subject he must justify his title to that place by being able to point at all stages of the classical course to its salutary effects. In the past Latin has enjoyed a form of protection in the schools because of the compulsory Latin requirement for university entrance and the demands of the Arts Faculties. This has enabled Latin to maintain a precarious foothold in schools where otherwise it might have vanished. The transformation of the First Examination into a subject examination, however, may start a new trend. True, the universities at the moment are supporting Latin strongly; yet no one can foresee with certainty what the future holds. The classical teacher in any event would be unwise to base his case on so uncertain a foundation. The purpose of this section will be therefore to determine what aims the classical teacher must set himself to justify the place of his studies in the curriculum and what should guide him in the prescription of those aims.

The definition of terms need not detain us long. In its widest sense a course of Classics is understood to imply the learning of Greek and Latin, together with some knowledge of the literary and historical backgrounds of Greek and Roman civilization. To some extent Classics may be taught in a history lesson. Courses are planned which involve the reading of the Classics in English translations, or which deal with the subject-matter but not the language of ancient literature. In the following pages, however, Classics will imply a course of study in which the learning of the language is the central feature. It will be convenient, too, frequently to speak as if the only language learnt by the pupil was Latin, which indeed is often the case; and where middle school Classics are concerned Greek will not be assumed unless it is named. The curriculum (without further qualification) must be understood to be the curriculum of a secondary grammar school to which pupils come at eleven years of age. The teaching of Classics to pupils over thirteen will also have reference to entrants to the independent schools. What applies to the upper middle school in a grammar school must frequently be held to apply to the middle school of an independent or public school. It will be appreciated, moreover, that while the methods employed for mixed schools or girls' schools may be largely similar to those mentioned here, the authors have had the boys' school predominantly in mind.

To return to the classical teacher, his paramount aim must be to provide a course whose value must be easily demonstrable if not self-evident at every stage, both to the pupil and to others, in order to justify its retention in the time-table. This will be no light task. The stimulus of the compulsory subject may well have been removed. Latin lacks many of the superficial allurements that make pleasant the other avenues of learning. It is no longer fashionable in the educational world to expect pupils to take on trust the pabulum vouched for by the voice of authority alone. Should the teacher therefore fail to prove his case, there will be a tendency for classical teaching to narrow down to a thin stream, provided only for the handful of abnormal boys who for some reason were not perfectly convinced at the age of twelve that they were destined by Providence to become inventive geniuses or world-famous scientists. The modern practice of leaving the choice of subjects to the immature judgement of a child (often reinforced by parental ignorance), where no definite lead is given by the school, works against Latin. The misleading habit of thinking in terms of innate 'aptitudes' (often mere auto-suggestion) accentuates the danger. But a calamity indeed it would prove if the classical side of a school became a numerically negligible minority, developing a sense of being cut off from the normal culture of the school, rapidly dwindling to an extinct species. Inevitably then must the classical establishment of the school be reduced until the narrow circle of boys becomes too expensive in staff allowance, and part-time staff must perforce be called in from the French and English departments to eke out a minimum time-table. This is not to disparage the valuable cross-fertilization that can occur when a French or English expert does a little Latin; there is, however, a danger of deterioration in classical studies if they are taught exclusively by specialists in other subjects.

The general aim of the teacher in providing a suitable course in Classics will quickly divide itself into a number of specific and concrete objectives which there is a reasonable hope of being able to reach at given stages. One effect of the modification of the external examination and its suggested postponement to the end of the school course would be to remove some of the precision from the immediate objectives. Near and precise aims are more likely to be realized than distant but admirable aims.

> That low man goes on adding one to one;
> His hundred's soon hit.

A boy at a preparatory school may aim at nothing better than learning a number of dodges to enable him to spot the constructions of the trickier sort in the sentences of a Common Entrance Paper. Radical readers of Board of Education Memorandum No. 116 may denounce these low aims as illiberal, unless of course they themselves cherish a tender affection for the gender rhymes of their youth. But if even these low aims have been realized, something fundamental to education has been achieved, namely, successful purposive effort. 'Glorious failures' are all very well, but teachers cannot afford to have too many of them. The road to Parnassus must accommodate other traffic as well as grammarians' funerals. Narrow, therefore, and trivial as the activities brought into play may have been, from the point of view of character, if not culture, they are far more beneficial than an unco-ordinated flirtation with alluring general courses that cannot lend themselves to the rigours of a serious examination. This is not to advocate the inhumanism of the humanities after the old style. Nobody wishes to reintroduce the pedantry of Donatus or Holofernes. Modern methods are usually better, but they must be applied to precise objectives.

It is essential to believe that a Classical course can be contrived which shall satisfy three requirements:

1. At each stage it must be appropriate to the mental development of the pupil.

2. At each stage it must realize perfectly definite aims: that is to say, it must be self-sufficient.

3. At each stage it must contain within itself the potentiality of future advance.

In other words, we have to believe that it is possible to make a success of a course in which the requirements of the dull and the bright boy, the junior and the senior, are met without sacrifice on anybody's part.

It may seem a truism to say that each stage of the course must be appropriate to the mental development of the pupil, for teachers are clearly forced to recognize the difference between an eleven-year-old and a seventeen-year-old mind, and would no more insult the latter with simplified Caesar than they would burden the former with details of Roman Imperial Government. It is clear too that each age group contains a wide range of ability. Teachers soon learn to adapt the pace of the lesson to the bright form, and insist on repetition and recapitulation for the duller boys. Nevertheless, some of the older Latin course books showed a remarkable blindness to the differing capacities of the different age groups, and it may be that here and there some teachers cling to the courses they themselves used when they were young through conservatism or lack of enterprise or blindness to the faults of a favourite book. Luckily there are few teachers who today do not realize the absurdity of lingering over the memorization of rare irregular noun forms when the time could have been so much better spent on, say, a dozen short sentences dealing with simple realities. A boy who has not grasped fully the fundamental principles of inflexion should not be worried with the ablative of *supellex* or the list of exceptions to the rule governing the genitive plural of third declension nouns. The old text-books which introduced difficulties from the outset on the principle that, as Latin is a hard language, youth must be taught to face the toughest problems resolutely from tender years were on good moral ground. Those text-books which go to the opposite extreme, and pretend that all Latin can be made very simple and very humorous in content, do great harm. Nevertheless, however morally justifiable a method may be, if its austerity is so repellent that the course becomes as it were strewn with abandoned wrecks, another method must be found. To do them justice the best modern books do avoid the austerities and superfluities of the old. Lodge's Word Frequency List is behind most of them. It is now generally realized that children react favourably to the content of their sentences; that the aridity of Latin is increased by dull and inanimate abstractions instead of lively and picturesque examples; that a sentence like *Reges servos sagittis vulnerant* is infinitely better than *Bella reges fortitudinem docent*.

Each stage of a course should have its own ends, realizable for the majority of those who take it. To plan a course based on the possible requirements of university scholars may mean facing the majority with a mass of detail whose 'uselessness' is only too evident if the studies are brought to a premature end; and it must be remembered that the 'uselessness' of Latin is one of the main arguments of its critics, while the unsuccessful students of Latin comprise its worst enemies. It will not be easy, but it is possible, to plan a majority course without sacrificing the interests of the few. The future Chancellor's medallist need not learn a different Latin from the other members of his class, but he will presumably learn it better. The ideal is to map out the course in definite stages, each self-sufficient when its own ends have been reached. If then for any reason a pupil discontinues Latin, there will be no need to say, 'Yes, we appreciate that you have learnt nothing that you can understand, but it would have started making sense if you had carried on into the Sixth Form.' If he had been set upon a course consisting of sensible stages with sensible objectives, he would have to admit that progress and profit were at no point beyond his reach.

Yet while there is general condemnation of the Procrustean policy of trying to adapt the average boy to the needs of the potential scholar, it would be a bad mistake to subject the really bright boys to any form of intellectual starvation. Each stage must contain within itself the potentiality of advance. It is assumed that there will always be plenty of material at the right intellectual level which would suit the needs of the clever boy as well as the medium boy. It is here that a teacher is often called upon to display a certain resourcefulness in improvization. Some manage to develop a system of extra private reading of an author for an exceptional boy whose facility at getting through his work would leave him with time on his hands. This might prove vexatious and inconvenient, but in the long run it is eminently worth while. In this way a smart boy can be laying the foundations of a loftier building in the future. Otherwise, a course devised mainly on the memorization of single words, with a preponderant stress on the translation of individual sentences, is apt to breed a certain superficial cleverness whose hollowness is only revealed later. There is in fact a type of pupil who, while displaying amazing virtuosity in the early stages of sentence writing, never seems to advance beyond the

Common Entrance level, so to speak, showing that to him Latin has represented a kind of cryptogram or cross-word puzzle rather than a language of ideas. To avoid the failure and disappointment which inevitably attends this form of arrested development, it must be clearly demonstrated at each stage that Latin is a language and as such was used as a vehicle for the conveyance of thought, not as a puzzle, a scientific exercise in deduction, or a branch of algebra.

When we turn to the subject of aims in the teaching of Latin, it is difficult to be precise without talking in terms of the syllabus. Yet there is a kind of general aim of which the teacher must always be conscious, less precise than the passing of a particular examination, more definite than the imponderables so often evoked by Classical apologists. The common factor of these aims is success, not necessarily examination success, but the success implied in the pupil's conviction at all stages that he is getting somewhere. For this reason the end of each stage should be preceded by recapitulation and revision with the object of pointing clearly to a natural division of the work, and in an attempt to leave those who are to be discarded from the course with the feeling that they were equal to their assignments at the level at which they were set. The aims can be considered under five headings.

(*a*) *Translation*. The most obvious test of success is translation. If a pupil cannot translate from Latin a passage of the difficulty he is accustomed to, his Latin master has failed with him. The end of the first two years should leave a boy able to translate at sight simple mottoes, inscriptions of the easier sort, and short sentences. Translation should be therefore set in the forefront of the curriculum. Many a boy who is hopeless at composition can nevertheless make a creditable shot at seeing the meaning of a Latin narrative. Moreover, besides being a sound linguistic basis for learning Latin, translation should also be treated as an exercise in English.

(*b*) *Composition*. At all stages a pupil should do some composition. But the passages set should be much more simple and easy than the Latin passages that the same pupil can turn into English. At first they should not merely be simple and easy: they should be short. For the young learner a six-word sentence is much harder to put into Latin than two three-word sentences. After all, a seven-figure number is the standard test for a fifteen-year-old intelligence. Linguistically immature people are incapable of maintaining uninterrupted the thread of attention demanded by a long complex sentence. If oral composition is attempted, so much the better.

(c) *Reading aloud.* Throughout the course the pupil must be trained in reading aloud, but by the beginning of the third year a boy should be able to read connected Latin with some degree of fluency and understanding after it has been read by the master. Though he may not be at once alive to the balance and emphasis of a rhetorical piece, a middle-school pupil can often reproduce in elocution a certain dramatic effect. Dramatic readings and competitions can be an attractive and useful feature of the work at this stage.

(d) *Background.* No teaching of Latin can be considered adequate unless constant reference is being made to the background of civilization from which the language comes. This is especially important where there are legacies from the past to our own literature and civilization. Without the habit of allusion to the life and times of ancient Rome the whole stuff of the language tends to lose colour and become meaningless. A boy who has to learn *Consul uterque* must know why consuls were thought of in pairs. It is better that background should be the subject of frequent reference and allusion than a theme for set lessons. The teacher who avoids background is, however, robbing Latin of much of its content.

(e) *Sense of style and logic.* Except indirectly these may be said to be desirable rather than essential. It is true that the keen classical teacher will be anxious to awaken in his pupils' minds at all stages an awareness of the pattern of words and the patterns of thought. Logical considerations continually come into play in translating at sight from Latin, and there is a good deal to be said for considering certain features of style and rhetorical patterns on the same level of importance as grammatical constructions in understanding the meaning of an author. A boy who has had some training in the simple patterns of rhetoric would find less difficulty in translating *Ducunt volentem fata, nolentem trahunt* than a boy who knew more about participles but less about rhetoric.

To be effective these five aims should be consciously integrated with the requirements of the curriculum, and separate tests of proficiency given at various levels. The pupil himself should be aware of the aims he is expected to bear in mind, and to test progress a uniform test of a kind easily marked should be available for use terminally. If given simultaneously to a number of forms, after a short period of revision, these standard tests not only could stimulate competition between form and form, but might act as a yardstick for comparing one year with another.

Whilst we admit that greater unanimity as to these ends and aims would further promote the advancement of classical studies, yet of course there cannot and ought not to be any interference with the right of the teacher to be individual in his methods. Man teaches man, not method pupil. The history of classical scholarship is bejewelled with famous classical teachers. With some of their tenets we might now passionately disagree; but they were fine men, great personalities, distinguished scholars, and finally became something of a legend; they were devoted to their calling and their Sixth-Formers never forgot that they had once been their pupils. It is not for the giants that rules are necessary.

II

JUNIOR AND MIDDLE-SCHOOL LATIN

1. AGE OF STARTING LATIN

'Adeo in teneris consuescere multum est.' (VIRGIL)

OPINIONS no less than practice differ widely on the question of the best age at which to begin Latin. The Common Entrance Examination at 13 +, and keen competition for entry to the public schools, has often resulted in preparatory schools making almost a premature beginning with youngsters of nine years of age— a policy viewed with grave doubt by many teachers in both public and preparatory schools. On the other hand the projected plans of some education authorities, anxious to avoid differentiation between 'types' of pupil before the age of thirteen, include curricula which seem to imply the postponement of any language teaching, and in any case of Latin, until thirteen—a policy which has led the Classical Association to pass a resolution deploring a late start to Latin. If weighty support were forthcoming for both these extreme views, there might well be a danger of a high standard of Latin becoming the perquisite of a few schools, specializing to the exclusion of other subjects. The consequent identification of Latin with either a social class or a particular type of school would be a result unwelcome to all liberal-minded educationists. However, the bulk of the grammar schools in the country agree on the age of eleven or twelve, i.e. in the first or second year of the grammar school course, as being the most suitable. The choice between these will be largely determined by the adoption of the four- or five-year course to the Ordinary Level of Latin in the General Certificate of Education. The respective merits of these two courses will be argued later in this chapter—for the moment it will be sufficient to consider problems connected with the start.

Most language teachers are agreed that up to a certain point the earlier a beginning is made the better. The point in question will be determined not only by other demands of the time-table but also by a desire not to put too great a strain on immature minds. Nevertheless, the plasticity of the young in the habit-forming age gives the teacher an opportunity to mould his pupils in the right way, and to lay the secure foundations necessary for the thorough mastery of any language. If this is neglected, endless trouble will be incurred later on. It is the experience of most teachers that much of the memory work required in the early stages of Latin, the learning of declensions, conjugations and the like, a task often quite cheerfully performed by young boys, becomes a much more laborious process and much more distasteful if delayed until later. In fact, it can be asserted with some confidence that despite much that has been written by older writers, whose memory of childhood days is perhaps more picturesque than reliable, young children positively like their grammar work, and stand in no need of the unnecessarily elaborate artifices devised by some 'courses' to sugar a pill that is really not unpalatable. These considerations suggest that the best age for beginning Latin is 11+. Here, however, a difficulty arises. Most children coming into the secondary schools at the age of 11+ begin either French or another modern language, and voices have been raised in protest against the simultaneous commencement of two languages on the ground of the confusion it is alleged to cause. This is exaggerated. There are manifold possibilities of correlation, and opportunities to satisfy an awakening interest in language, especially now that formal linguistic training plays a less important part in primary schools, should be multiplied wherever possible. Indeed, some modern language masters assert that the routine drill in formal grammar, which Latin masters feel that they must give in the course of the first year, constitutes so valuable a preparation for any language study that they would welcome an early start to Latin even if it meant postponing the start to French. Some schools in fact begin Latin at 11+ and French at 12+, and the staffs of these schools speak of the beneficial results of this practice. On the whole, however, it seems hardly necessary to postpone either—what confusion there is, is mainly temporary and superficial.

The selection of pupils to do Latin is a process that may take place at the beginning and subsequently during the course. As we are dealing with an academic grammar school, whose pupils are all supposed to be reasonably intelligent, there is no *a priori* reason why all entrants should not be taught Latin, and indeed some schools do in fact give all boys a grounding in this subject. Yet it is only in the minority of schools that the course is continued for all, right up to the Ordinary Level of the Certificate of Education, and for most there is an original selection followed by a further weeding-out. The best of all methods is that all should begin Latin in the first year of their course, but at the end of the second year unsuitable pupils should drop Latin. Some schools vary this arrangement by allowing their pupils to drop Latin at the end of the first year, but it may be doubted whether this allows sufficient time for a true estimate to be made, since so little English grammar is learnt in the primary schools, and therefore much of the first year has been spent on teaching English. Another common method is for pupils showing linguistic ability after one year of a modern language course to start Latin in the second year. It has already been objected to this that it entails a later start and necessarily a shorter course. There are still others who devote two or three periods a week in the first term (or part of the first term) to elementary grammar in English to give a grounding in the basic concepts of parts of speech, parsing, and analysis of simple sentences. Success in this course is used as a prognosis of ability to learn Latin.

The methods of selection employed in the schools are very numerous and varied. It is hardly possible to speak of any general practice. Inquiries from a number of schools showed that in a third of the schools Latin was not dropped, in a third Latin was dropped by some pupils at the end of the second year, and in the remainder at the end of either the first or the third year. Normally, either the most capable boys are chosen for Latin or those with most linguistic ability. The recommendation of the master, the wishes of the parent, and the wishes of the boy (in that order) appear to determine the selection of the boy for Latin. It is rare for a complete cross-section of a school to be set to this subject.

2. Course for the First Two Years

There is no unanimity about the order in which the various features of accidence and syntax are to be introduced to the young learner. Courses which concentrate on the learning of the tenses of the verb first both in English-Latin and Latin-English appear ill at ease until they have got beyond the narrow limits of the first declension in the nouns; on the other hand Latin wears a baby look if it is confined to the present tense even though it runs the whole gamut of the five declensions. Yet there is much to be said for concentration upon one thing at a time in the interests of sound learning. Text-books vary so widely in the manner in which they face this and other similar problems that it will be convenient to consider the first two years as a whole, leaving the question of the order to the individual taste of each teacher. By the end of the second year the pupil should have learnt:

ACCIDENCE

Nouns: five declensions with common irregular forms.

Pronouns: personal; interrogative; demonstrative; relative.

Adjectives and adverbs including interrogative and demonstrative, with common irregular forms.

Comparison of adjectives and adverbs with common irregular forms.

Numerals: cardinals 1–1000; ordinals 1st–100th.

Verbs: four conjugations, active and passive all moods; deponents; *esse, capere, ferre, velle, nolle, malle, fieri, ire.* Principal parts of common irregular verbs.

Prepositions: common prepositions.

SYNTAX

First year. Simple sentence: statement, command, prohibition with *noli*, questions.

Common case usages: subject, direct and indirect object, possession, place and time. common prepositional usages.

Second year. Simple sentences: exhortations and wishes for the future
(to be introduced when the subjunctive is learned).
Subordinate clauses: relative clauses; adverbial clauses
(purpose, result, time (with verb in the indicative));
noun clauses[1] (indirect statement, indirect command,
indirect question).
Participles: uses, including the ablative absolute.

It is necessary to explain that while the accidence is best presented as a total amount of work to be accomplished by the end
of two years, the division of syntax into first and second year's
work has been made because it is advisable not to overload the
first year's work with too much syntax. Where much new
material has to be assimilated in the form of declensions and
conjugations, it is wiser to keep as far as possible to the simple
sentence in the first year. Of the syntax in the second year it
must be emphasized that the subordinate clauses should be handled
only in the simplest possible forms. There is in fact a distinction
to be drawn in the learning of any new construction according to
the degree of familiarity with the construction that the pupil may
possess. Thus, for instance, indirect statement, on first being met
in Latin, is capable of a ready explanation on the lines of the similar
form in English, e.g. 'I know him to be clever'. This is soon
appreciated, and when one or two examples have occurred, pupils
will have no difficulty in *recognizing* the construction for translation purposes. This is the first stage of the process, but he would
be a rash teacher who would claim that a construction recognized
is a construction known. The progress from this stage to that of
putting the most obvious form of the English accusative and
infinitive into the parallel Latin construction appears to be quite
a stride for pupils to take. A still further elaboration occurs when
the pupil is taught to transmute the Latin accusative and infinitive
into the English 'I know *that* he *is* clever' and again when he can
reverse the process and translate the English noun clause into the
Latin accusative and infinitive. It is only the first two of these
stages that we may reasonably expect to be reached in the second

[1] Only in the simplest forms, mainly as recognized in Latin-English translation.

year. Similarly, most of the constructions mentioned as forming part of the second year's work must be considered as having been only introduced to the pupils—they should be studied in greater detail and complexity in the following two years.

If the ground described above is covered during the first two years, the pupil must have appropriately graded reading material to accompany and illustrate his work in grammar and his composition. By the end of that time he should be ready to tackle with a fair degree of confidence reading matter which, although it may not yet be of the difficulty of an original text pure and unalloyed, may nevertheless serve as a bridge to the reading of a text. Yet even here it is important to remember that some of our pupils may be discontinuing Latin at this moment, and it must be our aim to leave them with some sense of achievement. The reading matter will therefore form an integral part of the course, and should on no account be confined to isolated sentences. The matter should be interesting, and related to the life, literature and thought of the past in such a way as to acquaint the pupil with some of the more salient features of the ancient world. Roman life, history, and classical mythology form the best subjects for treatment. The objection to confining all the material read to a single theme, e.g. the rise of Rome in Italy, is that it unnecessarily restricts the field of knowledge of the past. A pupil brought up exclusively on a series of extracts devoted to a single historical theme might in consequence grow up wholly ignorant of some of the great stories of classical mythology that it seems almost the obvious duty of a classical master to teach. The same might apply to Roman history or life. Many teachers have attempted to meet the difficulty that arises here by devoting specific lessons to the teaching of 'background'. This is not quite the same question as the one we have been dealing with, namely, the content of the reading matter in Latin first used for translation. Nevertheless, it may be appropriate to consider it here. It is better that at this stage the teaching of 'background' should be made ancillary to the main object, which in the first two years is the teaching of the rudiments of a language. 'One thing at a time' is the best wisdom in the early stages. Nevertheless, if, as some teachers assert, a weaker set begins to reveal its weaknesses early in the second year, and if it seems almost inevitable that a large proportion of a class must drop Latin, some attempt should be made by the teacher to give more background so that the pupils may not go empty away.

We do not wish in this chapter to lay down detailed instructions for each teacher. Methods highly satisfactory for one individual would prove wholly incompatible with the temperament and tastes of another. Within the four walls of a classroom everyone must work out his own salvation. Nevertheless, there are some vital precepts whose importance is such that they can bear repetition.

(*a*) The teacher must insist from the very beginning on an accurate and confident mastery of the elements, both of accidence and of vocabulary. The pupil must reach such a degree of knowledge that not only is he sure of himself, but his responses to questions on forms are quite automatic. The pupil should know his conjugations and declensions as well as he knows the English alphabet, and should be able to apply his knowledge as readily as he would apply his knowledge of the alphabet in looking up a word in the dictionary. Above all, he must be trained to rely on his own memory. Looking up a word or a verb-form in the back of the book can develop into such a pernicious habit that many pupils acquire lazy habits of thought, and they turn automatically to the back of the book for something they already know. It is thus useful from time to time to insist on exercises being done in class without the aid of grammars and vocabularies.

(*b*) To attain this mastery and confidence constant repetition and practice is necessary. It is a fallacy to suppose that such work need necessarily be irksome or dull. The use of the competitive stimulus is here particularly valuable. All practised teachers devise ingenious ways of turning grammar into a game, and these aids are not to be despised. Short written tests at regular intervals are necessary as a check on progress. The young teacher should never forget that the coordination between the hand and the brain is often immature in the young, when writing is required, especially when the manual skill of writing receives less attention in the early stages than it should. Oral work is in consequence often deceptive, and most teachers are familiar with the disappointment they receive when a class which is bright at oral work totally fails at the written examination.

(c) The introduction to an inflected language is difficult for many boys. Therefore it is important that elementary grammatical concepts should be really understood. It is unsafe to assume, particularly nowadays, that the pupil has any previous knowledge of even the simplest matters, such as, for instance, the meaning of terms like 'verb', 'subject', 'object'. Much help to one another can be given here by the teachers of English, Modern Languages and Latin. As much correlation as possible is desirable, and the adoption of a common nomenclature has its obvious advantages, but this should not blind us to the fact that there are important differences between the grammar of Latin and English, and that if the similarities obscure the important differences, serious misconceptions may arise.

(d) It is of great importance that written work in the early stages should be well within the capacity of the pupil and not too difficult. A sense of achievement must be carefully fostered at each point, and this can be best secured by ensuring that no work lies utterly beyond the experience of the pupil. The writing of exercises should be partly or wholly prepared by previous oral work. A thorough demoralization may result from complete failure in doing an exercise. It is well known to teachers of experience that if a task is set for homework that involves breaking new ground, all but the best are likely to produce work full of mistakes. Too often a deterioration in morale results, to the great detriment of Latin in the school.

(e) Much has been written about pronunciation, but more difficulty with the new pronunciation has been supposed to exist than is really the case. Pupils rarely need lessons in pronunciation. No attempt should be made to deal with the whole question at the outset. Peculiarities may be dealt with as they arise. New material should always be read aloud first by the teacher, and the pupil or pupils be asked to repeat the Latin. Not only is this an invaluable aid to translation, since it teaches the child the correct grouping of the words, but it enables pronunciation to be picked up naturally and without effort. It follows that the teacher must himself be impeccable in his pronunciation. It is a matter of regret that many teachers are less careful than they should be on this very important point, or are inclined to underestimate its significance. Carelessness in pronunciation inevitably leads to false quantities, and misspellings which in turn lead to mis-translations.

(f) The question of the time allowance for Latin gives rise to more depression and bitterness than perhaps any other single cause connected with this subject. It is unfortunately only too true that in many parts of the country teachers are being expected to teach Latin on a wholly inadequate time allowance. This causes feelings of frustration and failure. The successful teaching of a language requires that there should be fresh practice every day. So much of language teaching consists of habit training that to neglect this important principle is to run the risk of failure. It is therefore imperative that there should be five periods of 40 or 45 minutes, if possible morning periods, a week. Moreover, as individual work is an essential part of the course, the classwork should be reinforced by two periods of homework of, say, 30 minutes each, although this will vary from school to school. Some, for instance, would prefer three shorter periods of 20 minutes each. However that may be, it cannot be emphasized too strongly that an inadequate time allowance will lead to scamped or slipshod work, and failure in the end. There is a vicious circle here. Heads of schools who in the first place expect Latin to be done on short time, sometimes feel inclined, when examina-tion results fail to come up to expectations, to cut the number of periods further, on the principle that one cannot afford many teaching periods on so risky a chance. Where this unfortunate state of affairs prevails it would be far better not to attempt the impossible. Those teachers indeed who boast that on a three years' course they have been able to 'get their pupils through' on four periods a week or less, do the cause of Latin very little good, do themselves and their fellow-teachers a disservice, and the benefit they confer on their pupils is very doubtful. Short-cut devices and cramming may produce a superficial success, but the long-term effects are seldom abiding.

It may be useful now to assess the achievement of a pupil at the end of two years. He has learnt a great deal of formal grammar, and has been introduced to the principles of an inflected language. This is in itself no mean acquisition. If, in addition, he has been trained, however imperfectly, to look at a word twice before taking it for granted, if he has been taught to analyse mentally even simple sentences into subject, verb and object he has gained something difficult to assess by rule of thumb but none the less positive. But we may expect more. We may expect our pupil to make a fair attempt at translating Latin monumental inscriptions, epitaphs, and the like—to show a certain familiarity with the common Latin tags—and to have had a glimpse, however fleeting, of some aspects of the great civilization from which our Western culture is directly descended. Scoffers may say that this is not much, but it will compare not unfavourably with the achievements of many another subject in the curriculum. If our teaching methods are satisfactory we may feel that even if a pupil gives up Latin at this stage we have not wasted his time.

3. MIDDLE-SCHOOL LATIN

At the end of the second year there will be in most schools a sorting-out of pupils. Already they will have demonstrated the degree to which they are capable of going on with Latin. Ultimately there will prove to be four classes of pupils, the degree of precision with which the classes can be determined usually depending on the number of pupils from whom the selection can be made. There will be—

(a) Boys likely to pursue Latin to Advanced and Scholarship standard.

(b) Boys likely to take Latin as one of a group of Modern Subjects.

(c) Boys of mediocre ability in Latin, who would benefit by continuing Latin on less formal lines.

(d) Boys who would be better advised to drop Latin altogether.

The size of the school, its resources in staffing, and the strength of the Latin tradition in the school will frequently determine how far separate provision can be made for the first three classes. Many schools, able to cater for one stream only, will be forced to adopt a middle course designed to suit the greatest need of the greatest number. Boys in class (*a*) will be those who start Greek at this stage. Boys in class (*c*) will be those for whom a special kind of course might well be designed. Such a course would be planned on broader lines with a wider outlook than is usual for the more academic type. It would involve the minimum of composition that can be considered consistent with the maximum amount of reading of which such boys are capable.

Although the length of the course will have already been determined by the age at which Latin is started, it still remains to be stated that the bulk of the work which must be done before the boy can proceed to the Latin of Sixth Form standard can only with the utmost difficulty be crammed into two further years. The main body of the syntax, which has still to be mastered, calls for two years' work. The following year should be occupied with the reading of texts. Every teacher knows that the reading of Latin literature, not originally written for people with an imperfect grasp of the syntax of their language, can be painfully slow when new constructions have constantly to be explained 'en passant' in order to make any progress possible. Much of the poor quality of the work that is done at present on books prescribed by examination authorities is due to the fact that candidates are being asked to translate prematurely Latin of too great difficulty. They have not reached certain constructions in their course, no time is left by the exigencies of the time-table to allow of an adequate explanation, and pupils are tempted to rely on a memorized translation to scrape through an examination. Such evils spring from the desire to accomplish too much in too little time. A four years' course presupposes not only a generous allowance of time each week but also a severe economy in the presentation of material. The four years' course is a possibility, but an uncomfortable possibility. It is hoped that the five years' course will become the general one, and seven years for boys of promise. On this reckoning we must allow for the next three years to be covered by boys aged roughly 13–16 years.

It will be convenient to consider the work in divisions, although in practice they will of course overlap. (1) Grammar, (2) Composition, (3) Translation, to which may be added a rather comprehensive term, (4) Background. While the bulk of the grammar will be covered in the third and fourth year it will need constant revision in the fifth. Composition will proceed *pari passu* with the grammar. The translation is a process of development up to the reading of Latin authors in the original. The whole is illustrated and supported by constant reference to background as it has been previously defined.

(1) *Grammar*

(*a*) *Accidence.* Most of the Accidence will have been covered in the first two years. Nevertheless, the following points must be considered:

(i) There must be constant revision of the regular forms of nouns, verbs, adjectives, adverbs, pronouns, numerals, etc. Oral practice at the beginning of a lesson and a regularly recurring test make for thoroughness in these matters.

(ii) In the course of reading and composition some new irregular nouns will have occurred, nouns like *vis, iter, domus*, although the actual words will differ according to the course used. Care must be taken over these, as they are apt to be forgotten as not coming within the scope of regular declensions. In addition to the personal, demonstrative, interrogative, and relative pronouns, by the end of the third year the compound pronouns (*quisquis, quidam*, etc.), the pronominal adjectives (*nullus, alius, alter*, etc.), the remaining ordinal numerals, 100th–1000th, the distributive numerals, and the numeral adverbs must be learned. The remaining irregular comparisons of adjectives and adverbs must be completed. Principal parts of verbs are best learned as they occur in reading or in composition. Many teachers maintain that a classified list of verbs, by grouping verbs of similar form together, makes, as it were, the task of learning these verbs too easy, with the result that they do not stick in the memory. For this reason many prefer a casual or illogical list of verbs, or even an alphabetical list, to one arranged according to a system.

(*b*) *Syntax*. The bulk of the syntax is better covered in the third and fourth year, leaving the fifth year for revision and practice over the whole field. The order of syntax varies widely from course to course. Many prefer to reduce the amount of new syntax in the fourth year in consideration of the time to be spent in reading authors. Where a four-year course obtains, this becomes an inescapable necessity. The ability of the form will usually dictate the division of the work between the third and the fourth years. The following is a suggested division, though it is clear that the break might be made anywhere, and many of the constructions must be anticipated for purposes of translation. Some of these constructions will have been met before, some will have been previously handled in an elementary way.

(i) *Third year*. Participles; ablative absolute; sequence of tenses; final and consecutive clauses; direct and indirect command; infinitives; gerunds and gerundive attraction; supines; indirect statement; indirect questions; impersonal verbs.

Time, place, space; genitive of price, value, objective and partitive genitive; predicative dative and dative with intransitive verbs; ablative of origin, separation, association, price, respect, manner, comparison, quality, difference.

(ii) *Fourth year*. Gerund and gerundive expressing obligation; verbs of fearing; causal clauses; *qui* with subjunctive; *quin* and *quominus*; temporal clauses; conditional sentences; concessive clauses; comparative clauses and continuous oratio obliqua.

(2) *Composition*

(*a*) *Sentences*. Composition is a difficult but valuable part of the work. Defence of the practice of composition and some hints on method will be found elsewhere. In the third, fourth and fifth years the boy is guided from the simple sentence to the easy complex sentence. Care should be taken not to give sentences beyond the boys' capacity, and at first not without a good deal of oral preparation. As the years proceed the boys' degree of dependence on previous preparation, vocabulary, grammar and other aids must be systematically reduced. This is a difficult business, and calls for a good deal of discipline from without and within. It must nevertheless be insisted on, for without a certain degree of self-reliance and a dependable memory it is unlikely that a boy will make a good scholar. By the end of the fourth year a boy should be able to tackle with a fair degree of confidence a complex sentence testing knowledge of at least one major construction.

(b) *Connected Latin.* It is important to distinguish between connected Latin and Latin prose composition. Few will expect pupils in the first five years to have reached the degree of proficiency implied in the ability to translate a passage from an English author into Latin. Nevertheless, many like to vary the practice of setting for translation isolated sentences, with no related theme, by setting a connected story consisting of simple sentences in English. Some may object that the resultant Latin, even in a copy deemed 100 per cent correct, is likely for reasons of structure and style to be very unlike real Latin. But this objection is more imaginary than real. The same criticism indeed might apply to much of the 'synthetic' Latin deemed fit for pupils in the early stages to translate.

(c) *Free Composition.* Free composition has its ardent enthusiasts, and some interesting examples are occasionally exhibited. The letters written to *Acta Diurna* well illustrate this type of composition. While the more austere will shrink from the dangers of dog Latin, the added incentive that an occasional exercise of this sort gives can hardly be denied.

(3) *Translation*

The distinction between prepared and unprepared translation will count for little in the third year, where so much translation has to be done with the assistance of the teacher. At any rate, it is unwise to begin requiring the pupils to keep vocabulary books before they are old enough to be trusted to put down the word in its proper form. For the first two years the Latin has been 'synthetic'. Now a change has to be made to the reading of Latin which was not originally intended for children. This is usually done through the medium of a simplified author, e.g. Caesar. In the third year translation is called upon to perform at least three functions, and in spite of the skill with which many of these adaptations are made, it is hardly surprising that they are rarely equally successful in achieving all their objectives. The translation book of the third year must—

(a) Provide a transition from made-up to real Latin, i.e. it must be a simplified author.

(b) Provide material for the illustration of new syntax learnt.

(c) Provide some of the background of Roman history, literature and life.

It is clear that if these aims are kept in view more than one reader should be used. There is in fact an advantage in not keeping to one reader too long. There are numerous editions of simplified authors which are useful at this stage. The transition to verse is much more difficult, although often desirable at this stage for its content. A simplified Ovid has been published, but in general little has been done to ease the transition from the simplicity of Latin prose to the difficulty of Ovid and Virgil. It would be a good thing if more 'synthetic' verse found its way into Latin courses with a view to facilitating the introduction to Latin poetry.

In the fourth year a start should be made with unadapted texts. Caesar is traditionally useful at this stage, but it is now realized widely that there has been too little adventure in the field of Latin Literature. Not only Caesar, but also Cicero, Livy, Pliny, Nepos, Curtius, Erasmus, and Medieval writers can all provide reading of interest. In verse, selections from Virgil, Horace, Catullus and Martial are suitable. Opinions vary about Ovid, some finding his allusive style too difficult for boys. Some excellent anthologies of Latin prose and Latin verse are available, and the previous belief that an entire book of one author ought to be read at this stage finds less favour nowadays. Yet here a note of warning must be sounded. There must be sufficient substance in what is read to provide a whole continuous theme, in order that there may in the end be some sense of achievement. A diet of snippets is to be avoided at all costs.

More will be said later on the perplexing question of the technique of teaching translation and the difficulty of getting the full co-operation of a class in work of this sort. A distinction can be drawn, however, in the fourth year between the standard of the translation a boy might be expected to do at sight, and that of the translation of set books, i.e. already prepared and therefore to a certain extent remembered. Some are so suspicious of the value of translation as memory work that they favour the discontinuance of set books. It must be said that for one reason or another set books often give a false impression of the boys' ability at the stage when they are read. The amount of Latin to be attempted in the fourth year may be set at roughly 30–40 chapters of Caesar and 600 lines of Virgil, or the equivalent in other authors. The doing of formal 'unseens', that is, as a separate written exercise without previous preparation, in contradistinction to new Latin read in class, is perhaps best postponed to the fifth year. The danger in setting 'unseens' at too early a stage is that it may lead to demoralization among the less able. Some, it is true, prefer to begin earlier in the hope of getting in plenty of practice in unseens before the examination. Nevertheless, there is a widespread feeling that excessive drilling in the 'technique' of doing unseens is undesirable.

(4) *Background*

While it is generally agreed that a course of Latin which was treated as the acquisition of a language only would leave much to be desired, and perhaps would not wholly justify its place in the curriculum, there is less agreement on the method by which some elementary notions of the life, literature, and history of the Romans are to be taught. Some assert that a whole term of language teaching may be sacrificed to a historical course on these lines; others say that such information must be imparted incidentally in connexion with the actual reading matter. More reference will be made to this in chapters IV and V, but there seems to be justification for the view that if the value of Latin is to rest at all on its claim to deal with the origins of Western civilization, a course that left any adequate picture of the Roman civilization out of its reckoning could hardly be defended. In short, it may be urged that no boy should finish without a rough notion of the salient events of Roman history, the outstanding Latin writers, and the social, religious, political and military institutions of the Roman people.

Time allowance. It remains to speak of the time allowance. None of the principles mentioned earlier in the first two years' course will have lost any of their validity at the later stages. The work has become considerably more difficult and more exacting. It cannot be efficiently accomplished on less than five periods of 45 minutes with two periods of preparation, say, of 30 minutes each.

III

GREEK: THE EARLY YEARS

1. POSITION OF GREEK IN THE SCHOOLS

'Except the blind forces of Nature nothing moves in this world
which is not in its origin Greek.' (SIR HENRY MAINE)

THERE is ample and eloquent testimony to the value of Greek in
modern education. Whether studied *per se* as literature or because
it contains the germ of many of our literary forms, Greek is
recognized by more and more educationists as being worthy of
an important place in our educational system. The relevance to
modern times especially of the fifth and fourth centuries B.C.,
when the Greek world seemed to be confronted by many of our
problems in miniature, has captured the imagination of many
writers. The clarity of Greek thought is held up as a model of
lucidity for our pupils. It is claimed that the originality of the
Greek genius in science, mathematics, philosophy, as devisers of
political forms favouring the growth of freedom, as pioneers in
oratory, history and the drama, should serve to stimulate our own
youth to a like freshness of thought. As in the past great forward
movements in learning have taken their origin from the Greek
culture and civilization, so in our own day we may yet derive
new impulses from Hellas. Indeed, it must be owned that in
many respects Greek provides the classical apologist with better
ammunition than does Latin.

Yet for all this the hold of Greek on the schools is little more
than precarious. While it still forms part of the staple diet of some
of the public schools and older grammar schools, only a handful
of scholars here and there in the majority of our schools attempt
Greek. Of course it is important not to understate the position.[1]

[1] The number of candidates in Greek for the Ordinary Level of the
General Certificate of Education has in fact been fairly steady ever since 1953—
viz. (1953) 2469; (1954) 2311; (1955) 2232; (1956) 2380; (1957) 2412;

Wild statements to the effect that Greek has vanished from our schools are to be deplored. The efforts of Sir Richard Livingstone and others to give the humanities their due place in education, and Greek its due place among the humanities, have not been fruitless. Nevertheless, the gap between theory and practice still remains uncomfortably large.

One difficulty is that an expansion of Greek studies may often only be effected at the expense of Latin. This would be distasteful to many on other grounds than an unwillingness to sacrifice the substance of Latin for the shadow of Greek. It must be admitted that the theory of 'Greek instead of Latin' has its superficial attractions. The literature is easier, more varied, and has greater appeal to the young. This may be conceded without recourse to the not-too-innocent pastime of picking a Greek literary team to play a Roman. Without arbitrating between the two legacies, if Greek is to be the only classical language, we may doubt whether it has the same residual value for those who leave school, while for those who go on to the modern course it has not the same preparatory value that Latin can afford. Evidence is as yet meagre, but there is reason to believe that Greek does not abide in the memory so long as does Latin. History and Modern Language teachers are emphatic that they prefer Latin to Greek as an ancillary study. Some schools have experimented with a Greek course for all, followed by Latin for a selected few. A headmaster of a large school where this experiment was made felt himself compelled by the recent change in examination requirements, and in particular by the requirements of certain faculties at the universities, to abandon the experiment. His verdict was that while the best boys profited from the reversal of the usual Latin-Greek order, boys of less ability neither gained nor lost very much.

In a grammar school with a crowded time-table, practical considerations become paramount. Even so, practical considerations suggest that we should consider in this volume first and

(1958) 2519; (1959) 2601. It is misleading to give these figures as a percentage of the total number of candidates.

foremost the Greek course of two to three years begun after two years of a four- or five-year course of Latin. As hitherto practised, the two-year Greek course has come in for a good deal of criticism; experience suggests that, however selected the pupils may be, two years of Greek up to the required standard for the Ordinary Level of the General Certificate of Education is not enough. While the accidence and a certain amount of simple translation may be covered in the first year, the necessity of translating set books *pari passu* with learning all the necessary syntax and revising the accidence is productive of hurried methods and of cramming. It is to be hoped that a three-year course to this level will become the common practice.

2. SELECTION OF PUPILS

The selection of pupils for Greek calls for some comment. One important factor in the selection of pupils for Latin hitherto has been the universities' requirement of compulsory Latin for an Arts degree. This has meant in practice that some pupils of lower attainments still keep up Latin, which they might otherwise have dropped, in the hope of securing an Intermediate qualification, even though their main interests and capacities lie elsewhere than in Latin itself. This has acted as a check on the standard of Latin, and kept it reasonably moderate—some say, too low. In Greek no such forces are at work. Greek is regarded as a difficult study—often unwarrantably so, for many of its apparent difficulties are only superficial. In consequence, selection of pupils to do Greek has become a very austere 'seeding' process. Only the cream of our pupils have been doing Greek. When, however, the laws of percentage and the activities of examination statisticians are brought into play, pupils of quite high ability are failed in Greek. This has the resultant effect of making the selection process even more rigid. The gateway to Greek becomes narrower and narrower. The temptation to the universities to encourage an ever higher-mounting standard is great, and the schools have sometimes to take a wider view than do the universities. There may be more ways of killing a cat than by choking it with cream, but it must be owned that this lethal method is not wholly without its effect on Greek. If the numbers of pupils, in spite of this, have even slightly increased, it is only the enthusiasm and self-sacrificing zeal of our teachers that has made this possible. It takes no little courage for an intelligent boy to abandon a possibly easier alternative in favour of Greek, and when, as sometimes happens, results prove disappointing, the teacher of Greek is liable to incur criticism. Again, it has been widely noted that there is an increasing tendency for pupils in our Arts Sixths to ask to be taught Greek. Such boys had evidently been passed over earlier in their school career. The conclusion appears to be that in selecting our pupils for Greek we must cast our net a little wider, and welcome not only the potential scholars, but also some of the 'littler' fish. We may have to cater for those who will give up Greek after taking it to the Ordinary Level, for late-starters in the Sixth Form, for non-specialists, for scientists, for those whose ability may not be too great but whose aesthetic leanings incline them to love the highest when they see it, however dim that discernment may be. A howl of execration may be expected to greet any suggestion of lowering the standards, but we must be careful to see that such a howl does not come from quarters not wholly disinterested.

One more point arises before we can proceed to a consideration of the course. Young teachers, seeking to introduce Greek into the curriculum, are frequently asked by their heads, who must grapple with the time-table problem, to what subject Greek should be an alternative. A sample survey of schools suggests that in most cases at present the answer is German, and in some, Science. It is best that Greek should be an alternative to another language, as languages make similar demands on the time-table. If the rule in the past has been that the best boys do Greek and the rest German, the reason for this unsatisfactory state of affairs must be sought in the excessively high standard in Greek demanded by the examining bodies. A division on the basis of literary or practical interests may prove more acceptable. Some schools, whilst making a third language an alternative to Physics and Chemistry, wisely provide a General Science course (not necessarily for examination purposes) for their linguists in some of the available periods. Sometimes it is possible to effect a saving by borrowing from periods devoted to English Language, not so necessary for boys who are devoting so much time to language. The provision of some form of Science course for Greek pupils avoids leaving a serious gap in a boy's education for the modern world. The question is a thorny one, however, for it is clear that something must be sacrificed, and even in such a worthy cause the choice between evils is hard.

In spite of our criticism of the narrow gateway to Greek it must be conceded that some selection will be necessary. This will have an important bearing on the methods of teaching employed. Too often in the past there has been a complacent assumption that the aims and methods applied to the teaching of Greek are a mere reflexion of what is done in Latin. Thus the *Report on Classics in Education* (1923), p. 175: 'What we have said about Latin applies *mutatis mutandis* to Greek also.' Yet this is a casual view to take. The pace at which boys can proceed after two years of Latin—selected boys at that—is far more rapid, much more understanding of difficulties may be safely assumed, and a much more formal approach to grammar (which is the shorter method) may be undertaken. In fact the exigencies of a shorter course demand different methods. On the other hand, the greater mechanical difficulty of writing Greek, and the inescapable necessity of ensuring complete accuracy, demand a great deal of repetitive practice in simple sentences at the initial stage.

3. AIMS AND CONTENT OF THE COURSE

To come then to the general aims of a two- or three-year course. The first year should be sufficient to cover the accidence, some elementary grammar rules, and a certain quantity of reading of Greek of a concocted type usual in Readers. The second year will be partly devoted to syntax. Greek syntax is not difficult. Boys who have already grappled with the austerities of Latin syntax find about Greek constructions a natural and easy-going air that makes them readily comprehensible. Some teachers boast that they can get all Greek syntax on to a postcard. As an offset to this must be reckoned the huge bulk of Greek accidence—Rutherford gives sixty forms of the third declension—and the most commonly used forms are the most irregular. While, therefore, it is important that a beginning on original authors be made in the second year, the prescription of authors too difficult, or of excessive amounts for examination purposes, leads to all the evils of the set-book system, the cramming, the learning by heart, the acquisition of a rigidly *ad hoc* vocabulary. A book of Xenophon and 600 lines of Euripides is enough. Tradition makes Xenophon the first author to be read, and experience approves the tradition. The *Anabasis* is simple and romantic, excellent provender for boys at that age. Certain plays of Euripides, notably the *Alcestis* and the *Cyclops*, when edited, are suitable at this stage; but it is a fallacy to regard all Euripides as equally suitable. It seems that too little attention has been paid in the past by examining bodies to the suitability of the subject-matter of Greek plays, apart from the inherent difficulty of translating them. Philosophy, even in the simplest dialogues of Plato, has very little appeal to boys of this age looking out for a good story. Nor is it easy to explain the popularity with the examining bodies of the *Medea* of Euripides, so difficult and unsuitable at this stage.

A word must be said here about the suitability of Homer as a text-book for beginners. Experiments have been made in starting boys with Homeric Greek in at least one school in this country, and if the experiment was abandoned it was for reasons unconnected with the intrinsic merits of the scheme. Clyde Pharr of Vanderbilt University, in his book *Homeric Greek*, claims that Homer is simpler in vocabulary, style and idiom; that there are fewer forms to be learnt in Homeric Greek than in Attic; that all three persons are constantly used; that the sentences are short and simple; that the uncontracted forms lead naturally to the contracted forms later on; that the eminent literary quality of Homer makes him much more worth while reading in himself; that Homer leads naturally to the Greek dramatists and Herodotus. Furthermore, something has been gained at once, and there are no 'deferred returns' as there must be in studying the old way.

No doubt all this makes a very attractive theory. It seems fair to add that there are drawbacks mainly concerned with the reading and writing of prose, for not all will wish to confine the legacy to Greek epic and the dramatists with Herodotus thrown in. Many teachers would have to begin learning the grammar of Ionic Greek. Few examining boards seem likely to accept sentences written in Homeric Greek, especially with its simpler syntax. It is unfair to expect a boy to learn both Attic and Homeric Greek, and it is precisely this double requirement that in the past has choked the experiment. Yet it would be interesting to see a course worked out in this way with grammar and reading parallel, developing from Homer through Herodotus to Attic Greek.

The aims of the third year will be to read a wider range of authors, although for some set books may be the main consideration, and to consolidate and extend the pupils' knowledge of syntax. During this time the teacher will deal with Greek literature, history, mythology, thought, social life, and what is called 'background', incidentally, as the need arises in the course of lessons. At the end of the course it must be evident that it has fulfilled all requirements according to the capacity of the pupils, i.e. it has formed a complete course in itself, or it has served as a useful preparation for a Sixth-Form course of Greek Literature in translation, subsidiary Greek, Greek as a part of a group of modern studies, or Greek as part of the main classical course.

Content of the Course

(a) *First year.* Regular declension of nouns, adjectives and pronouns; regular and contracted verbs in full; -*mi* verbs, perhaps only in the indicative mood; adverbs, prepositions, etc., as occurring in the Reader and exercises; a few very elementary syntactical constructions. The Reader, while being based on a systematic sequence, will at the same time attempt to give some glimpses at the commoner stories of Greek literature and mythology. From the very beginning pupils will be urged to trace the connexion between Greek and English through derivatives.

(b) *Second year.* Revision of accidence previously learnt, and all basic syntax. The learning of grammar will be tested throughout by the writing of sentences, with a view to the consolidation of the work learnt. The reading of one book of Xenophon and the dialogue portions of a Euripidean play to the extent of some 600 lines.

(c) *Third year.* Further reading of books chosen from Homer, Herodotus, the Gospels, Thucydides and selected portions from Aristophanes (e.g. the *Knights*). Further syntax and sentences, with perhaps a beginning of continuous prose composition for advanced pupils.

Method

(a) *Grammar.* Although pupils will already, through Latin, have mastered the initial difficulties of an inflected language, and although considerable simplification can be effected in the Greek grammar to be memorized in the first year, yet constant repetition and revision are essential; a sure foundation must be laid at this stage.

(b) *Composition.* Unless extreme care is taken from the outset, a habit of carelessness can easily grow among beginners. It is, therefore, essential that numerous simple sentences be given, and no mercy shown for the omission of breathings, iotas subscript and the like. Only thus can accuracy in the future be assured.

(c) *Vocabulary.* One of the biggest difficulties of teaching Greek is the difficulty of getting pupils in a comparatively short time to acquire any satisfactory amount of Greek vocabulary. Boys are inclined to be satisfied with what is needed for the immediate purpose of translating the relevant portion of the set book. This is a matter that requires constant attention from the teacher.

(d) *Derivations.* Much enthusiasm for the study of Greek can be promoted from the beginning by a study of the derivation of English words from Greek roots. It is not necessary to plague boys with words they do not know in order to rouse this enthusiasm. Better explain a word like 'butter' than a word like 'aphasia'. Some teachers start with the words from the time-table, Mathematics, Geography, etc.

Greek accents form a great stumbling-block to the learning of Greek, and there is a school of thought that would abandon the use of accents entirely, on the grounds that they are a late invention, and if not functional, i.e. if they are not used in conjunction with pronunciation, serve no other purpose than a piece of dubious ornamentation. Where accents are commonly misplaced these arguments seem hard to counter. Others would use accents only where the accent distinguishes the meanings of words spelt alike.

There is a sterner school of thought which would not part with a single accent, while those who teach by the direct method claim that the accent is an integral part of the word, in that it aids pronunciation. It should be remembered always that accent marks pitch, not stress, a difficult thing for the average Briton to achieve. We recommend that accents should be ignored for the first two years, and gradually learnt thereafter.

Fuller guidance on the pronunciation of Greek is to be found in Appendix II (p. 220). The situation appears at present to be that the grammar schools and the newer schools have taken up the revised pronunciation almost solidly. The old-fashioned English pronunciation still lingers in the schools of an older tradition. While this leads to some perplexity in the universities, it does not appear to cause insuperable difficulties as one might suppose. In fact it is noteworthy that numerous people derive immense aesthetic enjoyment from poetry which they all pronounce in entirely different ways. While it might be difficult, and perhaps imprudent, to upset a tradition of pronunciation long established, there is no reason for any teacher breaking fresh ground with Greek in a school to start with the old-fashioned pronunciation. Statements that the commonly-used revised pronunciation is difficult for beginners to learn do not tally with experience.

The time-table requirement for Greek will be largely similar to that of Latin. In each of the three years, it will be necessary to have five periods a week, on the principle that a fresh practice must be attempted every day, and at least two homeworks a week will be required to cover the broad division of the work into two. To what extent the requirements of pupils who have begun earlier in their preparatory schools will differ is not certain, but in most cases these will form a minority.

It has been pointed out earlier in the chapter that a beginning of Greek will not always be made in the junior or middle school. Occasionally a Sixth-Former who can do so with profit will want to begin Greek, occasionally a non-specialist. Nothing could be worse than the attitude of persons who look askance at such enthusiasm, or who would like to make a privileged preserve of Classics for the specialist. To know a little Greek is better than to know none. There are other alternatives to deep draughts of the Pierian spring than a raging and unquenched thirst. For the Sixth-Former the content of the course will be much the same as that outlined above, except that a more rigid economy may be employed in doing exercises and learning accidence forms, and it will often be possible to substitute for the synthetic Greek of a Reader actual excerpts, sometimes consisting of only a line or two, from Greek originals. Adults appreciate the thought of Greek authors usually more than do the juniors. The Greek Testament is very valuable here, where the content is so familiar. Frequently a boy who has a vocation for the Church may be taught in this way. The amount of teaching necessary may not exceed three periods a week, as much may be left to individual study. Although remarkable things have been achieved from such beginnings, the aim of such a course need not be set higher than the ability to make one's way through a Greek text with the aid of a parallel translation. It was with such an object in view that Mrs Dora Pym, who achieved such exciting results with beginners in Greek at the Education Department of Bristol University, set forth in a published pamphlet a scheme for the teaching of Greek in ten lessons. Given the requisite enthusiasm in both teacher and pupils it is well worth while to acquire even such little Greek as sufficed for Shakespeare.

Nor is it too fanciful to envisage a cultural course of Greek which would prove both attractive and profitable to the Sixth-Form physicist, mathematician, chemist or biologist. Such a course must attend upon the production of a text-book designed for their needs, but a text-book whose vocabulary would consist of the names of plants and animals rather than abstract nouns, and whose aim was to bring before the reader's eye the Greek origin of mathematics, geometry, biology, mechanics, dynamics, astronomy and zoology, with all their attendant specialized terms, would be performing an enlightened function indeed. If the course could be made to lead to the reading of simplified selections from Euclid, Aristotle, Hippocrates, Heron and Proclus, the result might do something not only to remove the barriers which have sprung up between the various departments in our schools but also to demonstrate to the scientists that—as Gilbert Murray points out—'the conception of Truth as an end to pursue for its own sake, a thing to discover and puzzle out by experiment and imagination and reason...has perhaps never in the world been more clearly grasped than by the early Greek writers on science and philosophy'. Such an experiment would not be an easy one. It would require the right text-book, about three periods a week in the Lower Sixth, and a sympathetic and broad-minded teacher. Given these conditions, an enthusiast might strike out a new line which would make educational history.

For it may be claimed that the majority of teachers of Greek are endowed with a sense of mission and high purpose. Battling against heavy odds in a cynical and materialist world, they can be forgiven for thinking that the survival of the ideals that the Greeks proclaimed is somehow wrapped up with the survival of the language itself. The survival of Greek can no more be entrusted to a small esoteric body of specialists than to the unabashed philistinism of those whose stock reaction to the word Greek is embodied in the maddening observation, 'Well it's all Greek to me!' We must, therefore, consider every new pupil in Greek, whether he learns little or much, as representing that degree of redemption from the darkness. For Greek, in the words of Dr Johnson's aphorism, 'is like lace; every wise man gets as much of it as he can'.

IV

TEACHING METHODS

1. THE TRADITIONAL OR LITERARY METHOD

'Id in primis cavere oportebit, ne studia, qui amare nondum
potest, oderit, et amaritudinem semel perceptam etiam ultra
rudes annos reformidet.'   (QUINTILIAN)

WHAT is frequently called the 'traditional' method of teaching
Classics is the method that was developed in the public and
grammar schools of this country during the nineteenth century.
Thus it is of no great antiquity, and some authorities, thinking
that the term 'traditional' obscures this fact, prefer to call it the
'literary method'. In the words of H. K. Hunt, 'The literary
method stresses the formal aspects of language study more than
other methods.'[1] Inevitably there have been changes. In the
present century reduction of the amount of time that can be
devoted to Latin has necessitated considerable modification in
detail. The basic principles, however, have remained unchanged.
They are these:

(a) *The accidence and syntax are learnt systematically from books
compiled for this purpose.*

The learning of accidence was originally regarded as an end in
itself. Lists of nouns classified according to their inflexions, with
all the exceptions thereto, were conned by rote with never
a thought to the likelihood of their occurrence in literature or
possible employment in composition. All verb forms were
studied alike with little reference to their frequency value. The
acquisition of gender rules and the like was held to be an exercise
for the memory worth while in itself. Much of this lumber has
now been discarded. The learning of accidence is limited with

---

[1] *Training Through Latin* (Melbourne University Press). To this invaluable
work the authors are indebted for much of the material of this chapter.

a view to its eventual application. Accidence is regarded as a means to an end—that end being the reading and writing of Latin.

The same is not, however, true of syntax. Syntax is still regarded as something to be honoured in its own right. It is viewed as an end in itself in so far as it (i) gives the pupil a logical training, and (ii) affords a foundation on which he can build the study of other languages. Attempts have been made to shake these beliefs by severely limiting the application of (i) and denying the necessity of (ii). The tide of opinion, however, seems to be running strongly in favour of the excellent groundwork afforded by the training in syntax acquired through Latin.

(b) *The pupil is introduced to the reading of continuous Latin gradually, and on the basis of accidence and syntax already learnt.*

In the Elizabethan grammar school Latin grammar was studied *in vacuo*. Any traces of this which lingered on through the nineteenth century have at any rate disappeared in the last fifty years. It would be safe to say that grammar is now nowhere studied divorced from reading and composition. The art of compiling specially constructed Latin passages, and of simplifying Latin authors without losing too much of the flavour of the original, has sufficiently advanced to enable us to introduce the pupil to readable and respectable Latin at an early stage. The numerous Latin courses now available to teachers of Latin show that this method is firmly established.

(c) *In the later stages of the course, proficiency in prose composition is aimed at just as much as proficiency in translation from Latin.*

Almost as soon as the pupil begins to master the elementary forms and constructions of Latin he begins translating English sentences into Latin. These sentences provide a means of applying the knowledge acquired, and test the soundness of that knowledge. The sentences may be wholly detached, may deal with a theme (e.g. the subject of the Latin read), or may be connected in meaning in such a way as not to be very remote from a piece of connected English. The 'traditional' method, besides leading the pupil on to the prepared and unseen translation of suitable Latin authors, aims also at bringing him to the stage of translating suitable passages of English prose into Latin that is idiomatically as well as grammatically correct. This involves translation of ideas no less than words, and is a vital point of the Latin course, as it provides training in clear thinking.

(d) *All the Latin read during the course is translated (either orally or in writing) into English.*

The advocates of the 'traditional' method hold that accuracy and precision can be sought only by translation of Latin into English. They do not believe that the simple reading of Latin, or the use of comprehension tests, are adequate linguistic substitutes. They are also not insensible to the valuable training in English that this method provides. The constant necessity to select the nearest English equivalent from the narrow or wide field of meaning provided by the Latin word is an exercise in English vocabulary work that cannot be rivalled.

(e) *The vocabulary introduced in the earlier stages is confined to words that will be of real use for the reading of classical Latin and for composition in the same idiom.*

In 1907 was published Lodge's *Vocabulary of High School Latin.* This list of words was drawn up upon the basis of their frequency in the classical authors most commonly studied in schools. This list has had a profound influence on the teaching of Latin, and most editors of courses following the traditional method keep as far as possible within the limits suggested by this list. Advocates of the word-order method also adhere to the principle, but the every-day vocabulary of the class-room required by those who teach according to the direct method can hardly be restricted to Lodge's list.

(f) *The provision of background information is kept largely separate from the linguistic teaching.*

There would not be found many teachers today who would maintain that their task is simply to teach the Latin language, or that instruction concerning the life, habits and thought of the peoples who spoke Latin lies outside the scope of their work. Yet such a view must have been widespread at one time; and even today there are some who, aware of the distracting influence of diversionary matter, prefer to keep background information for a separate lesson, carefully distinguished from strictly linguistic study. Many such teachers use special books to supplement oral teaching in this field, and there are many excellent little handbooks available for dealing with the life and society of Rome. There are also courses that aim at providing such information *pari passu* with, but distinct from, instruction in accidence and syntax. Those courses, however, in which linguistic and background instruction coincide, or are inseparably mixed, must be deemed foreign to the traditional method.

Accidence

In the learning of accidence the memory plays a vital part, and most teachers have little devices of their own which they employ to stimulate the memory of their pupils. 'Class chorusing' is a time-honoured practice by no means peculiar to the traditional method, though here a cleavage of opinion is to be observed. Some purists, recoiling from mispronunciation and misplacement of accent, condemn outright such horrors as *regó, regís, regít* and insist on *régo, régis, régit*. But many stalwarts stoutly defend the old practice, even in the teeth of the Board of Education Pamphlet No. 116 (p. 24). They say that the purpose of reciting grammar is to learn the inflexions, a consideration which supersedes all others. The verbal stress on the inflexion is a natural indication of its importance, which is, therefore, not lost on the pupils as it well might be if the grammatically unimportant stem were stressed. Co-operative chorusing is aided by rhythm, which is better when the inflexion is stressed. Nobody pretends that Latin thus chanted is being correctly pronounced. This is well appreciated by the pupils, whose normal pronunciation is in no way vitiated by the practice. Whatever view be taken of these claims, there is no doubt that class chorusing is a good way of learning. Other mnemonic tricks make a firm impression when performed in concert, e.g. raising the index finger at a 3rd declension ablative singular ending in -*i*, and describing a circle with the hand in the middle of saying *octoginta*.

The testing of accidence can be enlivened in various ways. Oral matches between teams questioning each other, a moving place system, pupils moving up or down as they answer questions passed around the class, quizzes and the like, all prove popular methods of getting routine work done.

Sentences

It is usual, and indeed it will be found prudent, to preface the writing of English-Latin sentences with much oral and black-board work. Formal grammar plays a less important part in the elementary stages of English teaching than it did previously, and the teacher who takes for granted a knowledge of analysis of simple sentences or of parsing will soon be in difficulties. One way of dealing with sentences is to insist on a short parsing of every inflected word before it is set down, e.g.:

Nom. sing. masc.   Dat. pl. masc.   Acc. pl. neut.   3rd sing. pres.
  Magister   *pueris bonis*   *praemia*   *saepe*   *dat.*

(The horizontal line marks a check for agreement
between subject and verb.)

Most teachers find that oral translation of Latin-English sentences is generally sufficient, and that a written translation is unnecessary.

Syntax[1]

After the four varieties of the simple sentence—statement, question, exclamation and command—have been learnt, most modern 'traditionalists' proceed to a systematic presentation of subordinate clause constructions. The systems of presentation vary; some work solidly through adjective clauses, noun clauses and adverb clauses; others prefer to group clauses in accordance with the mood of the Latin verb that they require—indicative, infinitive, subjunctive

---

[1] Some constructions are dealt with in greater detail at the end of this section.

with full meaning, subjunctive with weakened meaning; others allow the sequence to be dictated by the order in which the clauses happen to occur in the simplified Latin being read at the time. We would also point out that many subordinate clauses may be introduced imperceptibly, as it were, without the pupils being told that they are in fact using subordinate clauses. The simpler forms of relative clause and of final and consecutive clauses can be used in a manner so akin to their English equivalents that no special comment is called for, and pupils take to them naturally.

It is largely a matter of choice at what points the study of clauses should be interrupted to deal with other constructions, such as ablative absolute and impersonal passive. As for case-uses, the commonest are learnt during the early exercise work, and the rest introduced *passim*. The old way of working through all possible uses of each case before starting on clause-constructions has long been abandoned. Even so, most teachers could wish that editors of courses would spread their case-usages a little more evenly over their books. So often does it happen that a pupil begins to feel that he is making headway with the complex sentence, when suddenly he is becalmed for weeks in the doldrums of 'Dative Case after Verbs', 'Special Uses of the Ablative', 'More Special Uses of the Ablative', etc.

In the course of dealing with clauses, most teachers find it advisable to devote some time to the analysis of complex sentences in English. Once a pupil is trained properly to recognize whether a subordinate clause is playing the part of a noun, or adjective, or an adverb, it becomes much easier for him to distinguish between clauses of different function but similar appearance, e.g. between 'I know who did it' and 'I know the man who did it'; or between 'He knows that he is loved by all' and 'He is so good that he is loved by all'. In general, the pupil brought up under this method, when faced by a subordinate clause for translation into Latin, performs two operations: (i) he identifies the clause as of a particular type; (ii) he calls to mind, or looks up, the Latin idiom required for a clause of that particular type.

Reading of Texts

Pupils who have been accustomed from the first to oral work with Latin-English sentences, and who are gradually brought on to full texts by way of specially constructed passages and simplified versions, should not need this part of their studies to be impeded by an excess of analysis and parsing. The modern traditionalist avails himself of these processes when they appear necessary, but not as an automatic part of the translation of every sentence, as his nineteenth-century predecessor was inclined to do.

Much help is given nowadays by the teacher's preliminary translation of a chapter or passage into good idiomatic English, or by his reading of a 'crib' that satisfies this standard (e.g. S. A. Handford's translation of the *Gallic War*). Besides acquainting the pupil with the subject-matter in advance, this affords him a standard to which his own version should aspire. The modern teacher does not permit any suspicion of 'translationese'; e.g. he forbids English 'absolute' constructions and English historic presents, as being alien to present-day idiom.

When pupils are introduced to verse authors, care is taken from the first to make them realize that they are reading verse, and not prose cut up into strips. Average pupils can be brought to appreciate the rhythm of Latin verse by class-reading in chorus; detailed instruction in the finer points of scansion is deliberately postponed. While preliminary translation and pupils' versions are done in prose, good verse translations, when available (e.g. Rhoades' of Virgil), can be advantageously read to a class after a passage has been dealt with.

The conventional method of eliciting translation is to tell a pupil to read a sentence or sentences in Latin and then expound the meaning to the teacher and the class, with or without assistance from the teacher or from other members of the class. With a really good set of pupils, much ground can be covered this way and the interest of the whole class maintained continuously. But with the average large class of today, that includes a tail as well as a head, this method often results in either (*a*) desperately slow progress whenever a less intelligent member takes his turn, or

(b) employment of the abler pupils only, in an effort to cover the ground at a reasonable rate. In either case, the interest of the class as a whole is bound to suffer; and in the second, those pupils who are not invited to participate derive little profit from hearing work done at a pace that is too rapid for them to follow.

There is an alternative method which, besides being livelier, requires the constant attention of the whole class, and does not make undue or time-consuming demands on the weaker pupils; it has been found particularly suitable for use with junior classes. First, a sentence or short paragraph is read in Latin, either by a single pupil or by the class in chorus. Take as an example: 'Postridie eius diei Caesar, prius quam se hostes ex terrore ac fuga reciperent, in finis Suessionum, qui proximi Remis erant, exercitum duxit et magno itinere confecto ad oppidum Noviodunum contendit' (Caesar, *B.G.* II, 12, 1). Work then proceeds orally as follows:

Teacher: 'Postridie eius diei—R.' (The pupil R. translates these words; if he cannot, someone else is called on without delay.)

Teacher: 'Caesar—Z.' (Z., who is bottom of the form, obliges immediately.)

Teacher: 'prius quam se hostes reciperent—D.' (D., who is near the top, does his best, but says 'recovered'; whereupon A. is appealed to and succeeds in amending to 'could recover'.)

Teacher: 'ex terrore ac fuga—T.' (T. says 'from terror and flight'.)

Teacher: 'Any improvement—L.?' (L. produces something better.)

Teacher: 'exercitum duxit—X.' (X. translates.)

Teacher: 'in finis Suessionum—G.' (G. translates.) 'And tell us what else "finis" could have been.' (G. hesitates, gives a dirty look at his neighbour F. whose hand shoots up, and then remembers and gets out 'fines' just in time.)

Teacher: 'qui proximi Remis erant—P.' (P. says 'who were next to the Remi'; J., on invitation, gives an improved version.)

Teacher: 'et, and (that's easy enough for me)' 'magno itinere confecto—now's your chance—F.' (F. responds satisfactorily.)

58

Teacher: 'ad oppidum Noviodunum contendit—*V.*' (Even *V.* has sense enough to know that English requires ' . . . the town *of* Noviodunum'.)

The essence of this method is that the class is on the *qui vive* all the time, as no one knows when he is going to be called upon. If any pupil fails, there is plenty of time to give him another chance later on. When a whole passage has been worked out like this, there often remains sufficient time for one or more of the class to go over it again, giving a consecutive translation.

Unseen Translation

Instead of plunging the pupil suddenly *in medias res* during the year that precedes his first public examination, modern practice (as with prepared reading) leads him up gradually by means of passages specially constructed and adapted in respect of vocabulary, constructions and content.

In the early stages oral work predominates; here the technique illustrated above has been found just as applicable to unseens as to prepared passages. It lends itself to ensuring that a pupil is not befogged by the complexity of a sentence if it is dissected in this way by the teacher and accustoms him to learn the method of dissection.

When sufficient confidence has been gained, a start may be made on written versions of unseens that have already been worked out orally. From this point, the gradual elimination of previous oral work can be made to lead up to the production of written versions that represent the pupil's individual effort.

Written versions of this type are better set as class-room exercises than as homework or preparation tasks. The correct atmosphere should be ensured by rigorously banishing dictionaries and vocabularies from the 'unseen' period.

The following passage illustrates the kind of general advice that is given to the pupil:

Read the whole passage through slowly in Latin three times. At the end of this you should have some idea of what it is all about, and the precise meaning of some of the sentences or parts of sentences will probably be clear.

Then go through the passage again, sentence by sentence, trying to translate each mentally. If a word holds you up, try to work out what part of speech it is and what it is doing in the sentence; then translate the sentence, using 'blank' or '×' for the unknown word. You may have two or more 'blanks' in a single sentence; but the sentence itself or the surrounding context will often point out the only reasonable way of filling them.

When all else fails, you must make a guess rather than leave an empty space. But never write nonsense: an empty space is bad, but it is better than that.

Do not begin to write until you have mentally worked out the whole passage. As a general rule do not touch your pen till two-thirds of the time is gone.

More specific instruction might take the following form:

If you cannot at once see your way about a simple sentence, analyse it. First find the verb. Next look for the subject, unless obviously contained in the verb. Next, if the verb requires a direct object, look for it; if the verb is one that takes a genitive, dative or ablative, look for a noun or pronoun in the appropriate case; or if the verb requires an infinitive to complete its meaning, look for that. You thus get the skeleton of the sentence. Next try to build round it by looking for extensions of the subject (e.g. adjectives in the nominative, nouns in the genitive), and of the direct object. What still remains unaccounted for will be extension of the verb. You must not expect the stereotyped order, subject—object—verb, always to occur; it is very often departed from. Concentrate, therefore, not so much on the order of words as on their forms and endings.

Complex sentences naturally cause greater difficulty; but they can be treated in the same way as simple sentences, because a subordinate clause is, after all, only a group of words that is playing the part of a single noun, adjective or adverb. Before analysing a complex sentence, go through it and bracket all the subordinate clauses (including accusative-and-infinitive). Remember that a subordinate clause, once begun, must end before the main sentence can continue. After the bracketing, you will be left with your main sentence, which can be dealt with first; then work out each subordinate clause separately and put it in its proper place in the whole sentence, e.g. the relative clause must immediately follow its antecedent.

To find the meaning is only half your task. The other half is to express it in proper English. Translate literally when the literal translation fairly represents the Latin and reads well; if it does not, you must not hesitate to adapt and paraphrase. In particular, remember that, while the Latin idiom is to build up a complex sentence by means of participles, one or more subordinate clauses, and a single main verb, English prefers a succession of simple, or at any rate less complex, sentences. Do not hesitate, therefore, to turn Latin subordinate clauses into English main sentences: an English version that contains no more full stops than the Latin original is practically bound to be unidiomatic.

Continuous Prose Composition

The traditional method hopes to bring pupils, in the year preceding their first public examination, to the stage at which they can begin to think out the precise meaning of words, phrases and sentences in a suitable English narrative passage, and then translate it into Latin with some regard for the differences that exist between the two languages in respect of (i) sentence-construction, (ii) expression of ideas. Nothing ambitious is expected at the outset, but such a pupil can at least be taught (i) to combine two or three co-ordinate English sentences into a single Latin period (e.g. 'The consul received this news, realized that danger was at hand, and called his men back into camp'; 'Quibus rebus nuntiatis consul, cum periculum adesse intellexisset, suos in castra revocavit'); (ii) to recognize when English nouns should be represented by Latin clauses (e.g. 'my father's murderers', 'the presence of danger', 'the duration of his reign').

Some teachers make considerable use of the re-translation into Latin of carefully selected pieces of Latin that have been previously translated by the class into idiomatic English. Others base composition on reading in another way by constructing proses for which passages from authors read in class will serve as guides and models. Others, while they may admit such processes as an occasional change from routine, prefer as a rule to keep composition and reading separate. In view of the limited time that is usually available, we recommend the last method.

Free composition is very rarely practised as a class exercise; but in some schools the individual efforts of good Fifth-Formers in this direction have been found to be well worth encouraging.

It is claimed on behalf of the traditional method that:

(*a*) It aims at a clear understanding of the structure both of English and of Latin, and insists on seeking this understanding in a methodical and logical way.

(*b*) It insists on accuracy and exactness, and its processes show up slipshod and careless thought.

(*c*) It gives constant practice in the use of the kind of Latin that the pupil is going to meet when he comes to his Latin authors.

(*d*) It has been gradually codified, by long experience, and the systematic presentation of accidence and syntax in most books makes it the easiest method for the average teacher to employ effectively.

(*e*) It provides a more thorough groundwork for advanced course studies than is provided by other methods.

Imperfection in the use of the method, or in the text-books employed, may give rise to the following defects, which need to be carefully guarded against.

(*a*) *Excess of grammar-learning and exercise-writing in the early stages.*

There is now a large amount of suitable first-year and second-year reading matter available, and the up-to-date teacher will make full use of it, to ensure variety.

(*b*) *Wasting of time on rare words, forms and constructions.*

Kennedy's Gender Rhymes are a good example of the first; many supines in nineteenth-century grammars, of the second; and excessive exercising in the so-called future infinitive passive, of the third. The best modern books either purge these things or put them in their proper perspective.

(*c*) *Undue insistence on parsing and analysis during the reading of authors.*

This, of course, kills appreciation of content and style. It may have been a prevalent fault in the past, when there was plenty of time for it; now there is not, and it is fast becoming an unpleasant memory.

(*d*) *Use of 'translationese'.*

This was an incidental development from (*c*), and it was further fostered by the slovenly English of some old-fashioned exercise books. The modern teacher will have nothing to do with it, or with books that encourage it.

(*e*) *Neglect of spoken Latin.*

If the teacher does not make much use of reading Latin aloud, the fault is his and not the method's. Learning by heart of verse and prose passages already translated and understood is a most effective adjunct; this is quite easy to do by means of 'chorusing' in class.

(*f*) *Neglect of background information.*

This again means that the method is not being carried out properly. There are plenty of suitable 'background' books that pupils enjoy reading.

The Teaching of Constructions: some Illustrations

Every good teacher works out for himself his own method of tackling a new construction, and in the nature of things the method that appeals most to him is likely to be the best. Even the most skilful of teachers is, however, sometimes grateful for a hint dropped by another, and it has been thought worth while in the following sections to give by way of illustration a few samples of the detailed methods adopted by one or two experienced teachers in approaching new constructions.

Relative Clauses

In translating from English into Latin, the case of a relative pronoun presents real difficulty to many young pupils. A method of procedure which has proved effective is to insist that every English relative clause shall be lifted from its context and turned into a separate sentence by the substitution of a personal pronoun for the relative pronoun. The construction of the personal pronoun in the sentence thus formed will point to the construction of the relative pronoun in the sentence that is to be translated. Examples:

Original Sentence

I have sent for the boy *who* did this.
I have sent for the boy *whom* you wish to see.
I have sent for the boy *whose* brother did this.

Separate Sentence

He (the boy) did this.
You wish to see *him* (the boy).
His (the boy's) brother did this.

The study of these relative clauses is facilitated if pupils are given preliminary instruction on the difference between 'defining' and 'non-defining' clauses (e.g. as in H. W. and F. G. Fowler, *The King's English*, pp. 83 sqq.). This helps in distinguishing between 'The men whom he had called together' (*ii quos convocaverat*) and 'The men, whom he had called together...' (*viri, quos convocaverat...*), or between *Athenae, quod caput est Atticae*, and *urbs quae caput est insulae*.

Noun Clauses

In all cases the original simple sentence that the noun clause presupposes should be thought out. The tense of the indicative in the original direct statement will give the correct tense of the infinitive in a Latin indirect statement. In an indirect question the force of an English past tense thus becomes clear at once, e.g. with 'I asked where his brother lived' the direct question 'Where does he live?' points to *habitaret*, while with 'He could not say when they arrived' the direct question 'When did they arrive?' points to *pervenissent*. In indirect command it is important to decide whether the original direct command was a second person or third person one; e.g. 'He ordered the doctor to depart', *medico imperavit ut abiret* (original *abi*), but 'He ordered the doctor to be called in', *imperavit ut medicus adhiberetur* (original *medicus adhibeatur*).

Participle Constructions

The main difficulty that arises is the translation into Latin of an English expression that contains a perfect participle active. The often-given advice 'if in doubt, use *cum*' is a counsel of despair that is not calculated to produce idiomatic Latin. The following method of dealing with this problem is suggested:

The pupil should first answer the question 'Is the English perfect participle active transitive or intransitive?' He should then proceed on these lines:

Participle Intransitive

*I*1. Literal translation, if possible, by the perfect participle of a deponent verb. Example: '*Having advanced* to the gate, I tried to enter' (*progressus*).

*I*2. If this is impossible, no participle is available, and a clause (*cum, ubi, post quam*) must be used. Example: '*Having come* to the gate I tried to enter' (*cum...venissem, ubi...veni, post quam...veni*).

Participle Transitive

*T*1. Literal translation, if possible, as with *I*1. Example: '*Having attacked* our column, they were driven back into the woods' (*adorti*).

*T*2. If this is impossible, a Latin perfect participle passive should be used if one is available. This is the most complicated category, and it is dealt with separately below.

*T*3. Only when neither a deponent perfect participle nor a perfect participle passive is available must a clause be used. Examples: '*Having pardoned* the rest, he put the ringleaders to death' (*cum... ignovisset*; 'pardon' is transitive, but *ignosco* is not). '*Having learnt* the poem, he recited it without a mistake' (*cum...didicisset*; *disco* is transitive, but happens to be deficient in supine-stem forms).

Once it has been decided that *T*2 is the right category, further inspection of the sentence is necessary to see whether the object of the English perfect participle active is subsequently referred to by means of a pronoun.

(i) If it is not, then the mental replacement of English perfect participle active by English perfect participle passive will produce an 'absolute' phrase; therefore, the ablative absolute must be used. Example: 'Having captured the city, they returned home' (*urbe capta*; 'the city having been captured' is absolute, as 'city' is not subsequently referred to in the sentence).

(ii) If it is, then the first step is to replace the pronoun by the object of the participle, and translate the main sentence accordingly: the second step is to add the Latin perfect participle passive in agreement with the noun to which it refers. Examples:

'Having taken the city, they burnt *it*' (first step, 'they burnt the city', *urbem...incenderunt*; second step, *urbem captam incenderunt*).

'Having killed Hector, he dragged *his* body round the walls' (first step, 'he dragged Hector's body...', *Hectoris...corpus...traxit*; second step, *Hectoris interfecti corpus...traxit*).

'Having sent for the soldier, he gave *him* a reward' (first step, 'he gave the soldier a reward, *militi...praemium dedit*; second step, *militi arcessito praemium dedit*).

Participial catechism. The following catechism repeated *ad gaudium* has been found effective:

QUESTION	ANSWER
1. What part of speech?	1. Past participle.
2. Active or passive?	2. Active: if passive, go from 7.
3. Is there an active past participle in Latin?	3. No—except in the case of deponent verbs.
4. Is this a deponent verb?	4. No: if Yes, go from 7.
5. What must we do?	5. Change it to passive.
6. Can we do so?	6. Yes: if no, thus: (There is no active, and we cannot use a passive participle. What must we do? *Ans.* Use *cum*.)
7. Does it agree with subject, object, or indirect object, or any other word?	7. If Yes If No
8. What case must it be?	8. Nom. Gen. Acc. Dat. Abl.
9. Is there an unnecessary pronoun?	9. If Yes—
10. What happens to it?	10. Goes out.

Gerunds and Gerundives

A. *Gerundive Attraction*

The cardinal principles are these:

(*a*) The gerundive is part of the passive voice; so a Latin intransitive verb cannot normally have a gerundive.

(*b*) English transitive gerunds can govern objects without restriction; Latin transitive gerunds can do so in special circumstances only.

From (*a*) it follows that an English transitive gerund can and must be translated by a Latin gerund if the corresponding Latin verb does not govern an accusative-object. Examples: 'By sparing the conquered', *victis parcendo*. 'The art of using an opportunity', *ars occasione utendi*. (Exceptional gerundives such as *utendis* should form no part of a pupil's knowledge prior to advanced course work.)

The problem presented by (*b*) can be dealt with by teaching the normal ('gerundive attraction') construction as follows:

First step. In translating such a phrase as 'desirous of seeing the city', observe that the literal translation *cupidus urbem videndi* will not serve because it contains a gerund governing an accusative-object.

Second step. Change the English so that the object of the gerund stands in the same construction as the gerund did in the original form, and translate accordingly: e.g. start not with 'desirous of seeing' but with 'desirous of the city', *cupidus urbis*.

Third step. Add the gerundive, agreeing in gender, number and case like any other adjective: e.g. 'desirous of the city to-be-seen', *cupidus urbis videndae*.

The only exception worth emphasizing prior to advanced course work is that gerund + accusative-object is used in connexion with neuter words where the gerundive construction would cause ambiguity; e.g. 'desirous of seeing this', *hoc videndi cupidus*, because *huius videndi cupidus* would naturally mean 'desirous of seeing this man'.

It should be mentioned that a phrase such as *cupidus castrorum videndorum* represents Cicero's normal idiom. The fact that Caesar did not like repetition of *-orum* or *-arum*, and so preferred the gerund construction here, does not seem adequate justification for elevating his preference into a hard-and-fast rule.

(The more general use of genitive or ablative gerund + accusative-object, like Livy's *agros vastando*, should certainly be postponed to the advanced course stage.)

B. *Obligation Constructions*

Whatever may be the actual origin of the construction seen in *mihi eundum est*, it is reasonably certain that a Roman using present-day language would describe *eundum* here as a gerund and not as an impersonal-passive gerundive. Arguments for this are well set forth in the preface to Vol. II of Roby's larger *Latin Grammar*: and the adoption of this view for actual teaching purposes has the advantage of making the dative appear quite natural: 'there is a going for me (to do)', i.e. 'I must go'. (It can then be explained that this use of the dative was mechanically extended to gerundive obligation sentences.)

The following has been found a convenient sequence for teaching these obligation constructions:

(1) Start with the literal 'Carthage is to-be-destroyed', *Carthago delenda est* (with references to English words such as 'memorandum', 'agenda', etc., and 'Q.E.D.').

(2) Vary the English of such passive sentences—'Carthage ought to be destroyed', 'Carthage must be destroyed', etc. At this point, other tenses than the present indicative of *sum* can be introduced.

(3) Introduce the dative of the person obliged (postponing specific explanation till (6) is reached), still keeping the sentences passive— 'Carthage ought to be destroyed by Scipio', *Carthago Scipioni delenda est*.

(4) At this point bring in English obligation sentences of active form. Give the rule that such sentences must be changed into passive form before translating, and the warnings that this method can be used only when (*a*) the English obligation sentence contains an object, AND (*b*) when the Latin verb is transitive and can therefore have a gerundive. Example: 'Scipio ought to destroy Carthage' (='Carthage ought to be destroyed by Scipio'), *Carthago Scipioni delenda est*.

(5) Revise (1) to (4), and introduce the construction in accusative-

and-infinitive form. (It may be of interest to note that if the governing verb is not one of 'saying', omission of the infinitive *esse* is almost invariable; e.g. *tempus non terendum existimavit*, where the insertion of *esse* would be an offence against idiom.)

(6) Start on English obligation sentences with intransitive verbs, leading off with, e.g. 'I ought to go' (='there is a going for me'), *mihi eundum est*.

(7) Show that English passive sentences must be treated in the same way if the corresponding Latin verb is not transitive—'Force must be used' (='there is a using force'), *vi utendum est*.

(8) Bring back the dative of the person obliged by passing on to English active sentences of the same type—'We must use force' (='there is a using force for us (to do)'), *vi nobis utendum est*.

(9) Point out that when a verb that governs a dative is used, the presence of two datives MAY cause ambiguity. If such ambiguity would be caused, the ordinary agent-construction is used instead of the dative of the person obliged; e.g. 'You must persuade your brother', *fratri tuo a te persuadendum est*. If ambiguity does not arise, the two datives must stand; e.g. 'You must obey the laws', *legibus tibi parendum est* (*a te* here would be entirely unidiomatic).

(10) Revise (6) to (9), and introduce the construction in accusative-and-infinitive form, noting omission of *esse* as in (5).

Prospective Time Clauses

A. '*Until*'

The conjunctions meaning 'until' may be followed by a perfect or future perfect indicative denoting an action that did take place or will definitely take place. Examples:

'Until Marcellus returned, there was silence' (*donec...rediit*).
'I shall stay here until I know the truth' (*dum...sciero*). In this use *donec* and *quoad* are commoner than *dum*.

But to denote an action that is purposed or looked forward to, a prospective subjunctive is used, normally present or imperfect according to sequence. Examples:

'Let us wait until reinforcements come' (*dum...veniant*).
'They were waiting for reinforcements to come' (='until reinforcements should come', *dum...venirent*). In this use *dum* is far commoner than *donec* or *quoad*.

These prospective clauses are more easily understood by pupils if it is pointed out that the subjunctive in them has the same force as in an ordinary clause of purpose; *dum* + subjunctive is roughly equivalent to *ut interim* + subjunctive. As the pupil will have learnt to associate present and imperfect subjunctives only with clauses of purpose, it is important to leave unmentioned the occasional use of perfect and past perfect subjunctives in these *dum* clauses until the advanced course stage is reached.

B. '*Before*'

Ante quam and *prius quam* are ordinarily followed by an indicative verb; but *prius quam* (seldom *ante quam*) is followed by a prospective subjunctive if it is desired to denote that the action of the main verb takes place not before something does happen but before something has the chance to happen. Examples: 'We must depart before they come' (*prius quam veniant*); 'They burst in before the gates could be closed' (*prius quam. . .clauderentur*).

Again the similarity to an ordinary clause of purpose can be pointed out: *prius quam* + subjunctive is roughly equivalent to *ne interim* + subjunctive.

Conditional Sentences with Subjunctive in both Clauses

These furnish the one occasion on which it seems justifiable to spare some time on a rarely-used construction as a preliminary stepping-stone. If the use of *utinam* with present, imperfect, and past perfect subjunctive is mastered in advance, it is then easy to start off with a table like the following:

WISH	CONDITIONAL SENTENCE
(1) O that he may come! *utinam veniat!*	(1) If he were to come, I should rejoice. *si veniat, gaudeam.*
(2) O that he were coming! *utinam veniret!*	(2) If he were coming, I should be rejoicing. *si veniret, gauderem.*
(3) O that he had come! *utinam venisset!*	(3) If he had come, I should have rejoiced. *si venisset, gavisus essem.*

After observing that in these normal types the tense of the subjunctive is the same in both clauses, and that the English of the main clause always contains 'should' or 'would', plenty of practice is advisable before passing on to the following refinements:

(a) Variations in the English if-clause of type (1): 'If he were to come', 'If he should come', 'If he came'.

(b) If-clause and main clause referring to different times: 'If you had obeyed me then, you would not be in trouble now'.

(c) Use of imperfect in type (3) to denote continuous action or a continuous state of affairs in the past: 'If you had been alive then' (*si tum viveres*).

2. THE DIRECT METHOD

'Besides, 'tis known he could speak Greek
As naturally as pigs squeak:
That Latin was no more difficile
Than to a blackbird 'tis to whistle.'
(SAMUEL BUTLER, *Hudibras*)

Direct method, or rather the use of Latin as the medium of instruction, may fairly claim to have been the 'traditional' method of teaching the language, at least until the end of the eighteenth century. Its reapplication arose out of the dissatisfaction felt by many teachers in the early years of the twentieth century with the poor quality and unreality of much of the work done in Latin in school. The adaptation of direct method, which was recognized as practicable and was widely used as a method of teaching Modern Languages, to the teaching of Classics was due to the genius of W. H. D. Rouse, Headmaster of the Perse School, Cambridge, and of his staff W. H. S. Jones and R. B. Appleton. An account of their work may be found in the Board of Education Pamphlets, Nos. 20 and 28.

The movement spread fairly widely in this country, and direct method was enthusiastically adopted by a number of public schools and a larger number of grammar schools, both boys' and girls'. Despite the setbacks of two world wars, the movement, fostered in particular by the Association for the Reform of Latin Teaching,

6-2

has continued to flourish, and at present there is considerable interest in the method among teachers dissatisfied with their former teaching methods and keenly aware of the need for improvement if the teaching of Classics is to hold its own in the curriculum of the grammar schools.

Direct method, in brief, is an attempt to teach a foreign language in a way most closely approximating to that by which we learn our native tongue; that is, by imitation and by the gradual building up of a vocabulary and a method of expression directly associated with an object, an act or an idea that we ourselves have seen or experienced. On this method the pupils are led from the first to employ the language as a spoken tongue. The co-operation of the pupils can be secured because direct method appeals to two natural impulses, the impulse to understand and the impulse towards self-expression. Accordingly the emphasis is on oral work, particularly at the beginning of the course.

Direct method is built up on four major processes: imitation; repetition; association; and induction—in that order. The master will introduce the pupils to a particular point of accidence or syntax by a suitable demonstration of the point himself; this is imitated by the pupils and continually repeated by means of a 'drill' devised for the purpose, sufficiently frequently for the point to become almost automatic; parallels are then drawn and alternative methods of expression employed to encourage the association of ideas; and finally, under the guidance of the master, the pupils are led to induce the rules for themselves and to express them in words they can readily understand.

Grammar is thus taught inductively and not deductively; tabulation and learning by rote come after oral practice and not before. It is necessary to stress that tabulation, analysis of accidence and syntax, and learning by rote are as essential with the direct method as with any other method. A language of the complexity of Latin cannot be 'picked up', nor can the discipline of hard work be avoided. Constant testing, preferably daily, is essential to ensure that knowledge of the 'bones' of the language is not woolly or vague.

Translation into English as a means of learning the language is abandoned; for it is felt that translation is more of a test of English style than an aid to learning Latin. This is done partly to avoid the 'translationese' that is so often produced at an early stage, and partly to save time for wider reading. The pupil's comprehension can be tested by oral questioning in Latin, and by paraphrase in Latin, all of which means that more and more Latin is being heard and being used in the classroom. An occasional translation can be called for as a test, if any doubt remains about the pupils' comprehension, but as a rule this is not necessary. Later, translation must be taught as an art in itself, and this at a stage when the pupil is beginning to have some mastery of English style and can produce a translation and not merely a construe.

English-Latin sentences are used not for teaching grammatical or syntactical points but as a final process at each stage for testing the pupils' understanding of the particular point being taught. The chief composition work in the first two years is the continual use of Latin in the classroom. Every Latin sentence spoken by a boy on his own initiative is itself an exercise in composition.

Finally, it is important that the material used at each stage should be at the level of the pupils' understanding. In the early stages the subject-matter is drawn from the pupils' own world and is in as concrete a form as possible. That is to say that for a twelve-year-old boy *Magister discipulos baculo longo pulsat* is more of a living reality than *Regina insulam amat*. Not that boys mind dealing with the latter type of sentence—there is the joy that comes from getting a thing right—but it is important to take the 'stuffiness' out of Latin, to eliminate the later criticism so frequently heard, 'What I learnt in Latin at school was all about queens loving islands'. If the pupil is later to regard Latin as having something worth while to say, then it is important that at each stage the language should be a living reality and not merely a verbal jigsaw. Yet, as the course progresses, the school world must be left behind and be replaced by the realities of Caesar's and Cicero's world when the pupils are really ready for them.

The object of the first two years' work in Latin on the direct method is to teach the mechanics of the language, to teach Latin

73

as a 'technique' rather than a 'subject'. Accordingly background
—an essential part of the full Latin course—is incidental at this
stage and not a primary object. What is essential is that in these
two years the pupils should cover the main field of Latin accidence
and syntax, acquire a feeling for the language, and be ready at the
end of them to begin tackling a Latin author. A thorough treatment of classical background comes in the second two years
when, it is found, pupils begin to ask about it. Then the best
method of teaching it has been found to be through as wide
a range of reading as possible rather than by special background
lessons, although an occasional lesson of this type can be very
helpful.

The following is the outline syllabus of a four or five years'
course of direct method:

First year:

Accidence. All tenses of the active indicative. All five declensions.
Numbers. Pronouns. Infinitive. Present participle. Common irregular
nouns and verbs. All types of adjectives. Comparatives and super-
latives.

Syntax. The simple sentence. Relative clauses and simple conditionals
with the indicative. *Quod, quia, dum, post quam* and *ante quam.* Comparison. Time, place and space. Impersonal verbs with the infinitive.
Iubeo.

Second year:

Accidence. All tenses of the passive. Subjunctive all tenses, active
and passive. Deponents. Principal parts. Further irregular nouns and
verbs.

Syntax. The complex sentence: indirect command, purpose,
gerund and gerundive, indirect speech, indirect question, subordinate
clauses in *oratio obliqua*, ablative absolute, consecutives, verbs of fearing,
conditionals.

Third year:

Revision and expansion of the accidence and syntax of the first two
years. The transition to 'real' Latin. Original composition. Latin
debates. Repetition of Latin poetry. Latin authors, e.g. Catullus and
Caesar. Background.

Fourth year:

Unseens. Elementary proses. More Latin authors. The necessary work for an examination, if taken this year.

Fifth year:

If a fifth year is given, and this is to be urged, then further reading is possible and a slightly more generous time allowance can be given to each of the earlier stages.

Greek is usually begun after two years of Latin. The same principles are followed although naturally the rate of progress is much faster. The language used orally and the material read can be more literary since the boys are ready for it. In the first year the reading material will be made-up Greek, based on mythology and the famous stories of Greek history and literature, and in the second year Greek authors themselves. If a third year is available, and this is to be strongly advocated, the course can be less rushed, wider reading is possible and more time can be spent in exploring some of the byways of classical learning.

In the Sixth Form all the customary practices of Sixth-Form teaching will have to be followed. That is to say, a good deal of the work will be done in English, the teaching of prose and verse composition, of unseens, of ancient history and literature, and, if need be, of set books. In particular the art of translation, begun in the pre-Sixth year, must be developed; but even at this stage much of the reading can and should be done with commentary in Latin and Greek without the need for translation. It is here, more than anywhere else in the course, that the direct method approach will save time and enable a wide range of literature to be read. Few can hope to emulate Dr Rouse; but for what can be achieved at this stage, the teacher is referred to *Scenes from Sixth Form Life* by W. H. D. Rouse.

It is necessary to point out that, as in all methods of teaching Latin, there are a number of dangers and difficulties that the teacher must be on his guard against. There is, for example, the danger that the teacher will do all the talking in Latin. It is important that the pupils should use the language themselves as much as possible. Explanations of new words can usually be elicited from the boys once the principle of so doing is established.

It is necessary, too, that the teacher's pronunciation should be good. The important thing is not so much that every sound should be pedantically in accordance with the ancient pronunciation as that the teacher's pronunciation should be clear and should distinguish things that differ. This is particularly essential when so much of the work is oral. The so-called 'modern' pronunciation is therefore to be recommended both in Latin and Greek. In Greek the exponent of the direct method would advocate the pronunciation of accents, by no means as difficult as is often alleged.

There is, too, the danger of self-deception on the part of the teacher, the danger of assuming that things are fully known when they are only half understood. It is not enough that the class should be babbling infant Latin; constant tests both oral and written are necessary to ensure exact scholarship. On the other hand there is the danger that the teacher will expect perfect accuracy at once. Direct method is not a cure for all ills. Mistakes will occur on this as on any other method. It is important to remember that all conjugations and at least three declensions are met with in the first few weeks, and time is needed for all this to be thoroughly assimilated and sorted out. The teacher must remember the old precept *Littera scripta manet*. Mistakes on this method are for the most part made orally and are therefore more easily eliminated. Written homework, particularly English-Latin sentences, must be carefully prepared in class to avoid, as far as possible, the writing down of mistakes.

There is the danger of 'dog-Latin', and some more austere teachers have felt that they could not run this risk. However, this is not as common as might be expected, and can easily be discouraged by the teacher by taking the appropriate action at the first sign of any slapdash Latin on the part of the pupils. Free composition in the first two years is not wise policy, as the boys will attempt what is beyond them in vocabulary and idiom.

It is unquestionably true that direct method makes greater demands on the teacher. He must be alive all the time, stimulating and encouraging self-expression by the pupils. Lessons must be carefully prepared to avoid haphazardness, and the course must be planned as a whole so that seeds may be sown to bear fruit perhaps as much as a year or more later. Furthermore, the discipline in the form room must be both comparatively free and at the same time well under control so that order is obtainable immediately.

If direct method demands a lot from the teacher it is only fair to ask if the effort is worth while. Those who use this method would claim in the first place that by means of it Latin and Greek cease to be viewed as dead languages, with the consequent greater enjoyment of pupil and teacher. The essence of the method is variety, and where so much must be forthcoming from the pupils there is little risk of monotony and its deadening effects. Demanding as it does the active co-operation of the pupils, it stimulates spontaneity and encourages a constructive and independent frame of mind. Its training in association is a considerable help in the appreciation of literature, and it is undoubtedly true that its greater pace enables a wider range of literature to be read, without any loss in exactness of scholarship. Above all, the boys undoubtedly do enjoy their Latin, and are more ready to put up with the hard work that Latin must necessarily demand and without which no subject is worth while.

Direct method, professing as it does to be an improvement on other methods, must meet and face certain criticisms. It has often been said that direct method ignores the grammar. Nothing could be further from the truth. No method could succeed in teaching Latin if it tried to ignore grammar. Grammar must be learnt as thoroughly by this as by any other method; the difference is that learning by heart comes after practice and not before. It is true, however, that the advocates of the direct method, in common with most modern teachers of Latin, would postpone the learning of oddities, such as the genitive singular of *supellex*, if learnt they must be.

Another criticism takes this form: 'A word that needs several seconds to explain in Latin can be explained in English in one.' Sometimes English is essential, particularly when dealing with abstract ideas. There must be no hesitation about using English, prefaced by 'Anglice', if time really can, on a long-term view, be saved. Usually, however, the time is well spent, since Latin is being used all the time and the pupils are hearing and using more Latin for themselves. Moreover, a grammatical point can often be fixed in the pupils' minds for ever by a good explanation or example.

'The value of Latin is that it helps to improve the pupils' English; the practice of not translating into English must mean the loss of this.' The truth is that in the early stages the pupils' English is usually so poor that the result of translation is merely translationese, and a bad translation spoils rather than improves their English. The direct method teacher would say that it is better to keep translation until fairly late, when the pupils have some idea how to use their own language and can appreciate the difference between a good and bad translation. In fact it is the study of Latin as a whole that helps to improve English, not the isolated act of translation.

Again it is often asserted that the direct method means the employment of words that are non-Caesarian or non-Ciceronian. To this it can be objected that the aim is surely not to teach a 'Basic Latin', to limit oneself to words that occur in only two of the many Latin authors, and only to the commonest 1000 or so of these. It is true that if the subject-matter is at the beginning to be the world of the class-room, then some words will not by the nature of things be found on every page of the *Gallic Wars*. The risk of a so-called 'impurity' is worth taking for the gain in living reality. In fact the risk is negligible. There is little or no danger that such words learnt previously will mar the purity of pupils' Latin proses when they come to do them in the Sixth Form. For they will have long grown out of them, and every teacher knows from experience that even the commonest words need constant use to be remembered.

'What about derivations?' is a question often asked. The value of derivations is the spotting of one by a pupil for himself. It is of little value to tell a boy that 'lachrymose' is derived from *lacrima* if, as is so often true, he has never heard of the English word before and is never likely to use it. The delight in spotting derivations is as common under direct method as under any other method. 'Licetne mihi dicere Anglice? Please, sir, does "patriotism" come from "patria"?' 'Ita, Marce. Bene dixisti. Pergamus.'

'Only teachers taught that way themselves can do it.' It is true that it is difficult for beginners not taught this way themselves, but, if it is worth doing, it is worth the effort involved. In fact the difficulty rapidly disappears, and many teachers in this position have proved very successful with direct method.

'I began it with the second year but it wasn't at all successful.' While it is true that certain features of the direct method can be adapted to other methods, it is impossible to switch methods completely in mid-stream. Pupils initiated into Latin on other methods usually find it difficult to adapt themselves to the change, although the converse is, perhaps, not so true.

It is often argued that it is impossible to deal with literary, historical and general background if the lessons are conducted entirely in Latin. It is, however, surprising how much commentary can be done in Latin; but in this matter too, if English is necessary, then there should be no hesitation in using it. Occasional lessons entirely in English are to be recommended.

Finally, the Report of the Prime Minister's Committee on the Teaching of Latin in *The Classics in Education* (1923) found that direct method was not a panacea and could not recommend its general adoption. No method is or ever can be a general cure for all the ills of classical teaching. It is important to remember that direct method is applicable in as many ways as there are teachers, and one of its virtues is that it is not stereotyped. Many of its details can be adapted to other methods, and it is remarkable how many of the principal features of direct method, the modern pronunciation, the stress on reading aloud and on oral work, and the simplification of necessary accidence, are now common ground, shared by other methods.

The author of one recent non-direct method text-book has called the direct method a 'high adventure'. Its successes can bear comparison with other methods, and at the very least it is an adventure that deserves investigation.

3. The Word Order Method

What has been called the 'word order' method of Latin teaching may be considered a modern method, although some parts of the method are by no means new. It was developed in America on lines laid down by Mason Gray and Appleton in their *Teaching of Latin* (1929). The method had a great vogue in America, and text-books based thereon have proved very popular in this country.

The main principles are first, that pupils should be trained from the very beginning to take in the thought of the Latin in the Latin order, before translating, as a result of which the study of syntax is made subordinate to the comprehension of the reading matter, which must be provided in abundance. Secondly, the reading matter, in dealing with Roman life, tradition, heroic legends and classical mythology, is designed, with the assistance of ample illustrations, to make the pupil feel that he is in touch with a great civilization which has left its imprint upon his language, his thoughts and the world in which he lives.

The principle of taking in the thought of the Latin in its given order, and of suspending judgement on the meaning until the whole has been read, is one that has long had its adherents. By dispensing with the formal analysis into subject, verb and object, etc., so often insisted on by upholders of the traditional method, it seems to lay less stress on the learning of accidence and syntax, and to subordinate the learning of formal grammar to the understanding of the reading matter. Indeed, it is the reading matter which dictates the rate and sequence of introduction of new forms. It should be said that very detailed explanation usually accompanies each new form and construction. Nevertheless, although there is much emphasis in text-books using this method on parsing and on the completion of skeleton sentences, there is so much preoccupation with Latin-English that the proportion of English-Latin sentences is necessarily diminished, and translation into Latin plays a less important part than it does in the traditional method. On the other hand, with a wealth of reading matter, the pupil proceeds from specially constructed passages to passages adapted from authors, constantly building up a large store of 'background' knowledge.

The emphasis is on *reading* the Latin, preferably by the pupil and aloud. The teacher must frequently prepare the way by reading the Latin to the class, stressing the 'thought-groups' into which the sentences naturally fall, e.g. the group of words forming the subject, the object or the adverbial modifications. The general story must be kept clearly in mind, so that the translation of the thought-groups may fit the logical sequence. A second or third reading of the Latin may be necessary to enable the pupil to grasp the connexion. In the early stages it will often be enough to limit this understanding to the thought of a single sentence.

The difficulty in getting the thought of the Latin lies in new words and new forms of words. As for the latter, it is essential that constant drill be given in accidence and in such syntax as case-uses, so that there is instant recognition of the part played by a word or group of words in the thought of the sentence. 'The study of Latin may be said to be a study of endings' (Introduction, *Latin for Today*). As for the new words, there are three ways of solving the difficulty: (i) sensible guessing; (ii) English derivatives; (iii) related Latin words. Only when these methods have failed should the vocabulary be used.

When the Latin becomes more complex and the reading of a passage does not give all the thought, it is necessary to go over the Latin word by word or group by group, consciously determining the meaning of each new word by looking it up and noting the form and all the possible uses of a new word or group of words.

For the teacher using (for example) *Latin for Today* there appear to be these essentials:

(i) A thorough knowledge of the new lesson.

(ii) Ruthless determination to confine himself to essentials—this depends to some extent on the standard of the form.

(iii) An exact appreciation of the relative importance of the rather bewildering multiplicity of usages liable to be introduced into *any* lesson.

(iv) An insistence on careful work at all times—even more necessary than in the traditional method.

(v) Care that the whole class is taking part in the lesson, especially as in this method one pupil occupies more time than he would in other methods.

The advantages claimed for this method are as follows. In the early stages the interest of the pupil is roused by the abundant connected reading matter in a way that the disjointed and frequently artificial English sentences of the traditional method could hardly hope to achieve. The introduction of new words in an enlightening context is both a stimulus to sensible guessing and an aid to memory. The deduction of new grammatical rules and constructions from their previously observed functioning in the specially constructed passages is a more sensible and natural approach. The understanding of the Latin in the Latin order, when properly achieved, enables the pupil to read more rapidly on reaching his full-dress Latin authors.

Criticisms of the method are often laid less appropriately at the door of the method itself than of the text-books which exemplify it. It is not, for instance, essential to its success that each new construction should be accompanied by long printed explanations, as if all that was required of the teacher were an ability to read aloud. A mass of explanatory and, sometimes, diversionary material may often have only the effect of smothering the explanation, which should stand out prominently, in simple clarity. It is better usually to leave within the discretion of the teacher the amount of background material that is to accompany each step forward, for this will vary with the ability of the class—but it is bad policy to tell a class that sections of a book may be ignored. Again, where the reading matter dictates the sequence of the constructions, a haphazard order may result. One text-book, for instance, pokes sections on the dative and the gerund in between the present and the imperfect subjunctive. Another danger is that a large amount of simplified Latin, presented in the early stages to impressionable minds, will permanently 'obscure the Latin thought-pattern and the true genius of the language for subordination rather than co-ordination' (H. K. Hunt). At any rate, too long a lingering on the first and second declensions and on one or two tenses of the active verb for the sake of translation may weary that very interest it is hoped to arouse. Perhaps most serious of all is the lack of sufficient translation into Latin. Too often it leads to a slapdash attitude of mind, easily satisfied with the blurred appreciation of inflexions, an opportunist's grab at a few key-words in the sentence, and a happy-go-lucky attempt at stringing them together in some sort of sense that owes nothing to care and accuracy. In fact such carelessness may be traced to the method itself. For the principle of 'suspended judgement' unfortunately demands too great an effort from a very young mind, and if this effort is not forthcoming the consequence will be that wild guessing, based on an English word-order and complete neglect of grammatical form, frequently results. This is not to deny that, when the peculiarities of the Latin word-order and the idiosyncrasies of a flexional language have been thoroughly grasped, the principle of 'suspended judgement' will prove indispensable in the interests of translating connected Latin more fluently.

4. Some Do's and Don't's in Learning, Marking and Testing

1. Grammar must be learnt as thoroughly as multiplication tables, so that a required form may come to the mind without conscious searching.

2. Grammar should be chorused in class. Don't let too tender a care for correct stress spoil the rhythm of the chorusing.

3. The use of coloured chalks on the blackboard and an effective lay-out are powerful aids to memory.

4. Give a few minutes daily to the oral revision of grammar.

5. Homework for juniors should be mainly learning work. A high standard of achievement must be insisted on from the outset.

6. Test grammar occasionally by standing boys round the room, passing questions from boy to boy, moving correct answerers up, and giving marks for the final positions.

7. Have a thorough-paced system of marks as an incentive.

8. Mark oral work, and even translation, in your mark-book, telling the boy at the end of his piece the mark he has gained.

9. Ensure by your mark system that each boy gets his fair share of the translation.

10. Never allow a boy to anticipate that he will be put on to translate, but vary the pace between the fast and the slow.

11. Competitive games (e.g. Romani *v.* Barbari) may serve as a powerful stimulant. Questions may be set by opposing teams.

12. Give boys Latin names suggested by their own names, to increase vocabulary and knowledge of declensions.

13. Always have marks given up in Latin, occasionally multiplied by 10 or 100, or given in as ordinals or multiplicatives.

14. Never assume that your first-year Latin set is familiar with grammatical terminology, or indeed with any English grammar at all.

15. In marking sentences mark straightforward sentences at first either right or wrong, but later mark more difficult sentences with four or five marks, so that you may be able to differentiate between the kind of mistake made, and also hold out some hope to the desperate.

16. Go over exercises again on the board, and insist on corrections (the whole sentence) being copied out carefully.

17. English-Latin sentences can frequently be prepared at home and written out in class.

18. Preparation of new translation should involve the compilation of vocabulary of new words.

19. Vocabularies should be periodically inspected by the master, and any slipshod entries should earn a severe reprobation.

20. By the setting of periodic tests ensure that such vocabularies are thoroughly learned.

V

CLASSICS IN THE SIXTH FORM

'Mox cum matura adoleverit aetas
Sis memor.'   (VIRGIL)

THE abolition of the School Certificate Examination removed, at least for a time, the clear dividing line between the main school and the Sixth Form. Its successor, the examination for the General Certificate of Education, is at the time of writing in an experimental stage. The regulations have already been modified, and may be still further modified before the new system assumes a stable form.

Broadly speaking, however, we may expect advanced studies to begin in the fifth or sixth year of the secondary school course. It is the practice in most schools for boys to spend two years in a course leading to the Advanced Level in the General Certificate of Education. Some thereafter will spend an extra year in preparation for university entrance scholarships. It is on these assumptions that we describe the organization of classical teaching in the Sixth Form. We are aware of a school of thought which would claim that there is no essential difference between the Sixth Form and any other form in that it represents but the final stage of an eight-year course. While, however, it is still the practice for the majority of boys to leave at the age of sixteen, conscious and purposeful specialization will rarely begin before that age. This very fact, apart from the greater responsibility and freedom accorded to a boy's ripening powers, makes the problem of teaching in the Sixth Form an entirely different one. We make no apology, therefore, for giving a separate and special chapter to Classics in the Sixth Form.

1. Types of Sixth-Form Course

Pupils taking Latin and Greek may be classified in three main groups:

(i) Those taking Latin and Greek with Ancient History in a full classical course.

(ii) Those taking Latin (perhaps Greek in rare cases) at Advanced Level with 'modern' subjects, e.g. English, Modern Languages, History.

(iii) A few taking Latin as a qualifying subject for matriculation.

Difficulties frequently arise because in all but a few large schools with a strong classical tradition Group (i) is usually so small as to make it uneconomic or even impossible to teach it separately from Group (ii). Although boys in both these groups may be at the beginning of the Sixth-Form course of level attainment, boys taking Latin in a full classical course soon outpace their contemporaries taking Latin with modern subjects. This is to be expected, and it is desirable if they are to reach the high standard demanded from classical scholars. But it sets up such a strain in the class-room that where it is at all possible the two groups should be kept separate. Where nevertheless groups have to be taken in combination, it is desirable that compensation in the form of extra periods should be allotted to boys whose work is thus retarded. This is no trivial matter, for the bracketing is frequently longitudinal as well as lateral, and it is no unusual occurrence for Upper and Lower Sixth Classical and Modern to be taught in one heterogeneous clump. We realize that this is probably inevitable, and do not therefore complain; but it should be borne in mind that an allowance of twenty-one or twenty-two periods for the full classical course is in the circumstances a less generous allowance of time than would appear at first sight. There is always in fact a tendency to regard Ancient History as an appendage to Latin and Greek, and to give three subjects the time-table allowance of two. Lack of man-power may necessitate a cut in the teaching periods allotted to Ancient History, but the cut should never be accepted with complaisance.

For the guidance of those who are organizing Sixth-Form courses in Classics we suggest the following weekly allocations of periods:

(i) Full classical course:
Greek, at least seven taught periods.
Latin, at least seven taught periods if taken separately, but where there is much merging, ten periods of which at least four should be taken separately.
Ancient History, not less than four, but preferably six periods.
(ii) Latin (or Greek) as one of a group of modern subjects to Advanced Level, at least seven taught periods.
(iii) Latin (or Greek) to Ordinary Level as a qualifying subject for university entrance. Probably four periods is all that can be expected at this stage, although beginners will need a generous private study allowance.

(i) *Full Classical Course*

Language

If pupils have been rightly selected we may assume that the elements of accidence and syntax in both Greek and Latin have been mastered. In the first year amplification and revision (particularly of the Greek accidence) will, however, be necessary, and occasional tests on elementary grammar may be both revealing and salutary. Thus, although the tools should have been fashioned in the main school course, there will have been little time so far to put them to use. As a general rule, boys entering the Sixth Form will have read comparatively little unadapted Latin and Greek literature; their technique in translation into English, even if accurate, will rarely be fluent. Their knowledge of idiom and vocabulary will be small. Furthermore, save in a few exceptional cases, little if any genuine prose composition will have been done, for proses done in the main school course are usually groups of sentences composed to exemplify specific constructions and strung together in the form of a continuous narrative.

The two main objects of the first year's work will therefore be to give in the first place increased facility in the technique and art of translation. This will involve introducing pupils to some

87   7-2

of the masters of Greek and Latin literature, with whom they have had little or no acquaintance. The choice of books read will depend to some extent on the taste of the teacher and the aptitude of the pupils. It is desirable, however, that the choice be planned to fit in with and supplement later reading, particularly the books prescribed in the Certificate Examination for the following year. In the second place the aim of the teacher will be to bridge the gap between sentences or synthetic proses and prose composition in the proper sense of the term, that is, the expression in idiomatic Latin or Greek of the essential meaning of a passage of 'undoctored' English prose. Thus during the first year boys will have been introduced to the basic principles and technique of prose composition, further progress depending upon practice and the growing knowledge of Latin and Greek usage, idiom and vocabulary which comes from wider reading.

In the second year much of the time allotted to translation work will be given to the preparation of set books, but the teacher should resist the temptation to play for short-term safety by over-meticulous revision and re-revision in class periods. With an eye to the wide reading essential to the making of a scholar, he should find time to do something off the examination syllabus. Such reading may be utilitarian in purpose, as for instance the reading of other works by the prescribed authors in order to give depth to the knowledge of the set books; or it may be diversionary—the *Odyssey*, for instance, or some Herodotus. The set books should be tackled with precision and thoroughness, no mercy being shown to slovenly or inaccurate translation or woolly commentary. Nor is the intensive and analytic study of a work of literature necessarily a process of murder and dissection, as some would assert. Translation can be as much an act of creative interpretation as the playing of a piece of music, and like all creative activities it is enjoyed for its own sake. Suggestions on translation will be found elsewhere, but it should be said here that the teacher should, as far as possible, let his pupils do the work; the pride and joy of creation should be theirs.

In the hands of an uninterested teacher—and the mood is quick to communicate itself to the boys—syntax can become a bugbear, and at the best a dull cataloguing and labelling of dry bones. The process of pairing off parallel gobbets and dubbing them with the dusty titles of the grammatical hierarchy (e.g. ...*lapsus rotarum*; gen. of definition; cf. ...*clipeique insigne decorum*) is apt to become a mechanical technique of doubtful value. Yet it should not be so. Close examination of the way in which writers use, and vary the use of, the machinery of language to express the subtle moods and movements of the human mind and heart is as essential to a true assessment and understanding of their genius as is a close examination of the technical devices of the painter and composer for the fullest appreciation of a picture or a symphony. To study the peculiarities of Virgilian or Sophoclean syntax is to come to know more of the way in which a great mind thinks, feels and imagines. A boy who can appreciate exactly why Horace said 'impavidum *ferient* ruinae' may have penetrated deeper into the heart of Horace than another who can slickly reel off a parallel for a future indicative in a conditional sentence of remote supposition. In any case comments on syntax, context or subject-matter should always be expressed in correct and concise English. They can thereby be valuable as a training in the difficult art of expressing abstractions clearly and simply. Never allow slovenly stuff like 'IT is subjunctive of purpose because IT...'. All of this is, of course, counsel of perfection which the harassed teacher, sometimes a lone figure expected to be a sort of Admirable Crichton capable of tackling anything from a lame pentameter to an exposition of Alexander's Eastern campaigns, may feel to be a little unfair. Nevertheless, it is well to keep before one's eyes the ideal, however short of it one may fall in practice.

The second year in prose composition will see a gradual shift of emphasis. In the first year, while the basic principles of this branch of study were being mastered, the type of exercise given was not such as to propound too many difficulties to the beginner simultaneously. Thus it was better that the narrative kind of composition which did not make too many calls on the pupil's power of interpretation should be regularly set. During the second year, however, boys should be gradually introduced to passages which demand the expression of simple ideas. The pieces of English should slowly increase in difficulty until the boy is capable of making a fair shot at rendering into Latin or Greek certain political ideas, a little rhetoric, or a description of a man's character, behaviour and relations with his fellows. It is well to keep an eye on the prescribed prose authors at this stage with a view to using them as standard models, bearing in mind that Tacitus taken in large doses now might have a deleterious effect on the growing but still somewhat weakly organism of our pupils' Latin prose style.

Ancient History and Literature

In few schools do boys come into the Sixth Form with any systematic knowledge of Ancient History or antiquities. It is therefore desirable to devote part of the first year to a fairly general review of the ancient world, in which Greece and Rome may be seen in their setting as part of a larger whole. In addition to the formal study of history in the narrower sense, boys should be encouraged to read on their own and pursue individual interests making full use of the school, and other, libraries. In the second year the period studied will be that prescribed by the Examining Boards, a choice of a longer outline period or a shorter detailed period being left open to the teacher. Questions of method will be dealt with in the next chapter, but the advantages of choosing a period of history which can be illustrated from the prescribed books read need no elaboration.

Of literature it should be said that although the cramming of other people's criticisms and appreciations of literature is to be deprecated, boys in the first year should acquire a factual outline knowledge of the main literary forms and of their chief exponents. Thus we should not expect first year pupils to write critical essays on the style of Virgil. We should, however, expect them to know such facts of Virgil's life and environment as are essential to the appreciation of his work, the themes of his writings and topics such as the reasons justifying the statement that Virgil borrowed from Greek writers. Similarly, to ask for an essay in appreciation of the dramatic art of Sophocles is preposterous, and will receive the usual answer, an ill-assorted anthology culled from the works

of Jebb, Bowra and Kitto, and paraphrased into something that
the writer, with commendable modesty, feels is not too good to
pass off as his own. We should, on the other hand, expect our
pupils to know in outline the way in which the drama developed,
the function of the chorus, and the shape and mechanism of the
Greek theatre. This is not to deny, of course, that aesthetic
appreciation does often begin at this stage; but to be genuine it
must always be related to something that a boy is himself reading
or has read. In the second year the literature and those aspects
of ancient life, thought and achievement not covered in the formal
history course will be relevant to the preparation of the set books.
It will nevertheless be quite possible for some important feature
of ancient life to be accidentally omitted during these two busy
years, and it will call for all the vigilance of the Classics Master to
see that his charges are tolerably well informed on all that they
might be expected to know.

Having thus outlined the nature of the syllabus for the full
classical course in the first two years, we suggest the following
allocation of work, assuming seven periods a week for each
language, and give a sample two year reading course, adhering
to the principle that set books for the certificate examination
should not be started until the second year. It will be seen that
in the first year the emphasis is on variety. It is not, of course,
necessary to read complete books.

Allocation of work (assuming seven periods):

two periods reading and prepared translation of prose author;
two periods reading and prepared translation of verse author;
two periods prose composition and syntax;
one period for unseens—at first oral, later written.

(N.B. At least one more period for verse composition if it
is taken.)

Reading programme

First year. GREEK

First half of year

Selection from New Testament (once a week), selections from early
books of Herodotus.

Thucydides: The siege of Plataea and the Plague as described in II and III, or the Pylos episode in IV.

Homer: *Odyssey* (as much of VI, VII and VIII as can be done in half a term—two periods a week).

Euripides: *Medea* or *Alcestis* or *Iphigenia in Tauris*.

Second half of year

Plato: Selections from *Apology*, *Crito* and *Phaedo*.

Demosthenes: *Conon* and *Callicles*.

Aristophanes: Part of *Knights* or *Frogs* or *Acharnians* or *Birds*.

If possible a little more Homer—*Iliad* this time.

Second year. GREEK

Start with set books: Demosthenes, *Philippics* I and *Olynthiacs*. Sophocles, *Ajax*.

If time before revision of set books some more Homer and Herodotus.

First year. LATIN

First half of year

Cicero: *Catilinarian Orations* I and III or selections from *Verrine Orations* or *Murder at Larinum* (C.U.P.).

Livy: Selections from I, II, V, XXI, XXX.

Virgil: *Aeneid* II or VI with some of the *Eclogues*.

Second half of year

Pliny: Selections.

Cicero: Selections from letters.

Tacitus: Selections from *Annals* (e.g. the description of mutinies of the legions in Book I might be suitable at this stage).

Horace: Selected *Odes*.

Catullus or Virgil, *Georgics* IV.

Second year. LATIN

Set books. Cicero, *Pro Roscio Amerino* or Tacitus, *Agricola*; Virgil, *Aeneid* I or Lucretius V, 1–770.

'Off' Syllabus reading. A selection of 'silver' age Latin: e.g. Juvenal, Martial, Pliny, Tacitus (if Cicero be taken as set author).

Third year

No formal syllabus is laid down, but the three main aims for pupils of this year are:

(1) A ready command of the Greek and Latin languages as instruments for the expression of ideas. Prose composition and unseens of increasing difficulty will provide the training.

(2) Wide reading both intensive and extensive of classical literature.

(3) The study of Greek and Roman history not as an examination 'set period' but as a continuously developing theme with an organic unity. History in narrow sense to be more and more integrated with art, literature and life.

(ii) *Classics with Modern Subjects to Advanced Level*

In the Modern studies group it is usually Latin that is taken to Advanced Level in combination with other Arts subjects such as English, History or Modern Language. Taken thus as one subject, Latin is at a disadvantage in comparison with the full classical course because it is only part of a whole. The so-called classical specialist, working for a classical scholarship and intending to read Classics at the University, is not really a specialist at all. To be successful, he cannot confine himself merely to the mastery of a linguistic technique, but must become acquainted with the many-sided achievements, political, social, literary, intellectual and artistic, of two great civilizations. The Greek and Latin languages mutually complementary, and linked with their background, are more than admirable systems of formal training in the use of words; they become the living voices of a past which has never died.

Shorn of Greek, and without the liberal time allowance usually and rightly given to the full classical course, classical Latin is in danger of being studied merely as a language, isolated from what preceded or followed it, and not even related to its own age. The inclusion by some examining bodies of the outlines of Roman history in the Latin syllabus represents an attempt to provide background. So much, however, of the time allowance normally given to Latin must be spent on the language that the study of Roman history tends to be little more than a perfunctory cramming

93

of a minimum of facts necessary to answer the examination questions. Other remedies have been suggested, such as the omission
of prose composition from the syllabus in order to set free time
for wider reading, and some examining bodies offer alternative
syllabuses on those lines. We believe, however, that to abandon
prose composition would be to sacrifice a very valuable part of
the linguistic discipline of Latin, and that the compensation in
the form of wider reading would be slight. Some favour the
combination of set books in the original with Latin or Greek
literature in translation as a means of giving their pupils a wider
acquaintance with the Classics. Translations have their place, and
are to be recommended particularly as material for general reading
out of school; but we do not consider they should be included in
the Latin examination syllabus. In the first place we doubt
whether literature in translation is an examinable subject. Secondly,
if it is examinable, a treatment so different from that given to
Latin literature in the original will be necessary as to make of it
a different subject requiring its own separate allocation of periods.
These must not be shared with, and therefore subtracted from,
Latin.

There may be field for experiment in the integration or relating
of Latin with other subjects in the modern studies curriculum. This
matter is discussed at some length on pp. 7–14. Integration of
this kind, in any systematic and complete form, would of course
require a high degree of co-operation between the classical and
modern subjects teaching staff. Moreover, the linking of Latin
with other subjects in the teaching syllabus should be sanctioned
by a similar linking in examination syllabuses. This, of course,
brings us to the university stage, perhaps outside our immediate
terms of reference. We would, however, urge teachers of Latin
to do all they can in their own lessons and by co-operation with
teachers of other subjects to bring Latin back to the high road of
Western culture from the academic blind alley into which it
sometimes appears to have strayed.

The best guarantee of all that our pupils' contact with the Classics
is not confined to a cramming of the set books and the acquisition
of an examination technique for disposing of proses and unseens

lies in the qualifications and attitude of their teachers. Wherever possible Latin should be taught by those whose familiarity with the more general aspects of the ancient world will enable them, by way of digression, illuminating commentary, or advice on spare-time reading, to give their pupils at least a glimpse of the scene beyond the arduous grammatical slopes up which they so painfully clamber.

Turning to practical considerations, we are at once faced with the difficulty that has been previously mentioned, the merging of these pupils with those taking the full classical course, where the approach, the emphasis and the rate of progress are so different. Doubtless the merging occurs in other subjects too, but the problem is peculiarly serious in Latin, where the precise mastery of a difficult elementary technique is indispensable to any comprehension of the later stages. Since, however, there is unlikely to be any remedy for this state of affairs failing an improbable windfall of man-power, the most useful consideration will be the wisest disposition of mixed and separate periods. The first year will present fewer difficulties than the second. In general, it may be said that in Roman History the merging of the two groups may even prove a positive advantage, because while the classical boys can help the modern by reference to original sources, the modern boys can help the classical by reference to parallels from European history. In set books the work can be parcelled out in such a way that less preparation is demanded of the modern group, and the classical boys are put on to translate in the later part of the period— a rough-and-ready arrangement which is probably the best that can be achieved in the circumstances. In unseens and prose com-position, however, it is essential that the groups should be kept separate. Even more disastrous is any attempt to combine the first and second year in these lessons. The only solution is to teach the various elements separately. Administrators sometimes believe that efficient teachers should be able to do a neat piece of dove-tailing here, taking section A in, say, prose composition while section B in the same room is doing an unseen. Those, however, with actual experience of teaching in these conditions speak feelingly of the break-up of the class as a living organism, the divided attention of the teacher, the interruption of the rhythm of teaching and the loss of smooth continuity. This is surely one of those matters in which the voice of hard experience should be allowed to wind up the debate.

Allocation of work

Although the syllabus may have to be virtually the same as that for the full classical course, the allocation of work, assuming seven periods, will probably be:

three periods reading and prepared translation of authors; two periods prose composition; one period unseens; one period history.

While the choice of authors in the first year will, to some extent, depend on the examination syllabus, most teachers will try to adapt their reading programme so as to supplement the set books and give their pupils as wide as possible an acquaintance with the best of such Latin literature as they can tackle at this stage. For this reason the practice of reading the set books in the first year, perhaps in vogue in some schools, is not to be recommended. It may, of course, be inescapable in cases where the teaching periods are inadequate, or the human material is weak, or the date of the examination is so far advanced as to disturb the balance of the school year. But even in schools where the first and second year groups have to be taken together, so that the reading programme of the first year is necessarily limited to the set books of the second-year boys, it will be found advisable to change the set books annually so as to widen the range of the boys' reading as much as possible. The following list will suggest a choice of material for the first-year programme:

LATIN: Cicero, *In Catilinam.*
Caesar, *Civil War.*
Livy, Books I, II, V, XXI or XXX.
Horace, *Odes* III.
Virgil, *Aeneid* I, IV, V or VI; *Georgics* IV.
Ovid, *Metamorphoses* I.

For the guidance of schools taking Greek to Advanced Level as one of a group of Modern subjects, the following is a suitable list:

GREEK: New Testament.
Xenophon, *Anabasis* or *Hellenica* I and II.
Plato, *Apology* or *Crito*.
Thucydides, narrative portions of books II, IV, VI and VII.
Homer, *Iliad* I, VI and XXII; *Odyssey* VI, VII and IX.
Euripides, *Medea, Alcestis, Iphigenia in Tauris*.
Aristophanes: selections from the *Knights* or *Clouds*.

It is not likely that these books can be read in full, and it is suggested that a half a term be given to each, and that prose and verse should alternate. Opinions may differ on this, but it is probably better to have only one author in use at a time. In the second year the texts prescribed for the examination will occupy almost all the time given to reading.

In the later sections of this chapter dealing specifically with such topics as translation and Latin prose composition, the suggestions there made apply in essence to Latin with modern subjects as well as to the full classical course. Nevertheless, pressure both in and out of school from other subjects demanding a different technique, and the fact perhaps that boys taking Latin with modern subjects have not the same flair for language as the full Classic, will make some modifications necessary. Knowledge of vocabulary and idiom, for instance, will have to be built up under the systematic direction of the teacher, and not gradually from reading. For in the short time available the amount of Latin read will not be enough, nor its range sufficiently comprehensive, to provide a balanced body of knowledge. To the miscellaneous vocabulary of the translation lesson will be added examples of allied words and usages; and these will be systematically revised. Material for prose composition and unseen translation will be so selected as in part to repeat and in part to supplement what has been met with in reading. Again, if Ancient History is given only one or two class periods, a nicely calculated division of labour between teaching, learning and testing must be planned so as to ensure the most economical use of time.

(iii) *Classics to Ordinary Level as a qualifying subject for University Entrance*

Apart from classical specialists and those taking Latin only to Advanced Level, there will always be in any Sixth Form a number of other pupils having different needs. Those reading for Civil Service examinations, extra translation papers in scholarship examinations, or other professional qualifications will be fortunate indeed to receive individual attention. In practice they will be merged with the appropriate classes taking Advanced Level. It is better for a boy to read with a class a set book which he will not take in the examination than to work numerous 'unseens' on his own for individual correction—a soulless procedure and extravagant of the master's time. There still will be two groups, however, requiring special comment. In the first place there may be late-comers to the Latin course who begin Latin in the Sixth Form, and secondly that bane of all classical masters, the boy who either because he has eluded Latin in the early years or because he has been cheated of it, finds in his last year at school that he needs Latin for Oxford or Cambridge or as a faculty requirement.

To deal with the latter class first, it cannot be too strongly emphasized that, if a pupil has shown himself capable of proceeding to a university, to allow him to reach his last year at school before beginning Latin is completely indefensible. No doubt it is possible for such a one to acquire sufficient Latin by intensive cramming in his last year: but the cost is far too great. Not only must the pupil devote a large number of periods to it at the expense of wider reading in his main subjects, but in addition his Latin teacher cannot, under modern time-table conditions, give him the individual treatment that he requires except by sacrificing the interests of ordinary Sixth-Form Latin pupils. We do not therefore offer guidance for procedure in a case that should never be allowed to occur.

Even with late developers, it is extremely rare for the future university student to hide his light under a bushel past the age of 15 +. Hence, while we emphatically deprecate any arrangement that has deprived such pupils of Latin up to this stage, we concede the possibility of a late start provided that the course is spread out over at least two years. It is essential that beginners of this type should be taught separately: they need a streamlined course of at least five periods a week, giving them the elements of accidence, syntax and vocabulary to enable them to pass the usual type of Ordinary Level Certificate Examination or University Entrance Examination. Those who doubt the educational value of such a course should reflect that it can be a lesson in economy of time and concentration of effort on the attainment of a definite aim.

2. SPECIAL TOPICS IN SIXTH-FORM TEACHING

We have discussed so far the general organization of the various groups in the Classical Sixth Form and have outlined the syllabuses they may be supposed to follow. It now remains to deal with the teaching of Classics in the Sixth Form in further detail. It has been previously stated that the problem of teaching in the Sixth Form is materially different from that involved in teaching the lower and middle school. By its nature the Sixth Form presupposes boys of maturity and some fitness for the subjects of their selection. Much of the technique required for the training of immature minds in a class whose co-operation cannot always be taken for granted will therefore be irrelevant here. Much of the method of teaching a Sixth Form is self-evident and calls for no particular comment. This is not, of course, to say that the teacher makes no difference. The successful teacher of the Classical Sixth must always have a sound knowledge of his subject and enthusiasm and vigour in expounding it; he must always have wide interests and a lively grip on current problems; he must always have the right mixture of tact, humour and firmness in dealing with adolescent boys; and in so far as he falls short of these desiderata he will be the less successful in handling one of the most difficult branches of knowledge in the curriculum. Nevertheless, given the right sort of teacher, the best method will be that which will suggest itself to him personally, and which might be wholly wrong for another equally successful teacher. In these circumstances we think it best to forego any attempt to detail individual methods of teaching the Sixth, and rather to discuss in a series of sections a number of special topics bound to loom large in the teaching of Sixth-Form Classics.

3. TRANSLATION IN THE SIXTH FORM

'At least be sure that you go to the author to get at HIS meaning, not to find yours.'   (JOHN RUSKIN)

Written Work

There is not likely to be much difference of opinion as to what constitutes a good translation, in the sense of a piece of written work, a scholarship 'unseen, for example, but it may not be out of place to discuss some of its bearings. A Frenchman is said to have compared translations to wives: they were either 'belles' or 'fidèles'. The less cynical Sixth-Form master may expect both forms of excellence from his pupils. Nevertheless, he should have an order of priority to fall back on in doubtful cases, and priority is not hard to establish.

The purpose of a translation is to communicate meaning. If the appropriate style and emotion can be conveyed as well, so much the better, but fidelity comes first. Fidelity neither implies nor precludes literalness. Literalness, in its turn, need not reject elegance: 'And looking round about upon them all, he said unto the man, Stretch forth thy hand. And he did so, and his hand was restored whole as the other' (Luke vi. 10). This translation is clear, appropriate in diction and well balanced. The subject-matter being simple, a literal translation is the obvious choice, and elegance follows as a parergon. In a sense the antithesis between a literal and free translation is meaningless. Both are means to an end, and are to be judged as such: hence rules such as 'Never translate a word by its derivative; never translate *immunitas* by "immunity"' are out of place when applied to the finished product, however salutary they may be as rules for oral translation in form, which will be discussed later. Free or literal, a translation is good if it is faithful.

The sanction behind the preceding rule was probably a healthy dislike of 'translationese'. It should be hardly necessary here to stigmatize un-English expressions, such as 'Which things having been decided by him', or to legislate against the literal, and hence incomprehensible, translation of idioms. There are, however, one or two dangers that arise when an idiomatic style or technicality of vocabulary in the original author makes literal translation impossible. A very free translation may run the risk of being thought a paraphrase, a camouflage for ignorance of construction: where there is such a risk the translator must take it with his eyes open. Again, a free translation may tend to be too long. The reader's mind requires intervals between gulps of information, and if the balance of clauses has been overstepped, his comprehension flags. At this point it may be pardonable to protest against translations that try to drag in everything: all the points of grammar, all the implications of history, and all the sonorities of Gibbon. A synthetic extravagance may illustrate this vice.

'Omnium consensu capax imperii nisi imperasset'
(TACITUS, *Hist.* I, 29).

Expansionist rendering. 'The fitness of Servius Sulpicius Galba to assume the burden of Empire was, or rather would have been, universally conceded, had not his elevation to that lofty pinnacle, seven days after the death of Nero, revealed his incapacity.'[1]

It is doubtful whether the modern schoolboy is much given to such excessive expansion, though it may occasionally happen that a Sixth-Former, accustomed through prose composition to sweat down 'On the receipt of this disturbing intelligence' into plain *Quibus rebus auditis,* may, when it comes to translation into English, hope to acquire merit by a reciprocal verbosity. Some colleges are said to make war on what may be called 'brilliant' translations, preferring a plain and faithful elegance. Whether this is so or not, there is still a good deal to be said for not discouraging a promising boy from exuberance of style, which is always a symptom of vitality. But this is to anticipate.

[1] Compare the 'translation' quoted by Prof. Ronald Syme at Oxford (1948): 'Universally conceded to be an Emperor with a brilliant future behind him.'

Oral Translation

In making the above remarks, we had chiefly in mind the written translation, the finished product, the scholarship unseen, for example. This, in a way, is an end in itself, with its own excellences. We come now to oral translation, that is, the day-to-day practice of translating a prepared book in form. This is partly a means to the end of written translation, and as such should be consciously directed towards improving the standard of written translation. But it also has objectives of its own. These include the study of authors as documents or background for history, literature, and antiquities generally. Here, therefore, we enter upon debatable ground. Most masters will be in general agreement as to ends, but in discussing means and methods, we may say with Tacitus: 'opus aggredior opimum casibus, atrox proeliis, discors seditionibus, ipsa etiam pace saevum'—our subject-matter is rich in vicissitudes, stubborn battles, and mutinous factions, where peace brings no clemency. Moreover, whereas 'translation' as dealt with above was a thing and hence able to be dealt with objectively, 'translation' in our present sense implies an activity of a whole form, and therefore is enriched and complicated by various human elements.

The advocate of direct method may still reduce translation into English to a minimum; the word-order method may be continued, dropped, or adopted for the first time; and as was said above, many translation periods may owe much of their value to parerga: historical discussion, the collection of material for prose composition, study of the development of drama, etc. Last but not least, an unrivalled opportunity is given by the oral translation period for experiments in all kinds of renderings, in the course of which a skilled teacher may be able to bring out the best from different types of mind by different methods. Nevertheless, some general principles may be laid down.

(a) *Translation for its own sake.* At least some of the translation periods should consciously aim at producing excellence in translation as such, and the pupils should be quite clear when this is the main end in view.

(*b*) *Rigour.* In these lessons it is important to let it be seen that the pupils are expected to do the work. Form-spirit means a great deal. Where more than one year translate together, nothing can fire the ambition of the first year more effectively than the occasional hearing of a third-year boy who is put on to translate and does so successfully for several pages. Model translations by the master are excellent, but should not be overdone, or the form will take them for granted and make less effort themselves.

(*c*) *The unbroken whole.* If a boy sticks fast when translating, he should be taken off. Otherwise he should be allowed to go on to the end of his quota without interruption. All discussion of points of syntax, subject-matter, style or vocabulary must wait until he has finished. A boy put on to translate is thus on his mettle, knowing that he will be neither helped by prompting nor hindered by criticism. Prompting tempts him to prepare less rigorously next time: criticism makes him resentful now. Once he is in the middle of a long sentence he quite rightly feels that this is no time for the master to point out that 'thing' is a poor translation for *res*, or to hold up the flow by asking for an example of a similar potential subjunctive—what he wants is to be allowed to work his way to the end of his sentence.

(*d*) *Confidence.* Once a boy knows he will not be interrupted his oral style can be greatly improved. 'Ums' and 'ers' can be usually eradicated by the injunction to insert a silent pause instead—if pauses are no longer regarded as signals for intervention.

(*e*) *Different aims in translation.* Extending the principle hinted at under (*a*), it may be said generally that the pupil should always be aware of what rigour is expected of him when translating different books. Examples may illustrate.

A Sixth Form, whose History speciality this year is the early Principate and will be the Pentecontaetia next year, has eight periods a week in which to do four books. It is hoped to finish all four in the first term. Priorities and aims may be as follows:

(1) Virgil, *Fourth Georgic*. A set book, intensive study; emphasis on style of translation; frequent written tests.

(2) Thucydides I. This book will be useful as a document for those who will be doing this period for History next year; but a high standard of style in translation will be required, for Thucydides is a stylist as well as a historian.

(3) Tacitus, *Annals* I. As a stylist he cannot be neglected, and the bright boy may be encouraged to epigrammatize. Nevertheless, the form must realize they are reading the book as background material, and therefore the chief aim is to cover the ground, document their history notes, and familiarize themselves with the technicalities of constitutional, military, and provincial organization.

(4) Euripides, *Medea*. This is chosen to accompany work (in Antiquities periods) on Greek drama. Speed and enthusiasm is everything. Drama must be read quickly if it is to be dramatic. Moreover, unless the form gets well ahead with the play, interest may flag for another reason; Thucydides I, a long book, may demand an extra weekly period towards the end of the term, and the *Medea* will drop to once weekly.

(*f*) *Different methods in translating.* It is impossible to prescribe a single method of oral translation, and the cunning Sixth-Form master will ring the changes according to the particular aim he has in view. A passage may be taken 'as it comes' by the word-order method on occasion: perhaps to correct any tendency to jump over construction to a brilliant, stylish, and wrong translation, perhaps to teach the trick of preserving rhetorical order by inverting the subject (*Caesarem occidit Brutus*, 'Caesar's assassin was Brutus'), perhaps as an introductory technique for those who have not yet learnt to read and follow without translation. On occasion a passage already translated literally and dully may be worked over again with a view to exploiting the possibilities of English style. Or with the needs of individual boys in mind a master may preface an unseen passage with a near paraphrase of its subject-matter (for boys who are more interested in grammar and composition)—another time he may point towards the major difficulties of construction that will occur, with a warning to those who bend grammar to fit the desired sense that in this unseen the marks will go to those who solve the constructional difficulties. On another occasion, if he is fortunate in his form, he may require a translation in a particular style: Gibbon, Macaulay, or Shaw. If a verse translation is offered, he should praise the attempt, and be sparing in emendation, unless later in the term efforts are made to place it in the school magazine.

In short, different phases in a form's development and different reasons for choice of an author will suggest different methods in the practice of oral translation. However objectively it may be possible to assess the merits of a written translation as a thing, the assessment of the value of a particular approach to an author read in form will always remain a subjective one, best left to the teacher.

4. SIXTH-FORM LATIN PROSE COMPOSITION

Supporters of a classical education find one of their strongest arguments in the beneficial effects of Latin prose composition on adolescent minds. The processes, they say, of getting down to the fundamental meaning of an English passage, and of rebuilding the ideas into the complex structure of a Latin period, not merely inculcate a general sense of style, but sharpen the analytical and critical faculties in a way that is bound to make itself felt in all aspects of the student's work. Many even go so far as to claim an ethical value for Latin prose composition in that its discipline makes such demands on the absolute honesty of the student that Latin has a kind of psychotherapeutic value. Opponents of the Classics argue that there is no evidence that specific abilities can be transferred to other subjects, and that in any case the large majority of our pupils never reach the standard at which these forces are called into play.

Whatever may be thought of the first half of the critics' argument, the validity of the second is hard to deny. While certain analytical and synthetical processes are involved in the translation of English sentences into Latin, he would be a bold man who would claim for 'sentences' all that is claimed for Latin prose composition. If we believe in the values of Latin prose composition we cannot logically do otherwise than wish as many pupils as possible to share in those values. For this reason we should beware of a movement which would confine the exercise of Latin prose composition to the experts, to the potential scholarship winners, or to those who show an 'aptitude' for it. Education today is bedevilled by those who think that it is Education's business to flatter aptitudes rather than correct deficiencies. The plea that Latin prose is difficult is not a good educational reason for abandoning it. It may be that more gain comes from trying to do what one cannot than what one can.

Yet it must be conceded that much of the feeling of frustration connected with Latin prose is due to the teaching. The fact is that many teachers do not sufficiently train their pupils in the processes of thought which this exercise demands. It is not enough that a pupil should attempt a prose, and that a teacher should correct his copy and point out to him the merits of the 'fair' copy. The teacher must see the pupil's mind working. If it is one of the virtues of Latin prose that it compels the pupil to delve into the meaning of the English, the boy must see the teacher, and thereafter the teacher must see the boy, in the process of delving. This can only be done when teacher and class together construct a fair copy on the blackboard. Otherwise the tendency will be for pupils week after week to hand in proses which never read like Latin at all, not merely because of the errors, for these will be eliminated in the course of time, but because the pupil has never been told or is too lazy to go deep enough into the matter. The obvious gap between the effort he makes and the 'fair' copy dictated to him becomes a gulf that can never be bridged. Despair and apathy result.

Latin prose, then, is good for the Sixth, both for those taking it as part of a modern and classical group of studies. A passage of English should be given to the form to put into Latin. This should be done privately or at home in not less than $2\frac{1}{2}$ hours. It should be handed in at an appointed time, and returned marked to the form at the beginning of a double period. The returning of work individually to boys is excellent, but so wasteful of the other boys' time that it is a luxury few can afford. The double period (it cannot be less) should then be spent in the construction of a 'fair' copy on the blackboard. The boys offer their suggestions and criticize each others'. The final copy must be compounded of the master's and boys' suggestions. It must not be too good, though better than any individual effort in so far as it comprises the best that a co-operative effort can produce. The master should either have written his own copy, or (since life is short) have a good idea how a fair copy runs. By hints and suggestions, not too obtrusive, he can then help. Big dictionaries, of which there must be plenty, should be constantly consulted by the whole form. Records of the proses and fair copies should be kept. The compilation of vocabularies and phrase-books should be encouraged and supervised. Boys, in particular adolescent boys, develop a great feeling for style and rhetoric, if sufficiently stimulated. Whilst, therefore, in the early stages of continuous prose composition the pupil must necessarily be kept to proses of the narrative type, the sooner that he is introduced to proses which demand that the thought of the English rather than the actual words be translated, the better the boy will come to appreciate the value of this exercise, and even (dare it be said?) to like it.

5. THE TEACHING OF VERSE COMPOSITION

The teaching of Greek and Latin verse composition has been crowded out of the curriculum during the last generation in many schools, even where there is a strong Classical Sixth. It seems worth while to maintain it for the following reasons:

(1) An acquaintance with even the rudiments of verse composition familiarizes the pupil with rules of quantity and rhythm. Without this familiarity his reading of classical poetry and his enjoyment of its music must be defective.

(2) If, after mastering the rudiments, he tries his hand at translating some good English poem into Latin or Greek, the very difficulty of the task will give him a deeper insight into the meaning and beauty of the English.

(3) The boy who finds that he has a gift for verse composition will enjoy it as something creative. This gift is sometimes discovered in unlikely people and its exercise tones up the whole of their work.

The following suggestions are made for the teaching of verse composition:

(1) In the first Sixth-Form year all classical specialists should be taught the rudiments. One period a week for each language is enough for this. The process at first must be largely mechanical, but even at this stage stress can be laid on peculiarities of poetic vocabulary and idiom and on alternative methods of paraphrase and expansion. The passages set will usually be translations of lines from Greek and Latin poets, but sometimes the class may be invited to co-operate with the master in composing an original piece of verse. It does not matter how trivial the subject of this is, so long as it exercises the ingenuity of the pupils.

(2) After the first year, pupils who show no aptitude for verse composition should be allowed to drop it. Those who keep it up must be encouraged to learn by heart as much Greek and Latin poetry as possible. There is no greater help towards the writing of verse than a memory well stocked with the greatest passages of classical poetry. It should be observed that *all* students of the Classics should learn some Greek and Latin poetry by heart, but the future versifiers will need to learn most.

(3) The pieces set should, to start with, be similar to passages from the classical poets, and references to parallel passages in the Classics should be given so that the pupils can study them before attempting their compositions. At a later stage, pupils may be encouraged to try their hand at pieces of English poetry that appeal to them. A difficult but inspiring piece of English often produces better results than a flat, uninteresting passage.

(4) The difficulty of a pupil in the early stages of verse writing is that he is required to make bricks without straw. Every effort must be made to help him by suggesting ways of paraphrasing or expanding the original and by setting him on the track of suitable words and phrases. There are books on the market which do this very well. The use by the pupils of a gradus need not be discouraged, but they should be warned to check the authority for any word or phrase found in these books.

(5) In Latin verse, most teachers give more attention to elegiacs than to hexameters. Elegiacs are probably easier to write

when one has mastered a few Ovidian turns of phrase, but hexameters offer a much wider range of emotion and direct the pupil to finer models. If Virgil is more read by Sixth-Formers than Ovid, it seems a pity that they should not be given the opportunity to imitate, however imperfectly, the varied rhythms of the Virgilian hexameter. It may be, however, that the restrictions upon freedom imposed by the stricter laws of elegiac verse are a salutary discipline in the early stages.

(6) Most of the fair copies in books of compositions are far beyond the powers of the pupil. They may be used as models, but the pupil will often learn more if his own bungling effort is re-fashioned, with the teacher's help, into something which, though not brilliant verse, will at least pass as Latin or Greek. It is often more useful, if more difficult for the teacher, to work out a translation of a few lines on the board with the class, than to present them with a ready-made fair copy of the whole.

6. THE PROJECT METHOD

It is pertinent to any account of work done in a Sixth Form to mention an interesting experiment in co-operative work by boys of a Sixth Form, involving much use of the school library, which was attempted at a boarding school. Three periods a week were allowed for work on a projected theme, although in practice the boys used a great deal more of their own time. An essay on a theme linked with the classical work of the group, and offering a number of obvious subdivisions, was selected. A typical theme was Roman Britain. To ensure sufficient background knowledge of the work, every boy was required to read Collingwood's *Roman Britain*. The master discussed with the whole group the range and bearing of the subject as a whole, and found that it was not difficult to enlist the enthusiasm of the boys. The subject was then split into a number of sections—in this case:

(*a*) *Historical.* (i) Britain before the Conquest; (ii) History of the Conquest; (iii) Military Organization of Britain; (iv) Political Organization of Britain; (v) Social Life of Roman Britain; (vi) Later History and Evacuation.

(*b*) *Descriptive*, Archaeological Topics. (i) The Walls; (ii) Forts and Fortresses; (iii) Roads; (iv) Towns; (v) Public Buildings; (vi) Villas and Houses—types and examples.

Sections were then assigned to pairs of boys or individuals, care being taken to see that the more difficult work went to the abler boys. As far as possible, boys were allowed to choose the sections which appealed to them most. The boys had to write an account of their separate topics with a view to a corporate thesis. Sources were discussed with the master, and the rule established early that material for the work must be drawn from more than one source. Experience of this type of work shows that it is often necessary to warn boys against the wholesale 'lifting' of passages from books. A date was then fixed for the completion of the work. When the first draft was finished, the sections were handed to the master, who discussed and criticized them with the authors, finally circulating them when amended to the whole group. An editor was appointed, copies made, and all who shared in the writing of the thesis received a copy, with acknowledgments made for individual contributions. A copy was kept for the library. The work made inroads into the normal time-table, and was eventually discontinued for that reason. If, however, this kind of work could be assimilated to the normal curriculum, and, say, Greek History, Latin Literature, and the like could become subjects of comprehensive essays, there might then be less criticism on the score of time-table difficulties. A boy might do one co-operative and one individual essay a term, and thus cover many topics connected with the history, literature, and social life of Greece and Rome. The value of this method lies in its training in the use of books and the library, while at the same time it affords wide scope for personal initiative. Nevertheless, it must be admitted that it throws a great burden of organization and supervision on the master responsible, and in ineffective hands it might prove a disastrous failure.

7. THE USE OF TRANSLATIONS

On the general question of reading authors in translation, it must be admitted that as a rule a translation from Latin or Greek cannot give much more than the matter of the original. The manner largely defies reproduction in another language, and may in fact be transmuted into something that produces a quite different impression.

This is of course no argument against the free use of translations in order to introduce Greek or Latin authors to pupils with literary tastes who are not classical specialists (including those who know no Latin or Greek at all). It is clearly more desirable for such readers to obtain what they can from this method than to have no acquaintance whatever with ancient literature. But there are teachers in every generation who conscientiously maintain that classical specialist pupils who can appreciate something of the spirit of their authors in the original languages should not have that appreciation confused or vitiated by recourse to translations for any purpose whatever while they are still at school.

We would sympathize with this view to the extent of saying that when translations are used they should be chosen with discrimination. For instance, there are several excellent prose versions of Homer that seem to us less un-Homeric in tone than any existing verse translation: and while we might recommend Dryden's *Juvenal*, we should deprecate the use of his *Virgil*. In addition, when classical specialists are rapidly covering ground in this manner, they should be encouraged to make frequent references to a plain text of the author whom they are studying. Some (though by no means all) of the Loeb Series volumes are admirably suited for this purpose.

For the benefit of those who are still dubious, another method of rapid reading may be mentioned, which does not involve any use of translations. The class is given in advance the gist of a long passage of the author concerned; the passage is then broken up into sections, and each pupil is detailed to prepare one section, and translates it orally when his turn comes in class. This method has been used in our experience with effect, in double periods, for the reading of large portions of such authors as Homer, Apollonius Rhodius, Herodotus, Xenophon, Lucretius, Ovid, Lucan, Livy and Tacitus.

8. THE USE OF PRIVATE STUDY

'Numquam sis ex toto otiosus, sed aut legens, aut scribens,
aut meditans.'   (THOMAS À KEMPIS)

The term private study may describe all work done outside the class-room period, at home or at school, as a set class task or on the initiative of the individual. While, like charity, it may cover a multitude of sins, especially if its purpose be administrative convenience rather than educational advantage, yet the right conditions plus planning and a not too blindly optimistic faith in the inherent self-control and instinctive assiduity of youth may make of private study a time saver and a useful adjunct to the class-room period. Most important of all, private study is an essential element in the training which should be provided by an advanced course. For the boy is taught how to work on his own and cultivate individual interests.

Of private study done at home we need only say that conditions will vary according to the attitude of parents and their ability or willingness to provide a room in which the boy can work undisturbed by conversation or the B.B.C. If without appearing over-inquisitive the teacher can find out the conditions in which his pupils work at home, he will be able to avoid unjust criticism of individual shortcomings.

Private study periods in school are not uncommonly called 'free' periods by the boys, an epithet whose use is to be officially discountenanced by the authorities, but noted by them as a warning. For boys will be boys, even in the Sixth Form, and the Classics has at least one undeniable advantage over most other subjects, a crushing superiority in the weight and missile force of its dictionaries. Quiet, the first requisite, must be ensured either by supervision, or, better, by the provision of a room of such spaciousness and dignity as will produce the right atmosphere for study.

Given the right external conditions, quiet, space for reading and writing in comfort, and access to books, the boy will still need a good deal of guidance at first, if he is not to spend the period in aimless browsing or, more probably, on work intended to be done at home. In the early stages of the Sixth-Form course he must be shown how to make use of the private study period. This can be done by giving him a fairly definite programme of work, which should be frequently checked. The programme, however, should allow of, and indeed encourage, variation. Furthermore, and this is particularly important at the beginning of the advanced course, the work should be within the scope of the boy's un-aided efforts and sufficiently interesting or stimulating to hold his attention.

These last considerations are particularly important if we try to make our pupils read Greek or Latin on their own in private study. If any such reading be set to beginners in the Sixth Form, it must be easy and obviously attractive. Homer and Herodotus might be prescribed at this stage after an introduction in class periods, and apart from their inherent charm, these authors are admirably suited to rapid reading, a habit which may do much to engender in our pupils a feeling of confidence in their own powers. Other authors which we might suggest in the early stages are Euripides, without the choruses, Aristophanes with Roger's translations, and the third book of Apollonius Rhodius' *Argonautica*. Classical Latin literature, with its essentially adult thought and content and its elaborately periodic style, has less to offer for private reading in the early stages. Caesar is usually (not always!) straightforward enough to read unaided. He might be followed by Catullus, the *Catilinarian Orations* of Cicero and selections from Pliny. More advanced pupils, particularly those preparing for scholarships, will, of course, be expected to tackle a much fuller programme. Lastly, a record of all Greek and Latin read, either in or out of school, in private study or in the class period, should be kept by the pupil and the teacher. A balance can thus be preserved and duplication or gaps avoided.

Private study will often be spent in the reading of books in English about classical subjects. Such reading, which may range from the consultation of works of reference on matters of detail to the perusal of major works of criticism, interpretation or appreciation, should in the early stages be mainly concerned with the more factual and concrete aspects of Roman and Greek life and achievement. If, for instance, the class is reading one of Cicero's forensic speeches, time could be saved if the master asked his pupils to acquaint themselves with the details of Roman legal procedure and court routine by consulting the appropriate books of reference in the private study period. Similarly the construction and mechanics of the Greek theatre, the actor's dress, the arrangement of the chorus and the organization of dramatic festivals, constitute ample material for individual research to supplement the reading of a Greek play in class. Of course boys must be told in outline what facts they are to look for, the theme or framework into which they are to fit, and the sources of information locally available.

Of works of literary appreciation and interpretation we need say little. The private study period is obviously the time when they should be read. Their place, however, is rather later in the Sixth-Form course, when boys have already read enough Greek or Latin literature to turn to such works for stimulation, and not merely for ready-made second-hand opinions and potted knowledge. We would, of course, encourage as early as possible a reading of books whose purpose is to give a general picture of ancient life, such as *Roman Panorama* (Grose-Hodge), *Schools of Hellas* (Freeman), *Cicero and the Roman Republic* (Cowell), *The Greek Commonwealth* (Zimmern)—to mention a few examples.

The above suggestions are meant to cover the whole Sixth-Form course, but emphasis has been laid on first-year work. For it is at this stage that the boy needs guidance in the use of unaccustomed freedom from continuous class-room discipline. Given the right training to begin with, the problem of private study should solve itself in the second and third years.

Although the foregoing topics have already served to illustrate the width, depth and richness of the Classical Sixth's curriculum, so important do we consider the teaching of Ancient History,

Life and Literature that we reserve our remarks on them to the succeeding chapter. Nevertheless, it should already be apparent that work in the Classical Sixth represents the full flowering of a growth that has been subjected to a culture difficult to surpass—as indeed has been borne out by the history of some of our famous schools. It would be a sad day for this country if it were to allow its Classical Sixths to become a mere memory of the past.

VI

ANCIENT HISTORY, LIFE AND LITERATURE

IT will be clear from the many references in other parts of this book that the study of Ancient History, Life and Literature can play a large part in education today. It is this portion of the classical curriculum which, more than any other, is valuable to every scholar and justifies its inclusion in the syllabuses of all types of schools. For there is in this study the possibility of a revival of interest in learning, since we may trace to Greek and Roman origins so much that is familiar and commonplace in our modern world—in literature, language, politics and even science. But in this chapter it is the classical student whom we have in mind, and we seek to give some guidance in the teaching of Ancient History, Life and Literature to the classical forms of a grammar school.

1. ANCIENT HISTORY

'What is all knowledge but recorded experience and
a product of history?'   (CARLYLE)

The widest application of Ancient History is its place in the progress of mankind and its relation to modern times. For this purpose the term 'Ancient History' must be held to cover the story of man from prehistoric times, and it is desirable that, as far as time permits, the position of Greece and Rome in world history should be emphasized; especially must the debt of Western civilization to Greece and Rome be made clear and advantage be taken of the opportunity which Ancient History offers to see in small compass many of the problems of our own days, to examine them without emotional bias and to evaluate the success or failure of the attempts made to solve them. But when the study of Ancient History is undertaken for the purpose of examination, it is the historical content which is of prime importance. If a defence of this attitude is needed, it may be maintained that there are periods, like the fifth century at Athens or the last days of the Roman Republic, whose intrinsic importance and interest are amply sufficient to justify their study.

In most schools Ancient History is part of the first year of the History syllabus, but the period covered is usually too long for any but the briefest treatment of Greece and Rome; the use of classical stories in the lower forms is helpful. The Sixth-Form specialist must therefore start afresh, but for the others this work in the first year is to be welcomed as giving a glimpse, however dim, of the glories of the past. There is scope, too, for the teacher of Classics in the middle and lower school to introduce Ancient History as a 'background'; in particular the story of Roman Britain surely deserves special attention, and there is available a wide range of photographs and film strips to illustrate it, while many schools are within reach of museums or sites of excavations.

The intensive study of Ancient History is usually the concern of the Sixth Form. In some schools, it is true, Greek or Roman History is offered for examination at the Ordinary Level, but in the interests of general education it is not recommended that Ancient History should replace the study of Modern History at this level. The course in the Sixth Form should be of three years, if the history of other civilizations than those of Greece and Rome is to form part of the syllabus; but in most schools it corresponds to the two years allowed for the Advanced Level examination, with possibly a third year for scholarship candidates. There is considerable divergence in the number of periods a week given to the course, but it is desirable to have at least two periods for Greek History and two for Roman History. In many schools, especially the smaller ones, it is necessary to combine both years of the Sixth Form in these periods; this combination should not be required if the number of periods is fewer than two a week for each subject. If Ancient History is taken at the Advanced Level as a separate subject, it must be given its allocation of periods as a full subject.

In both Greek and Roman History the requirements of the examination at the Advanced Level are usually a long period for study in outline and a short period for special study which is either additional or alternative to the outline period. Where there is a choice between an outline period and a special period, the majority of teachers prefer the longer period, for it provides the opportunity of a wide review of movements and events, and avoids much of the detail that is rather the affair of the history specialist. The periods usually set by the various boards, whether for outline or special study, are considered in the main satisfactory. We believe that a special period should be within the outline period, where both have to be taken. As it is desirable that in the first year of the Sixth-Form course some knowledge should be gained of the history outside the period chosen for study, some general text-book of Ancient History should first be read; it may be simply a short history of Greece or Rome, or, when more time is available, a book which includes the earlier civilizations.

Apart from the choice between the longer period for general study and the shorter period for special study, something may here be said on the selection of main periods. In schools interest has been traditionally centred on Greek History to the death of Alexander, and on Roman History to the death of Augustus.

Although boys should be made aware of the broad outlines of the Hellenistic period—even if only to enable them to understand the relations of Rome with the Eastern Mediterranean—few would recommend it for inclusion in a school examination syllabus. The issues are so confused and the general tone so different from that of classical Greece, that, in the limited time available, any detailed study would prove a serious distraction from the all-important lessons of the sixth, fifth and fourth centuries B.C. For in these centuries, undistracted by the sometimes irrelevant complexities which seem to make up the intricate pattern of life in the modern national or supra-national state, we see the working out of basic moral and political ideas illumined by the writings of men who combined outstanding literary genius with the advantage of having lived in, and even of having taken a leading part in, the events and issues they describe and discuss. The pre-eminent value of classical studies lies in this coincidence of great events and great minds.

Similar arguments might be adduced in favour of studying Roman History to the death of Augustus rather than the imperial period. The story of the rise of Rome to mastery of the Mediterranean world and of the conflict brought about by the strain of adapting an outworn city-state constitution to the task of administering an empire has the intrinsic appeal of dramatic completeness. It is a story with a beginning, a middle, and an end; a story not of the impersonal workings of a vast administrative and military machine, but of the revolutionary effects of the rivalries and ambitions of individuals. It may be said, too, that the last years of the Republic are of peculiar interest to the student of the Classics 'because its literature is largely the first-hand record of human reaction to contemporary events.... The writers of the time were the leading men of action, or their intimates. Cicero personally helped to shape the great events of his day. He was also a sensitive man and a skilful writer.... His letters and speeches take us right into the heart of things, and let us know, with a directness and a certainty unattainable by even the greatest of historians writing of a past age, exactly what was being said and felt by the very man who shaped and caused the events we are studying. Caesar, too, and Sallust...describe matters in which the one took a leading part and with which the other was intimately connected.'[1] It may fairly be said that an Advanced and Scholarship course in Latin must include the reading of a good deal of Cicero; if it also includes a study of the later Republican period, then history and literature explain, complement and illuminate each other in an integrated whole.

On the other hand it must be admitted that he would be a poorly equipped student of ancient Rome who had little knowledge of it under the Emperors. The story may not be so colourful as that of the rise of a small city-state to the control of the entire Mediterranean region and its hinterlands. It does not include the defeats of Carthage, of invading barbarian hordes, of vast Hellenistic kingdoms, nor the temporary rending of Rome's dominion by long and savage civil wars—Marius and Sulla,

[1] 'The Classic and Roman History: a Defence of Tradition', by D. G. Bentliff, in *Greece and Rome*, vol. v, no. 13 (October 1935).

Pompey and Caesar. But the period of the Principate offers us something perhaps more civilized and more noble—the spectacle of steady efforts to consolidate the vast ramshackle power, to extend and maintain the widespread Pax Romana; herein too is included the Romanization of Gaul and Spain and, to some degree, of our own island; later comes 'the Golden Age of the Antonines'; later still, if the student can spare the time, the crumbling disintegration of 'Decline and Fall'. For those who delight in dramatic vicissitudes, there is always A.D. 69 and its portrayal in Tacitus' *Histories*.

The earliest part of the history of this period should have particular appeal to the present post-war generation. Wars and disasters, it is true, continued, but the main problem was the administrative one of building a stable and peaceful community after the distractions of the last century B.C. and of trying to create a unified Mediterranean regime. It must not be forgotten that it was the Principate, much more than the Republic, which established in Western Europe the abiding influence of Imperial Rome. If one of the main strands of our civilization is the Hellenic, the chief weaver of that strand is Rome of the Emperors and its heirs and imitators. The triumphs of the period are those of the organizer, working quietly and patiently, not the coups of the soldier or the diplomat. There is the effort, too, to set up a government above class or party. It is true that the first Princeps owed his unrivalled power to the general eagerness to welcome anyone who promised relief from the insecurity and bloodshed of the recent past, and that many of his successors, even if one discounts most of Suetonius' gossip, were hardly worthy of their high office. Yet none the less the early Empire was an astonishing regime, and no one interested in the government of mankind can afford to disregard it. It had to try to answer questions not unlike those of today, and even if it did not permanently succeed, there is lasting value in the solutions it attempted.

Two minor reasons for preferring this period may also be mentioned. One is literary; it will encourage the reading of Tacitus; the other is more important. It is the period of Roman Britain; and the study of our own land, perhaps of our own town, under another civilization has a fascination of its own.

The most important claims of Republican and Imperial history may perhaps be satisfied by a compromise policy which, at the time of writing, is followed by one examination authority. The period prescribed at Advanced and Scholarship Level yearly alternates between (1) the Republic and Principate down to A.D. 14—with special emphasis on the period 150 B.C. to A.D. 14; and (2) 90 B.C. to A.D. 138. Many boys take the examination in two successive years first at Advanced and then at Scholarship Level; they thus twice cover the period of the Revolution and will also have studied the earlier history of the Republic and the greatest years of Imperial Rome.

Methods of Teaching

Something may be added here on methods of teaching Ancient History at Advanced Level. It has already been emphasized that this subject, which is of great value, requires an adequate allowance of time; it cannot effectively be treated as mere background to the linguistic study of Greece and Rome. (This, of course, does not preclude the selection of reading matter in the language periods on historical as well as literary grounds. The advantage of meeting in the original a primary source for history, such as the first book of Thucydides, or of Tacitus' *Annals*, should be plain.)

The pitfalls on either side which beset the teacher of Ancient History are superficiality and cramming. His pupils must never imagine that the chief qualification of a historian is a gift for writing glib essays or for mechanical reproduction of dictated notes or of the gist of a text-book.

The examination itself will mainly, if not entirely, consist of a series of short essays, of which the form, as well as the content, is important. Clearly these must be practised, but not to the exclusion of everything else. The first task of the pupils is to learn the facts, which they can do by reading a good text-book outside the class-room. But this task must be broken up for them into specified and manageable sections; and perhaps the Ministry's *Suggestions for the Teaching of Classics* (1939) is too optimistic in its statement that Sixth-Form pupils may be expected to get up the facts for themselves. Occasional tests, whether in the form of 'one-word' answers or brief essays without the book, should not be dispensed with, especially in the first year. But the Ministry rightly say: 'The teacher's function is to supplement or illustrate or interpret the outlines given in the text-book.' The writing of essays impresses the facts on the writers' minds; it also reveals their misunderstandings and limitations, and essays should therefore be written before, and not after, any notes or discussion of the topic which may seem desirable. The teacher cannot fill the gaps till he knows what the gaps are. For this the method of producing notes by a co-operative effort, similar to that recommended elsewhere for the production of a fair copy of a composition, is much more stimulating than mere writing from dictation.

It is advisable that early in the course there should be a brief description of the geographic and economic background of Greece or Italy, for this is often assumed or referred to only incidentally even in the best text-book. Later on, a period or two should be devoted to a brief outline of epigraphy. Special topics in the period ('projects'), such as religion, trade, warfare, slavery, everyday life and so on, can be allocated to individuals for research, and in due course the researchers should be given a period in class in which to share the results with their brethren. If time allows, let there be a few periods when the master shows films or lantern slides or reads pseudo-Xenophon's *The Old Oligarch* or excerpts from Plutarch or Suetonius. Biography, it may be added, is one of the most comprehensible forms of history. Historical novels should not be forgotten, but the wisest time to recommend them is at the beginning of the holidays. Variety is the spice of life and the stimulation of interest a primary duty in a Sixth Form, as indeed at all levels. It is important too to make comparisons between ancient and modern problems and their solutions, and between conditions then and now. The danger here, however, is that of trying to increase reality by the introduction of modern labels and catchwords. It is *not* advised that Spartacus be regarded as a less successful Lenin or Themistocles equated with Winston

Churchill or Gaius Gracchus with Aneurin Bevan ! One advantage of the study of Ancient History is, or should be, that the judgement is not influenced by the emotional prejudices that so easily creep into our study of modern times.

The essentials for the teacher are sympathy with his pupils, a clear picture of his aims and a wide and deep knowledge of his subject. He, and if possible his pupils, should have access to a good library. Granted these, sufficient has been written on method.

2. LIFE

Before reaching the Sixth Form pupils will have gained a certain amount of knowledge about life in the ancient world in a more or less unsystematic way during the course of their ordinary Greek and Latin lessons. Some may also have read books that give an elementary summary of such background knowledge; and in addition many will have listened to lectures or talks, probably accompanied by visual aids, about particular topics in this wide field. In some cases this will have been reinforced by visits to museums or to the sites of Roman remains.

In general, however, the Sixth-Form entrant knows a good deal about the languages in which he is specializing, but not very much about the people who spoke those languages; and the study of Ancient History alone will not be adequate to redress the balance. It is therefore desirable that some effort should now be made by the teacher to open more widely a few doors on such subjects as Greek and Roman art, architecture and religion, and also on some aspects of the daily life of Greeks and Romans. There is no time for intensive teaching of these subjects, nor would it be desirable even if there were: what the pupil wants at this stage is a lead, followed by guidance on further private reading about any topic that arrests his interest.

The following are suggestions for single-period talks, with visual aids where possible:

Art. The Parthenon; Greek sculpture and Greek vases; Roman busts and Roman relief sculpture (e.g. Arch of Titus); Greek and Roman coins.

Architecture. Greek temples and theatres; Roman public buildings; Roman town and country houses.

Religion. The Delphic Oracle; Athenian festivals; 'mystery' religions; Roman state religion and private beliefs; votive and sepulchral inscriptions.

Social life. Greek dramatic performances; Greek athletics: Roman sports and amusements; Greek and Roman writing materials and books.

Other subjects would be similarly handled with reference to relevant passages, in the original or translated, from ancient authors; e.g. procedure in an Athenian or Roman court of law; procedure at Roman elections, and at meetings of the senate; education of an Athenian, Spartan or Roman boy; a day in the life of an Athenian or Roman; treatment of slaves in the ancient world.

One department, that of ancient philosophy, has not been mentioned. Though it is true that this has occasionally been studied to some extent at school, it is surely far better left to be dealt with by the more mature mind of the undergraduate. This does not of course preclude the reading of a philosophical text such as Plato's *Phaedo* by a good Sixth Form for its literary value and intrinsic interest.

3. LITERATURE

'Books are not absolutely dead things...they do preserve as in a vial the purest efficacy and extraction of that living intellect that bred them.' (MILTON)

It is in the first place essential that pupils who specialize in Classics should, during the course of their Sixth-Form work, acquire an outline knowledge of the histories of Greek and Latin literature. This can be done during private study periods and pupils' spare time if they are introduced to some of the excellent manuals that are available. The names of Murray, Rose, Mackail, Wight Duff, Bowra and others will at once occur to the teacher in this connexion; and experience has shown that sixteen-year-old pupils of the right calibre will read such books with pleasure, and will be able, on their own, to obtain from them sufficient knowledge to act as a basis for further study. The acquisition of outline know-ledge should not be subjected to testing by means of written work: in particular, it is wholly undesirable to call upon a pupil to reproduce second-hand opinions of the subject-matter and style of authors whose works he has not read.

After such a foundation has been laid, or even before it has been completed, it can be built upon in several ways that will call upon the teacher's assistance as well as continued private reading by the class.

(a) More Detailed Study of Particular Authors or Works of Authors

To take Virgil as an example, it is difficult to see how anyone who has read in the original a couple of books of the *Aeneid*, an *Eclogue* or two, and perhaps a few lines from the *Georgics*, is in a position to appreciate the author's work as a whole, or even that part of it, the *Aeneid*, with which schoolboys are most generally concerned. Some teachers, realizing this, endeavour to supplement their pupils' knowledge by getting them to read books in English about Virgil, or by reading extracts from such books to them. This procedure at this stage is—quite literally—preposterous. Before he reads or hears what other people have to say about the *Aeneid*, a pupil should read the whole, or at least a great part, of the *Aeneid* for himself: and of course the only way in which this can be done in school is by covering most of the ground in a good verse translation. Then, and not till then, he will be able to turn to Sellar and Glover with profit.

The same procedure can be followed with most of the front-rank Greek and Latin authors. The set-book periods, or rapid class-reading of a text in the original, provide the starting-point: more of a particular work, or selection from an author's other works, can then be read in translation; and finally the critics and appraisers can be allowed a hearing. It will often be desirable for the teacher to take the class through a summarized biography of the author, not forgetting to link up the author and his works with the general history of the period in which he lived.

(b) Study of Special Literary Genres

Some of these (e.g. Attic Orators, Roman letter-writing) are well catered for by existing books of selections. Others (e.g. Greek Tragedy, Roman Historians) are too wide to be studied in their entirety at school, though we see no reason why a good third-year Advanced-course class should not discuss particular questions that arise within them; for instance, a comparison of the part played by the chorus in Aeschylus, Sophocles and Euripides, or of the narrative style of Caesar, Livy and Tacitus.

There remain plenty of themes that could well be handled by Sixth-Formers with their teacher's help. The following are three examples:

(i) *Pastoral poetry*. Selections from Theocritus in the original and in translation, followed by the *Lament for Bion* and then by some of Virgil's *Eclogues*. Next, passages from Calpurnius Siculus and Nemesianus could be introduced in 'unseen' periods; and the course would be wound up by readings from English pastoral poetry.

(ii) *Speeches in ancient historians*. Examples from Herodotus, Thucydides, Livy and Tacitus. Quintus Curtius could also be included with profit if accessible.

(iii) *Ancient biography*. Start with some Cornelius Nepos (in the original) as an example of 'potted' biography; including in particular his *Life of Atticus*. Continue with selections from Plutarch and Suetonius in translation as examples of popular or journalistic biography. Conclude with large portions (in the original) of Sallust's *Jugurtha* or *Catiline* and Tacitus' *Agricola* as examples of historical monographs cast in the biographical form.

(c) Study of a Character as Depicted by Different Authors

Ancient literature affords plenty of opportunity for this, e.g.:

(i) Medea—in Euripides, Apollonius Rhodius, Ovid (*Met.* VII and *Her.* XII) and Valerius Flaccus (if accessible).

(ii) Electra—in the *Choephoroe* and the two *Electra*'s.

(iii) Socrates—in Aristophanes, Plato and Xenophon.

(iv) Catiline—in Sallust and Cicero, contrasted with 'special pleading' by moderns on the other side, such as J. Lindsay (*Rome for Sale*) and Beesly.

(d) Study of Modern Scholars' Views on Problems of Classical Literature

While it must be repeated that the reading of books about Greek and Latin authors should be entirely subordinated to the reading of the authors themselves, the classical specialist pupil may well be invited to consider certain problems discussed by modern authorities, and to reach his own conclusion on them. In the Greek field the most obvious example is the Homeric question, which could be discussed after reading Murray's *Rise of the Greek Epic* on the one side, and Bowra's *Tradition and Design in the Iliad* on the other. As another example, Verrall on Euripides is positively enthralling to young readers, particularly his essays on the *Alcestis* and the *Andromache*; and the same can be said of his theory of the *Agamemnon*. Always provided that the other side of the picture is well and truly presented to the class, we can think of few more exhilarating experiences for teacher and taught than one 'Verrall' period a week for half a term. With Latin literature, 'vexed questions' of fact, such as the authorship of the *Appendix Virgiliana*, do not come within school range: but on the question of taste it is still stimulating to read to a class something of what has been written about the respective claims to pre-eminence of Catullus and Horace or of Lucretius and Virgil.

VII

CLASSICS IN THE SECONDARY
MODERN SCHOOL

'Non omnia possumus omnes.' (VIRGIL)

By suggesting the inclusion of Classics in the curriculum of secondary modern schools we may be thought to be betraying our ignorance of hard facts and to stand revealed as educational faddists. To accept this judgement would be to confess to a narrow conception of classical studies, and also to make too sharp a distinction between the capacities of pupils in different types of schools.

It is true that the study of Latin and Greek is of itself an educational discipline of the highest value. It is also true that it is not possible fully to appreciate the beauties of classical literature or to understand the thought and attitude to life of Greek and Roman writers except by reading them in the original. Yet much of the ancient heritage can be enjoyed without a knowledge of Latin and Greek; and our belief in the value of that heritage as part of our spiritual, cultural and intellectual defence against the new barbarisms is sufficiently strong to make us feel that we should fail in our duty if we did not make some suggestions for its wider diffusion.

Furthermore, there is a very wide range of mental ability in the secondary modern schools, providing a borderline, or even an overlap, between them and the grammar schools. Much, therefore, of this chapter may very well apply to those many pupils in the less academic streams of the grammar schools who do not learn Latin or Greek and are, therefore, in danger of being cut off from a knowledge of Greek and Roman civilization.

It is undoubtedly an opportune moment to consider the curriculum of the modern schools. The length of school life has been increased by one year by the 1944 Act, and it is intended, as soon as financial and other conditions permit, to extend this by a second year. There are two important consequences of this; the obvious one that there is one year, and possibly two, to occupy with something that is educationally worth while, and the other, the very great development in maturity of mind after the fourteenth year, a development which, whatever its limitations in the academic field, will be intolerant of the old and elementary and in search of something new and enlightening. The main and admirable theme of the latest Education Act is secondary education for all, suitable for the aptitudes and abilities of the pupils. The word 'secondary' must be given its true and proper meaning if not merely full, but any, benefits are to accrue from the time, labour and expense entailed. It must have a wider content if it is to justify itself. It must be given a broader outlook and more far-reaching experience. It must try to provide a better understanding of human aims and endeavours. It must do whatever is possible to develop interest in something more than football pools and cinemas, and make every man, whatever his intellectual calibre, as worthy a citizen as possible, aware of his heritage and responsibilities.

Nothing could be more fatal to these aims than a compulsory continuation of school instruction in which interest has begun to wane. It cannot be denied that when 'elementary' education was the lot of most children up to the age of fourteen, very many of them began to chafe and look forward to their fourteenth birthday as the day of deliverance. The more rapid advance in maturity at that age makes the full use of it the more imperative if the extra year is not to be wasted. Repetition, or even continuation, on similar lines will increase restlessness and more than nullify any advantages gained by the lengthening of school life. Putting the old subjects in a new dress is only a partial solution; children are fairly acute at penetrating disguises, and once the gaff is blown it is the end. It is fortunate, however, that the mental growth that produces the dangers also provides a means of circumventing them, for it makes it possible to take an interest in and respond to topics and subjects that would have had no appeal a year or so earlier. We hope to show that the Classics can provide these interests.

1. The Scope of Classics in the Modern School

It is acknowledged that the mental calibre of the pupils in the secondary modern school will be of a lower level, generally speaking, than that of those in the grammar schools. This will be particularly the case where there is a generous provision of grammar-school places. It is indeed noticeable that in such areas there is a more thorough 'creaming' of the modern schools than before the raising of the school-leaving age. Many parents previously declined grammar-school places because they entailed an extra two years at school, whereas now it may be only one, and whether the 1944 Act likes it or not there is still some sort of cachet attached to attendance at a grammar school. This being so it will clearly be useless to try to foist on to such pupils a course of instruction in and appreciation of the higher beauties and values of ancient thought and achievement. We mention what may seem to be obvious, but the danger exists when a young and in-experienced teacher fresh from college, where he has perhaps dabbled in ancient philosophy or literature, deludes himself into thinking that deep thoughts and ideas when put into basic English become less deep. Admittedly some of the most important and valuable legacies of Greece and Rome are in the realm of ideas and the abstract, but they are incomprehensible even to those pupils of fifteen to sixteen in grammar schools who are of a sufficiently high intellectual standard to be taking Classics in the accepted sense. Most of their time up to that age is spent in the comparatively restricted and definite field of mastering the elements of language, and wisely so.

Obviously it will be equally useless to attempt the study of the Greek and Latin languages, which demand an analytical and methodical mind, and powers of concentration and memory beyond the reach of most. There is, indeed, some controversy about the wisdom of introducing even modern languages into the curriculum of secondary modern schools; but the very fact that they are being attempted in some is, in one respect at least, a good sign. It does denote recognition of the fact that something different is needed. The trouble is that such enterprise is often

CLASSICS IN THE SECONDARY MODERN SCHOOL

a more or less accidental fulfilment of the need. It just happens that there is someone on the staff with some knowledge or qualifications on those particular lines, and it is very tempting to use him to add variety—possibly a look of distinction—to the timetable. The educational value of such a proceeding will depend on numerous factors that may have had little consideration, but it has the appearance of supplying a need. There are cases where Esperanto has been introduced into secondary modern schools, but one may wonder what cultural or practical value any of the guinea-pigs find in that. Anything more artificial or less likely to have any natural points of contact with the pupils' present experience or future lives it would be difficult to imagine. Even the so-called living languages are dead unless they have a bearing on the life of the learner, if they do not add something to his appreciation and understanding of the things with which he comes into contact.

What of the so-called 'dead' languages? Is there not a far greater connexion between the languages and civilization of ancient Greece and Rome and our modern life and times than between the latter and our contemporaries just across the sea? It is a paradox that people who inhabited more distant lands two thousand years ago should still live in our language and our customs, and maintain contact with our daily lives, but it is this truth that compels us to suggest—state would, perhaps, be a better word—that there is a great deal in the Classics that could be usefully employed to enliven and enlighten pupils of the age and mental calibre found in secondary modern schools. There is plenty of material which has the necessary appeal, is factual and concrete, has the glamour of the past while illuminating the present, and the additional interest that springs from novelty. Here, in short, is a storehouse that could well be utilized in the difficult task of making that longer period of school life pleasant, interesting, useful, and possibly welcomed.

We shall endeavour later in the chapter to go into greater detail with regard to some material that might be used and suggest methods of using it, but it may be appropriate here to mention briefly some of the points on which our claim is based. It is an

131

axiom in education that so far as possible what is taught should be linked with what is known or what is met with. The Classics provide ample scope. There are endless possibilities in the English language, not only in roots and phrases taken from Latin and Greek, but for showing the real meanings of English words, making them live by means of the picture behind them. Incidentally it is a great aid to spelling when a word ceases to be an apparently arbitrary collection of letters, and some of the vagaries of our spelling and pronunciation would be explicable with a knowledge of the Greek alphabet. Then there are, so to speak, the artificial modern words, scientific terms, trade-marks, etc., that are met with every day, and from there it is but a step to familiar mottoes, inscriptions and the abbreviations in chemists' shops. Science becomes much easier and more interesting when its terms have a meaning, and considerably more interest could be aroused in modern scientific beliefs and theories by an elementary knowledge of those held by the ancient Greek philosophers. Boys are quite surprised to find that not even the atom is new. The Olympic Games have even more appeal if something is known of their origins and the rewards of the early victors, and boys are keenly interested to hear of hockey, draughts and other modern games as played 2500 years ago. For the older pupils the study of simple political development and local government can be enlivened by contrast and comparison with those in Athens in the fifth century; and legal procedure, with its insistence on fair play and justice in democratic countries through the ages, could be illustrated by accounts of famous trials in Athens, Rome and Britain. All children are interested in the lives, at home and at school, of children of other lands and earlier days. All these things have a close connexion with the world they know, or should know better, and all of them shed light, promote understanding and give an added interest.

Stories are always popular if they are adequately told and have intrinsic interest, and many are the lessons that can be drawn from them and the points that can be unobtrusively made. Nowhere is there a greater store of tales appropriate for all ages. There are stories of travel and adventure in actual or legendary lands, stories of achievements of worthy heroes with worthy aims, of the clash of personalities who come to life far more quickly and vividly than most of the figures of modern history, of the struggles that have gone on throughout the ages to gain or maintain freedom from tyranny and oppression. There are causal myths, the simple ideas of which always gain an added interest by reason of their arising from mystified inquiring minds, so closely akin to those of children. Here, in short, are stories for all moods and all purposes, stories that are full of interest, excitement, instruction and example. In addition they are clothed in the glamour of distant ages. Without them there is a danger that familiarity with many picturesque allusions such as 'the Wooden Horse', 'the Sword of Damocles', 'the Gordian Knot', as well as knowledge of cultural folk-lore that is an important part of our Western heritage, may indeed be lost for ever. Already fears have been expressed more than once that a generation may be growing up to whom such phrases as 'Job's comforter', 'a mess of pottage', 'a shibboleth' have become meaningless through neglect of the Bible. It would be a tragedy if, as a result of a craze for modernism or through mere default, the vocabulary and range of ideas of future generations should be permanently impoverished.

Nor need these stories remain merely word-pictures which may or may not be interpreted into something approaching accuracy. There is a good supply of illustrations showing the life, dress, buildings, weapons, etc., of ancient times. There may be, in the case of the Romans, local relics and associations. There is also scope for practical work in drawing and the making of models. There may even be opportunities in some districts of taking part in actual excavations and having the unforgettable experience of unearthing some relic of a bygone age, or of being on the spot when it was found. That, of course, would be a possibility for a very limited number of fortunate folk; but for all there is in the Classics an opportunity for a new, enlivening and satisfying experience, for a widening of outlook and a shedding of light in many and unexpected places. It is an unfortunate tendency in our times to take things for granted, to be satisfied with at best a semi-understanding; the very unexpectedness of this source of enlightenment makes its acceptance more welcome and more sure.

Such is a brief outline of the types of material available for teachers who wish and are able to make use of it. The material is excellent; what is demanded of the teacher? The most important quality is enthusiasm, and the greatest need either a wide and intimate knowledge of his subject or a knowledge of where to find what he wants. The teacher in a secondary modern school will probably not be a Classics specialist. It is not at all necessary that he should be. It is, in fact, high time that the Classics specialist ceased to regard this great heritage of the past to the present as a perquisite of those with a natural linguistic gift and the opportunity for developing it. To take a broader view would not only vastly strengthen the position of the Classics in the public regard but would also be of great benefit to education and the community as a whole. Classical scholars are so commonly regarded as a race apart and their pursuits as being concerned only with the distant, and somewhat dusty, past, that it would indeed be a novel experience for them to find themselves greeted with a respect that was due to gratitude and not veneration tinged with awe.

We may be prejudiced, but we find it difficult to imagine that anyone who has been put in contact with this abundance of riches would not be enthusiastic; and we know from experience that that certainly applies to the pupils, even if it is presented to them in a far from perfect form. It is, in fact, the pupils' eagerness that is likely to lead to difficulties. It is encouraging when children bombard one with questions in their search for further knowledge, but it is also embarrassing if one neither knows the answers nor where to find them. Fortunately, children are, on the whole, accommodating and will be quite happy if the information is eventually supplied, but one must be fairly wideawake to avoid some of the pitfalls, particularly, one might mention, in matters of derivation, which have an awkward habit of leading one into unexpected places. In other fields it is easier to keep on well-defined lines, whether one's interests are mainly in the literary, the scientific, the historical, or even the wider one of general applications of Greek and Roman customs, ideas and institutions. Which of these aspects are preferred by individual teachers will, of course, depend on their personal tastes, and what use is made of them depends on the capacities, environments and temperaments of their pupils. It is, therefore, impossible to be dogmatic about the choice to be made, or how the material should be used. It is possible to make suggestions, far from exhaustive, as to both, and to state quite definitely that there is something for all tastes and interests, and that an introduction to the sources available will be followed by an enthusiastic response on the part of all who feel the need for a breath of fresh air and the added interest of a new approach.

2. THE EQUIPMENT OF THE TEACHER

We must now consider how far the teacher in the secondary modern school is being equipped to carry out these suggestions. It is probable that at present the only contact with the Classics that most students entering the training colleges will have had, if indeed they have had any, is the acquisition of some Latin and even more elementary and indeterminate Ancient History at the grammar schools. At the training colleges it is possible that further contact may be made in one or more ways. Their course in the Theory of Education may include a study of Plato's *Republic* where it is concerned with education; they may come across Homer and Greek drama in translation in a comprehensive course in Literature; they may, in a History or Social Studies course, have traced developments in some field from the earliest times to the present day.

That is the most that can be expected, and it is not very much. In fact, what there is of it may, from a teaching point of view, be more dangerous than useful. For the conceptions given are rather for the adult mind; excellent indeed if the student, when he becomes a teacher, is not tempted to use the contents of his college note-book as the basis for a series of lessons for a class of under-sixteens. Those subjects were meant for his education, not for theirs. If he thinks a mere simplification of presentation will

10-2

render them suitable for consumption by the immature, his class will be bored and he disillusioned, and disinclined to make any further experiments with the Classics. That would be a pity when there is so much that could be used if only he remembered that, to be suitable for pupils of this and lower ages, topics must be not merely simply expressed but concrete or picturesque, and/or have some clear connexion with the present or things within the pupils' own experience. Mention of this danger is not meant as a criticism of the training colleges' schemes. They are to be welcomed whole-heartedly, both as certainly widening the students' conceptions and possibly sowing seeds of interest that may develop into the fruits of inquiry. What we should like to see, indeed what we must see if the Classics are to figure as we believe they should in the education of the masses, is a great development in this con-nexion on somewhat different lines. We are confident that experi-ments such as we suggest would have far-reaching and beneficial effects on both the teaching and the taught.

The moment at which this question is raised seems doubly appropriate; there is a growing realization that if secondary education for all is to have its fullest meaning and value it will need a different approach and content from the former elementary type; and secondly the training colleges throughout the country have been brought by the establishment of Institutes of Education into closer contact with the universities. The consequence of the first is a state of fluidity in the modern school curriculum and methods, a period inviting experiment. The latter we believe to have been a very wise decision from every point of view; for our immediate purpose it is providential. The Institutes are central bodies guiding and regulating the training of teachers in all the training colleges and departments in their respective areas, not ruling them with a dictatorial sway but providing means for the interchange of ideas. They are enlightened bodies composed of men and women representative of different fields, all with the cause of education at heart. Not only are they concerned with the actual training of teachers in the colleges, but by lectures and conferences they are developing and increasing their educational influence outside them, among teachers already in the schools, members of education authorities and others whose interests lie in that direction. Their power is, therefore, very great and should become greater. Their university connexions and the quality of their directors and deputy-directors should ensure that breadth of outlook that is necessary if education is to be guided along lines that will produce results commensurate with its cost. It is, therefore, to them that we appeal to encourage in every possible way the fullest use that can be made of the material to be found in the Classics.

This will mean not only that such material should be given a more regular and extensive place in the education of the student, thereby arousing his interest in its intrinsic value, but also that the selection of material and the methods of its presentation appropriate to the different actual or mental age groups should be an integral part of the teachers' training course. There will, of course, be greater opportunity to do so as the length of the period of training is increased, as it is hoped it quickly will be. As it would be far from fair to confine all these good things to the teacher in embryo and thereby rob some children now in the schools of an interesting and educative experience, we earnestly urge that demonstrations and lectures should be arranged, and exhibitions and conferences held by the Institutes for the benefit of teachers already in the schools. This might, indeed, be a useful first step, the results of which could provide some indication as to the most suitable shape, contents and methods of the full training course. There would have to be certain differences in the case of established teachers but we are confident they would respond to the call of the new with the same enthusiasm. As they will be in a better position to realize what they have been missing that is only to be expected.

If we have given the impression that the introduction of the Classics into the modern schools would be a complete innovation we apologize. There are some such schools where there is a study of classical subjects, and the success achieved in them, or perhaps we should say the interest aroused by them, proves that those who consider that the life of the Greeks and Romans is too remote from the life of children today to justify its inclusion are wrong, because they either do not know their subject well enough, or have presented what they do know badly, or have not really thought about the possibilities at all. These are the faults we desire to see eliminated, and that can be done by learning, training and instruction. Those modern schools that include a study of classical subjects do so on the basis of either or both of two major principles: that much in the life of the Greeks and Romans was great in itself and therefore deserving of study, and that a great deal of our life today has its origin in Greek and Roman times and a study of this heritage will increase the children's understanding of life and be truly educational. In these cases the use of the Classics is probably due to the happy chance that there was somebody available with an interest in the subject and a realization of its possibilities. We believe it is almost criminal that such things should be left to chance, and are anxious that all should have the opportunity of widening their outlook and increasing their understanding by making some degree of contact with an imperishable age.

We know that while the curricula of modern schools may be in a fluid state they are not elastic; we know also that in the training colleges there is overcrowding of curricula and syllabuses and a consequent disinclination to take on anything extra. If there can be an allocation of time for the teaching, or training in teaching, of specific items under the general heading of Classics, such as some periods of History, simple forms of social development, life in ancient Greece and Rome, Classics and the English language, etc., so much the better; but perhaps we should make it clear at this stage, in case there has been any doubt, that we do not suggest that the only way advantage can be taken of the subject is by labelling a certain number of periods in the time-table 'Classics'. It is indeed undesirable that it should be regarded as a subject in the usual sense of the term either in the schools or the training colleges. It is not so much a subject in itself as a source from which spring all manner of teaching and educational aids in a wide variety of subjects. Regarded as a subject it might tend to become isolated from the rest of the curriculum, whereas its main characteristic is its ability to play a part, and an illuminating part, in dealing with other subjects. We therefore suggest an increase in the use of classical material on the lines indicated later in the chapter, its substitution in some cases for something less effective, or its addition in other cases where it may have an important part to play, but has hitherto not been included in the scheme of things.

3. SUGGESTIONS FOR POSSIBLE LESSONS

It is not within the scope of this book to provide ready-made courses or schemes of work for either schools or training colleges. Local circumstances and interests are of many different kinds, and it is on these that any enthusiasm must be based. The conditions vary considerably in different types of institution and, therefore, the best that we can do is to give illustrations of when the Classics would be helpful, suggestions as to how the material could be used, and indications, by no means exhaustive but sufficient to whet the appetite, of where material may be found. We have sufficient faith in our case to believe that the teacher will be encouraged by results to undertake further research for himself.

Before doing so, however, it might be as well to emphasize that the lower their intellectual calibre the less capable are children of grasping abstractions or facts unrelated to their experience or emotions. They learn almost entirely through the senses. They learn by living, and associate what they experience with their own lives in a very direct way, and if there is no direct contact it is very difficult for them to learn. Like younger children they also learn by copying, even if they do not fully understand what they are copying, and are quite happy collecting lists of special instances and separate items, without any desire to generalize or draw conclusions from them. In short, they are intellectually immature, and in some respects will remain so for long after they leave school. On the other hand they mature quickly both physically and emotionally and in those respects are often older than their age.

For the not so old there are the stories the popularity and value of which have already been mentioned. One might suggest those of Demeter and Persephone, Jason and the Argonauts, Orpheus and Eurydice, Atalanta, Theseus, Perseus, Midas, Hercules, the story of Troy, the *Odyssey* and the *Aeneid*. It will probably be found that these stories are much more effective told than read, even from such books as Kingsley's *Heroes* and *Tanglewood Tales*. The same applies to the stories that come under the heading of legitimate history, for the personality of the teacher, himself enthusiastic and full of the spirit and atmosphere of the tale, will make a much more appreciative audience than the possibly more literary effort of a recognized author. The teacher's words are free from distracting influences and alive, whereas the author's have to be translated into a living force.

It is, of course, in the English language that one finds the closest everyday connexion between Latin and Greek and modern times, and here there will be ample opportunities for enlivening and enriching things that would otherwise be of no particular interest or significance. It is often found that the less academically minded grammar school streams find derivations and all the picturesque odds and ends an even greater source of surprise and interest than do those who are better able to cope with the difficulties of language construction. That this enthusiasm is not, as the cynical might suspect, due to relief from the need for mental strife, is proved by the questions they will ask and their readiness to spend a great deal of time in research out of school hours. It is a genuine interest; and anything that will promote a spirit of inquiry in legitimate directions is more than desirable, as it possesses both a negative and a positive value.

With a little research and an intelligent use of such a book as *Latin Words of Common English* (Johnson) anyone could soon have a useful knowledge of the real meaning and origin of words that would be a constant source of interest whether explanations were given casually as the words happened to occur, or deliberately in what might be called a lesson on words. There is a place for both methods, and enthusiasm can certainly be aroused for the second one by a few preliminary hints as to the next group or groups to be tackled. The hints may, probably will, start some false hares, but everything will lead somewhere, and one of the merits of this type of lesson is its conversational informality.

When there are so many possibilities it is not easy to select one as an illustration, but a very interesting and instructive lesson can be given on the occasion of a local or general election, when everyone is familiar with the canvassing of candidates. The word 'candidate' is much more colourful when one has a mental picture of the Roman seeker after office parading the city clad in a super-white (*candida*) toga, and 'rival' has more meaning when its association with *ripa* (river bank) is clearly seen. And what is canvassing but 'going round' (*ambitio*) soliciting votes, and who would do it if ambition did not urge him on? From this point there naturally develops, if it is so desired, an account of Roman elections to the various offices of state, and possibly a series of lessons comparing and contrasting ancient and modern methods of local and national government.

Such series of lessons could be developed with a reasonably good stream in a secondary modern school, and the link with the days of old would lend additional interest to the present. But even those whose literary experience is confined to comic or thriller picture-strips will be interested to know that *alias* and *alibi* are merely Latin words meaning 'at another time' and 'at another place' respectively. There is ample scope for all to find something that will give a new and interesting sidelight on things well within their experience. Perhaps a few more selected at random will prove the point. 'Plus', 'minus', 'maximum', 'minimum', 'gratis', 'tandem', 'junior', 'senior', 'major', for instance, are common enough and are pure Latin. Other words provide puzzles. What is the connexion between 'cardinal' and a hinge? What has 'gland' to do with an acorn? How is 'fine' in all its meanings connected with end? How does 'retort' come to mean two such different things? What links 'deliberate' with 'lb.' or 'petrol' with 'petrify'? What really is a 'companion' and why is it unnecessary to speak about a *private* secretary? What process is envisaged by 'calculation'?

The last one introduces a topic for a lesson on the abacus, arising from the difficulty of working with the symbols used before the advent of our Arabic numerals—a lesson that is always found to be entertaining—and then, of course, it is interesting to know how the Roman numerals came into being, and why 4 on clocks is IIII. There is, in fact, no end, and a little enterprise can give colour and meaning to what are otherwise merely uninteresting words. It is, indeed, surprising to find how flagging interest can be revived by some diversions on these lines.

So far we have only mentioned Latin, but Greek also plays its part and many peculiar-looking words—and not all of them unfamiliar to the common man—become more reasonable in appearance to those with some knowledge of the Greek alphabet. ('Alphabet' is itself a good example.) In addition to this advantage there is the light that is thrown upon their meaning. Mrs Dora Pym, in a letter to the Bristol Institute of Education's *Journal*, wrote of the interest and understanding aroused among children in a secondary modern school when she gave an explanation of the form and meaning of the word 'character' by reference to its Greek origin. That is an excellent instance of an awkward collection of letters becoming a living word. 'Hymn' soon accounts for its 'y' and 'n' when transferred to Greek characters, and it is not difficult to define a gramophone when 'telephone' and 'telegram' are understood—nor that horrible hybrid 'television'. Children soon recognize the characteristic peculiarities of English words derived from Greek, and when they see the corresponding Greek letters it will not be long before they want the whole alphabet. It is not difficult to learn or to write, and the pupils will be thrilled to copy it together with the English equivalents.

One could enumerate Latin and Greek prefixes and their effect on the root word—it is particularly useful as an aid to spelling to know that 'anti' is Greek for 'against' and 'ante' Latin for 'before'—but these are probably fairly widely dealt with. One could urge the advisability of teaching the actual words of which i.e., e.g., cf., ad lib., N.B., etc., are abbreviations, and one could mention the interest and enthusiasm aroused by collecting Latin mottoes, inscriptions and phrases, things that are, perhaps, not themselves so valuable as the spirit of inquiry engendered. There is also a field for observation and research in the advertisement columns; Saxa salt, Lux soap, Somnus bedding, Aquascutum raincoats, Cuticura soap, etc.—and what is Bovril but Latin Oxo?

But above all let us encourage the development of the word sense, a desire to know what words really signify; let us do something to check the present tendency to take everything for granted at its face value, the superficiality that bids fair to be the hallmark of the times. Let us try by any means to inculcate the idea that everything we have, even the words we use, are the result of the lives and thought of countless generations. And this is one way of helping to achieve that aim.

The deeper significance of the history of Greece and Rome is in the realm of ideas, demanding for its comprehension some power of abstract thought, some ability to reason from the particular event of a particular age to the general pattern of events in all ages. It is fortunate, however, that, like great works of art, music and literature that have stood the test of time, the history of Greece and Rome contains not only depths to be sounded by the mature and experienced thinker, but also much that has an immediate appeal to the young and the unintellectual. As a commentary on the foibles of human society *Gulliver's Travels* commands the serious attention of adult minds; it is also (subject to censorship) a first-class children's book. Read the voyage to Lilliput and Brobdingnag when you are young, and Swift the teller of the traveller's fairy tale will charm and draw you back when you are older to admire the brilliant and bitter genius of Swift the satirist.

So must we approach the history of Greece and Rome in the modern schools—by way of its stories. We must choose those stories—and there are many in ancient history—which appeal to the young. What, then, does the schoolboy like to read? Queer tales of foreign lands? In his descriptions of Egypt and the Middle East, Herodotus will provide plenty of these. The deeds of Horatius and Regulus, of the Spartans at Thermopylae and of the Athenians at Marathon, are exciting enough and moreover are first-class examples of heroism in the fight against tyranny. Our schoolboy also likes intrigue, secret messages, gangsters, bloodshed and something to make his flesh creep. Introduce him to those amiable rogues Histiaeus and Aristagoras (the slave's branded head is as good as invisible ink or secret codes); quench his thirst for blood

in the Marian and Sullan massacres, or in the waters of the
Assinarus. If he wants gangsters give him a glimpse of the Rome of
Clodius, Milo and Catiline. Stories of escape always fascinate, and
few are better than the story of the escape from Plataea, while
Thucydides' description of the plague is gruesome enough for
any taste.

Of course the mere presentation of highly coloured and, in
many cases, lurid pictures is not enough. In fact much of the
material mentioned above is of itself unedifying, and might suggest that the Greeks and Romans were not at all nice people.
Backed, however, by a simple account of who the Greeks and
Romans were, where and when they lived and what they did,
these stories would arouse interest by showing that the ancient
world was very much alive with people in all essentials the same
as ourselves, some good, some bad, some heroes, some rogues.

Appeal to the eye would do much to make the course successful,
and we might hope that a considerable extension of teaching about
the ancient world in the modern schools would make commercially
attractive the production of a far fuller range of visual aids than
is at present available. Here are some suggestions of the sort of
material we have in mind:

(1) Large photographs, or film strips, of the Italian and Greek
countryside.

(2) Wall pictures or film strips of Roman houses and articles
of everyday use—including clothes and armour—in Greece and
the Roman world.

(3) Pictures or models of ships.

(4) Films of famous episodes such as the battles of Thermopylae
and Salamis (the story of Themistocles' message to the Persians
would make excellent dramatic material); the stories of Regulus
and Coriolanus.

Nor should aural aid be forgotten. Broadcasts to schools might
include dramatized narratives of famous episodes, while the strip
cartoon can be used to tell the story of Greece and Rome. Also
necessary would be a wide range of freely translated and freely
paraphrased selections from the ancient writers. Last, and most
important, the teachers would have to be enthusiasts with that

full knowledge of their subject which would make a clear and attractive exposition possible.

Perhaps one of the easiest and most effective ways of making the ancient world real to the secondary modern school pupil is by bringing him into contact with the everyday life of the Greeks and Romans. A teacher anxious to introduce his pupils to this would, however, probably be well-advised to start by tackling a number of 'projects' in which Greek and Roman life play only a small part, e.g. those which trace the development through the ages of a topic such as transport or housing, before attempting a project dealing exclusively with the ancient world. In this way the life of the ancient world can be shown to be relevant to modern life, whereas to attempt a full-scale portrait of ancient life on its own without any preliminary studies might make the subject seem remote and alien to the child.

When such preliminary work has been done, a good starting-point for an exclusively classical subject might perhaps be found in 'Schools in the Ancient World'. Comparison with the pupils' own life and surroundings is easy and immediate. There are few children in any type of school who will not be interested to hear of the boarding-school life of the Spartan boy with its iron discipline, its prefectorial and fagging system, its floggings for the slightest offence, the nastiness of the school meals—the Spartan broth which prompted the stranger's remark that he now understood why no Spartan feared death; of the Athenian boy's education, μουσική and γυμναστική with all that that meant; of the Roman boy travelling with his pedagogue to school often before it was light, and munching his breakfast of bread or a bun as he went to be initiated into the mysteries of the abacus-board and to learn his lines of Virgil and Horace. 'Ancient Education' need not stop here but could be developed to deal briefly and simply with the higher education of a Greek or Roman, the Sophists and Socrates (both rich in anecdotes) and the Roman study of oratory. Another allied topic might be 'Sports, Games and Amusements in the Ancient World' with pictures and descriptions of the Olympic Games, chariot racing, gladiatorial contests, wrestling and boxing, and less public recreations such as draughts, knucklebones, dicing, hoops, the form of blind-man's buff known as 'bronze fly', hockey and even tennis ('recommended as a gentle exercise for the elderly'). Other topics might be 'Housing', 'Dress and Hair Styles' (an interesting film-strip has been devised by one girls' school on this), 'Slavery', 'Military Service', 'The Romans in Britain', 'A Day in the Life of a Greek or Roman', 'Trade, Commerce and Coinage', 'Ships and Naval Tactics in the Ancient World', 'Christians under the Empire' or 'Life in the Catacombs' (which might be co-ordinated with Scripture lessons); and 'the Greek and Roman Attitude to Religion' might be dealt with in a very simple fashion. As some of the most important contributions of Greece and Rome to Western civiliza-tion are Democracy, Law and the principles of Government, an ambitious teacher might profitably try to deal with the Athenian Assembly and Law Courts—many amusing anecdotes could be culled from Aristophanes—and the Roman Senate and Provincial Government. This would have to be made as concrete as possible, perhaps by holding a mock meeting of the Assembly or a mock Roman trial.

All this will of course demand a very enthusiastic teacher who is prepared to undertake a good deal of background reading if he is to satisfy the innumerable questions that are bound to arise when the children's interest has been stimulated, e.g. what materials were ancient clothes made of, what food did the people eat, how was marble for the Parthenon quarried, moved and chiselled into shape? (These are actual questions asked in one school where such an experiment was tried.) There are a number of good standard books of reference available for the teacher, and much useful background information can be obtained from such historical novels as *Freedom Farewell* by Phyllis Bentley, *Black Sparta, The Blood of the Martyrs* and *The Conquered* by Naomi Mitchison, *Nicanor of Athens* by O. F. Grazebrook, *I, Claudius* and *Claudius the God* by Robert Graves, and *Theras, the Story of an Athenian Boy* by C. D. Snedeker. Some of these books or suitable parts of them the children themselves will enjoy reading or having read to them. There are, too, a number of useful film-strips, wall-maps, charts, collections of coins and realien—reference to which is made elsewhere in this volume under Visual Aids (pp. 189–196)—but many more aids of this kind are needed. Some models can, of course, be produced by the children themselves if time is available. Visits to museums and, if possible, Roman sites in this country are, of course, obvious aids in establishing this contact with the ancient world.

These are only a few suggestions, and much thought will be needed for their working out in practice. So much will depend on the teachers themselves and the pupils they are teaching. It is most important that not too much should be attempted, that the teacher should have available an abundance of illustrative material and stories to tell, and that developments should not be forced if the enthusiasm is not there, but grow naturally from the particular tastes and interests of the class itself. It is important too that there should be plenty of things for the children to look at and handle, but it is no less important that these photographs, film-strips, etc., should be of the very best quality possible. More harm than good is done by dingy photographs or poor reproductions, so common in the older text-books, which make the ancients appear not only dead but incredible.

The following passage is quoted from a report of what actually happened recently at a secondary modern school in the west of England:

A project was planned on 'The Theatre' with a class of B-stream girls. They began by bringing pictures from home showing all kinds of things to do with the theatre; these happened to include an illustration from *Picture Post* of a Greek play then being performed in London. The material was then displayed and fell roughly into two divisions, (*a*) plays, (*b*) theatres. It was then decided to plan an exhibition for the end of term, and also to have one or two plays written and acted by the class.... After groups had been formed to investigate the theatre at different periods, the teacher led off by giving a talk to the class, with blackboard illustration, about the Greek Theatre and Greek plays. The children were so fascinated by the form of a Greek tragedy, and especially by the possibility of using a chorus, that thenceforth the term's work was devoted entirely to the Greek theatre.... At the end of the term, one of the plays that they had written in English on Greek themes was acted. The story of Perseus was the one chosen and, though

147

the girls could hardly remember their parts from day to day, they had really made something of their own, rudimentary though it was. The other plays they had written included one about Orpheus and Eurydice: the sadness of this story appealed to them, and a good deal of research had to be done by the teacher about Greek flowers, as they were anxious to introduce the right 'local colour' into their play.

This should be sufficient to dispel any doubts about the practicability of introducing the subject of the Ancient Theatre and Ancient Drama to classes in this type of school; and in addition it suggests an obvious method by which the subject may be handled. Further information can be obtained from chapter IX and the books listed in the Bibliography (p. 198). We are sure that pupils of this type, by composing and acting their own simple plays, will gain a better appreciation of ancient stories and legends than by meeting them in a purely literary shape: in fact, another sentence of the report already quoted runs: 'In the same school at another time the story of Perseus, when read in a "literature" lesson from Kingsley's *Heroes*, fell absolutely flat.'

If this is accepted, the question then arises whether such pupils can be induced to take a step further forward, and act in an English version from actual ancient plays. It is not suggested that this could be attempted without a considerable amount of preliminary abridgement and simplification to suit the needs of the class. But we feel that any teacher who is prepared to take the trouble that would be involved will find, as far as Greek Comedy is concerned, plenty of genuinely humorous material in Aristophanes' *Clouds* and *Frogs* that is simple enough to appeal to the dullest pupil. To attempt to draft a Greek tragic drama for this purpose would, no doubt, be quite impracticable with most of the plays; but Euripides' *Iphigenia in Tauris*, with its well-knit and exciting plot, would seem simple enough to offer scope for an experiment on these lines.

Although Egypt was the first Western nation to leave enduring architectural records, as in the pyramids and temples, it was the Greeks who made the outstanding contribution to the development of architecture in the perfecting of the orders: Doric, Ionic and Corinthian. There is an abundance of photographs of Greek temples, theatres and other buildings, from which to study this type of architecture, amongst them the following: the Parthenon, the Erechtheion and the Theseion in Athens, the temple of Poseidon at Paestum, the temple at Segesta, the temple of Concordia at Acragas, the temple on Sunium.

The Romans copied the Greek orders with some modifications, notably a new composite order for columns of exceptional strength. They also introduced the semicircular arch, which was of Etruscan origin, and its use can be widely illustrated. The temples in the Forum of Rome, which was developed from the Greek market place and the Maison Carrée at Nîmes, are examples of the Greek styles, and the Arch of Titus shows at its highest level the combination of the composite capital and the arch. The aesthetic value of the arch when many times repeated is best illustrated by the exterior of the Flavian Amphitheatre, or Colosseum. Outside Rome, there are many examples of this arch-form, notably the Pont du Gard, near Nîmes. The application of this form to private buildings is to be seen in the houses of Pompeii. Some mention of the materials used by Roman builders should be of interest, especially the use of concrete, which was of extraordinary strength, and the practice of facing walls with triangular bricks divided by layers of tiles, with a further covering of stucco or marble slabs.

With the quantity of models available, it is natural that Roman architecture provided the dominant style in the Renaissance, and the revival of this style in the nineteenth century gives the opportunity to observe the classical orders in every city and almost every town in this country. The comparison with the originals can be made an instructive study. The present century has evolved an architecture which is more truly expressive of modern ideas and culture; examples of this are, of course, to be seen everywhere, and they can be supplemented with photographs of modern buildings in Europe and America. Although the classical style has been abandoned, the lesson can be taught that architecture is an ever-changing mode of expression, which faithfully portrays its time.

All examples of ancient architecture mentioned above, and

many more, can be shown to pupils by means of photographs and illustrations from the many books dealing with the subject. The use of the epidiascope is obviously to be recommended. For the modern examples, there will be few schools so situated as not to have buildings accessible for observation and comparison with the classical models. Where possible, pupils should be given individual tasks of observing a specific building and later describing it to the class.

Few cities and towns are without examples of statuary of some kind, which might well prove the starting-point for an excursion into the history of sculpture, in which the contribution of the Greeks and Romans would naturally occupy a pre-eminent place. Children are notoriously blind to sights to which they have become habituated, and the introduction to such a course might well take the form of drawing the attention of pupils to

> ...things we have passed
> Perhaps a hundred times, nor cared to see.

Why, for instance, is the group of figures in the market-place carved in white stone? Why not coloured? Why are they undressed? Children can be brought first to think about things they have taken for granted. They can be encouraged to observe other statues in the neighbourhood. Then, when their curiosity is fully roused, they can be told something of the progress of sculpture through the various stages of its development.

As in architecture, Egypt historically is the starting-point in sculpture, and it is remarkable as exemplifying a conventional religious art which was virtually unchanged for four thousand years. By the frequent use of pictures, British Museum postcards and film-strips, children can be brought to see the technical advances which one generation was able to make upon another in portraying the human figure in three dimensions. They will observe the strides made from the first stiff formalized figures, still strongly influenced by Egypt, with bodies barely distinguishable from the first terminal carvings. They will note the conventional style of the Lion Gate at Mycenae, the Artemis of Delos, the statues of the Branchidae Temple and the reliefs on the temple at Selinus. They will laugh happily at the quaintly grinning Korai excavated on the Acropolis, but they will be learning something of the sculptor's struggle for mastery over his material. The idealized athletes of the fifth century should awaken a response in boys, at least, with their admiration of physical prowess, and though, perhaps, it would be expecting rather much to ask them to distinguish between, say, the elegance and refinement of Phidias and the earlier grandeur and solemnity, nevertheless the frieze and the pediments of the Parthenon have sufficient inherent interest to attract them to the glories of the classical style. Copies of Myron's Discobolus always appeal to boys, especially if contrasted with photographs of statues of modern disc-throwers. Nor should a class have any great difficulty in appreciating the new turn given to sculpture in the fourth century. The new humanistic, emotional and personal type of sculpture is notably exemplified in the works of Praxiteles and Scopas. Copies of their statues still exist, the Cnidian Aphrodite, the Satyr, the Apollo Sauroctonus of Praxiteles. The statue of Niobe and her children is an example of the end of this period. The Hellenistic age is represented by the Laocoon group, the Aphrodite of Melos, the Apollo Belvedere or the Nike of Samothrace. All these statues are so famous in world history that it is almost the inalienable right of children to be told something about them. But the value of visits to museums to see copies of statues in the round, to reinforce a knowledge that might otherwise be solely dependent on pictures or photographs, cannot be overstressed.

It may be that the children will have a sense of anticlimax when they turn to Roman sculpture, which is so largely an imitation of the Greek, but there are many examples of portrait busts and historical reliefs, which are almost exclusively Roman branches of sculpture. The earlier busts lack life and spirit, but later busts appear more natural. Nevertheless, the teacher would be well advised not to linger over this branch of art, unless the children have a particular interest in the person whom the bust represents. A more fruitful field of study may perhaps be found in the historical reliefs of the Ara Pacis Augustae, the Arch of Titus, the Arch of Constantine and similar arches.

Modern sculpture has shown revolts from classicism and returns to it, but a study of the Greek models is still of utmost importance for the appreciation of recent works. The teacher would do well to refer to the carvings of recent sculptors such as Rodin and Epstein, until he feels he has reached a point at which he can say that at least a basis has been provided from which, if they care, they can form their own estimate of the achievements of modern sculpture as exemplified in the statues once displayed on the South Bank and in Battersea Park.

In this chapter we have done little more than hint at the material available in the classical field for developing interest in, and a better understanding of, many things in the modern world, and for bringing a new vitality into the lessons and school activities of the quite ordinary child. In addition to stories, mythical and factual, of which it is impossible to have too large a stock, we have touched on the largely classical basis of the English language itself; on numerous everyday expressions and literary allusions; on the foundations of literature and history in the making; on the interests, activities and life of peoples living in a more simple world but having much the same natures and characteristics as ourselves; on possibilities of extending the scope of handicraft and dramatic work; on the early stages in the development of architecture and sculpture, some acquaintance with which may promote at least a realization that in some form or another these arts are with us still.

The field is wide, and we do not suggest that any one teacher will necessarily be able or desire to cover the whole of it. We do hope we have indicated sufficient possibilities from which each may choose according to his own particular bent. We are confident that whatever line is chosen deepening interest will lead to further research, and further research to ample reward.

VIII

EXAMINATIONS

'Ὁ δὲ ἀνεξέταστος βίος οὐ βιωτὸς ἀνθρώπῳ.' (PLATO)

1. THE JUNIOR AND MIDDLE SCHOOL

CHARACTERISTIC of the Latin and Greek languages, and, we would venture to add, prominent among their virtues as instruments of education, is the fact that to learn them one must master a body of precise knowledge. The forms of the accidence and the basic rules of the syntax are fixed and absolute, providing the pupil at each stage with a clearly defined goal towards which he must direct his efforts, and an infallible yardstick by which he may measure his progress. For these reasons Latin and Greek—at any rate up to Sixth Form level—are not only eminently examinable subjects, but subjects in the teaching and learning of which appropriate examinations play an important, if not essential, part.

We do not, however, use the word 'appropriate' idly. For the very precision which marks the elements of Latin and Greek inevitably reveals any failure to make the examination correspond exactly to the particular stage of the course with which it purports to relate. At each stage teacher and pupils must be consciously aiming at 'specific and concrete objectives' (see above, p. 16), and the examination must test attainment of those objectives and no others. Furthermore, the attainment of the objectives should be so far within the powers of the majority of the class or group being examined as to give the average pupil the impression that a reasonable degree of success depends not on his being very clever or very lucky, but on his paying attention, taking care and working hard. This is particularly important in the first two or three years; for small boys are sensitive to injustice, and poor performance in an examination containing difficulties with which they have had little or no chance of dealing is likely to lead to discouragement and bring the subject into disrepute.

Not only should the bulk of the examination be limited to material with which the majority of the candidates are thoroughly familiar, but the material itself should be presented in a familiar form. There is perhaps not much room for variety in the first two years of Latin (after all there are not many ways in which one can ask for the genitive singular of *rex*), but experience shows how even slight differences in expression will confuse the boy of twelve or thirteen. If, for instance, a class is for the first time being tested or examined on the conditional clause, the inclusion of the sentence 'Had you come yesterday you would have seen me' would be unfair. All but the brightest boys find it hard enough to understand the difference between the various types of conditions when expressed in the most straightforward form, and the omission of the conjunction is an unfair complication, unless, of course, the teacher has had time to give his pupils practice not only on the basic types but on the variations. Passages for translation into English should contain only those words which have been frequently encountered in the reader. Furthermore, the subject-matter and style (or should we say length and complexity of the sentences?) must be similar to those of the material of the reader. The teacher with a taste for epigram or neat anecdote who fancies himself as a Latinist may amuse himself in composing a snappy passage for translation; but the first- or second-year examinee will neither see the joke nor understand the Latin. The time to be clever with your class is when you are teaching them, not in the examination when you cannot help them to understand the products of your wit.

The number of questions and the marks allotted to a particular section of an examination should be proportionate to the emphasis given at that stage in the teaching to the facts or processes to which the section relates. Much, for instance, of the first year of Latin is usually spent on the learning and reciting of declensions and conjugations, and on mechanical drill in the accurate and facile application of the rules of agreement. A first-year examination paper will, therefore, for the most part test ability to write out declensions and conjugations correctly and to effect with accuracy the agreements of case, number, gender and person. Sentences will be of the simplest kind, and so composed that almost every word tests knowledge of a separate and definite point.

We do not, however, suggest that an examination should be so completely limited in scope that the majority in the middle of the class could by working hard get as many marks as the minority at the top. Without the incentive of a reward in the tangible form of higher marks in the examination, boys (the younger ones at any rate) may not extend their energies fully; keenness may be blunted and interest lost. Moreover, to set an examination that did not pick out the good from the average or mediocre would be to ignore another of the principles established in our first chapter—that each stage of the course should contain within itself the potentiality of future advance. The degree to which the best pupils should be given the chance of showing their superiority will vary with the composition, in terms of ability, of the class or group being examined. As a general rule, the paper or papers should be so composed that the majority of the class can tackle anything up to three-quarters of the questions with confidence, and with the feeling that they are dealing with something familiar. The other questions will be more selective, giving a chance to those who deserve it to reap the reward of special ability and industry.

In the first two or three years of Latin, examination papers should start with questions testing routine memory work—a few conjugations or declensions to write out. This will give the paper a less formidable appearance to the weaker pupils, who will be at once confronted with something they can do with a reasonable amount of confidence. Difficulties should come near the end. As a sample which to some degree illustrates this method we append a paper set for boys aged eleven to twelve, half-way through their first year of Latin.

Examination set half-way through First Year

1. Decline: Marks

    (*a*) in the SINGULAR ONLY (all cases)—*servus* ⎫
    (*b*) in the PLURAL ONLY (all cases)—*rex*   ⎬ 8
    (*c*) in the SINGULAR ONLY (all cases and genders)—*pulcher* ⎭

2. Give the Latin for:

    (*a*) A long war (accusative)   ⎫
    (*b*) Of the unhappy sailor   ⎪
    (*c*) For the Roman soldier   ⎪
    (*d*) With a large arrow   ⎬ 12
    (*e*) Of the small boys   ⎪
    (*f*) Many burdens (accusative)   ⎭

3. Conjugate in the SINGULAR ONLY:

    (*a*) Present tense of *paro*   ⎫
    (*b*) Future tense of *moneo*   ⎬ 4
    (*c*) Imperfect tense of *sum*   ⎭

4. Conjugate in the SINGULAR *and* PLURAL:

    (*a*) Perfect tense of *laudo*   ⎫
    (*b*) Future perfect tense of *timeo* ⎬ 6

5. Give the English for:

    (*a*) Ubi habitas?   ⎫
    (*b*) Saepe ambulabam   ⎪
    (*c*) Quem docuisti?   ⎬ 10
    (*d*) Servi laboraverunt   ⎪
    (*e*) Numquam timebimus   ⎭

6. Give the Latin for:

    (*a*) Good-bye, Sextus!   ⎫
    (*b*) From the inn   ⎪
    (*c*) He was fighting yesterday ⎬ 9
    (*d*) I shall beat Tullius   ⎪
    (*e*) Woe is me!   ⎭

EXAMINATIONS

7. Put into English:

(a) Salvete, pueri! Quo hodie festinatis?
(b) Ad ludum ambulamus; sumus discipuli.
(c) Quis discipulos docet? Orbilius est magister noster.
(d) Pueros ad ianuam ludi exspectabit.
(e) Timesne Orbilium, Tulli?
(f) Ita vero! est enim plagosus et saepe ignavos verberavit.
(g) Magistrum igitur timemus.

21

8. Put into Latin:

(a) The good slaves were adorning many tables.
(b) The soldier has terrified the unhappy farmer with an arrow.
(c) Yesterday the sailor was telling stories to the girls.
(d) Once upon a time the Romans laid waste the fields of the Gauls.
(e) Why will you praise the new freedman?
(f) He has worked for a long time in our country house.

30

9. Rewrite the following sentences, putting correct endings on the incomplete words:

(a) Agricol... nautas timet.
(b) Reg... bonum laudatis.
(c) Cur festin..., Sexte?
(d) Miles mult... onera portabat.
(e) Heri pueri magistrum tim....

10

110

Of the 110 marks, 49 can be obtained on the first six questions. The seventh question is a close adaptation of the material of two lessons in the text-book used. The theme is continuous, but the question is made to look simpler by being split into separate sentences, each on a separate line. The last two questions (8 and 9) are likely to prove the most difficult. Taken in a large grammar school whose annual intake of approximately 180 boys all start Latin in the first year, of whom only about 90 continue the subject after the first year, papers of this type have produced the following results:

40% and over obtained by more than 90 boys.
50%   ,,   ,,   about 80 boys.
60%   ,,   ,,   over 60 boys.
80%   ,,   ,,   over 20 boys.
90%   ,,   ,,   about 10 boys.

Thus of the boys who will continue Latin the great majority can obtain 50% or more of the total marks. Yet the examination is selective enough to allow only a very few to obtain 90% of the marks.

The same principles should be observed all through the course up to Ordinary Level. The examination syllabus should always be well within the powers of the majority of the class or group for whom it is set; and the paper should be in such a form as to make them feel that they are not being trapped into displaying their ignorance—like the victims of the gloating housemaster in *Young Woodley*—but are being given a chance to show that with honest effort they have mastered a definite task.

'All very well!' the schoolmaster critic may exclaim, 'but we have to get these boys through the Certificate Examination. However much we should like to vary our methods and our syllabus to fit the varying capacities of our pupils, we have to prepare them for a test imposed on them from outside.'

In reply we would admit that the School Certificate Examination (the predecessor of the Ordinary Level Examination for the General Certificate of Education) was in the early years of its existence sometimes unsuitable as a test for schools. The universities, who controlled the examination, naturally tended to model the syllabuses and papers on their own entrance tests which the School Certificate was to replace. Thus all candidates were forced to take an examination which stressed, by making compulsory, the academic disciplines, notably the Mathematics and Latin (or at any rate a foreign language). Failures, caused partly by this academic bias, have over a period of years persuaded examining bodies in consultation with teachers to modify the examination to a form more suited to the average pupil in the grammar school. It is important in this connexion to remind newcomers to the profession—and perhaps others—that there is close liaison between the schools and the examining bodies. Representatives of both sides meet regularly to discuss the suitability of syllabuses and papers in the light of comments sent in from individual schools. But for this machinery to work effectively there must be comments. Reform comes from the organized expression of reasoned public opinion. In particular, full use should be made of the facilities provided by the Association of Assistant Masters for the forwarding of detailed criticism—constructive as well as destructive, favourable as well as adverse.

Our schoolmaster has to prepare his boys for an examination which may be external, but which he and other schoolmasters have the power, if they will use it, so to adapt to the ability of their pupils that the G.C.E. Examination (like the internal examinations) will form an integral part of the school course. He and his fellows must, however, decide what it is reasonable to expect of the average grammar-school pupil after four or five years of Latin; and to aid them in making their decisions it may be useful here to review the examination in its present form and to comment on some variations and alternatives.

2. ORDINARY LEVEL EXAMINATION IN LATIN

In the past Latin was normally taken in the School Certificate Examination as a matter of course by all who had continued the subject beyond a preliminary one or two years. The candidates could be divided into three main groups:

1. Those who proposed to leave school after obtaining a School Certificate. Apart from any educational merits, Latin had for them the utilitarian value of being one of the subjects which could help them to make up the number of passes or credits necessary for the award of a certificate.

2. Those who needed a 'credit' in Latin as part of a qualification for entrance to the Universities of Oxford or Cambridge

THE TEACHING OF CLASSICS

or for admission to an Honours degree course in arts subjects at other universities, or as a professional qualification.

3. Those who would continue to study Latin in the Sixth Form either in a full classical course with Greek, or with other Arts subjects in the 'Modern' studies group.

Thus the School Certificate Examination was taken at the end of the fourth or fifth year of the main school course by all three groups, both by those (in Groups 1 and 2) who would discontinue Latin after the examination and by those (in Group 3) who would take it up to Higher Certificate or university level.

Since the introduction of the General Certificate of Education in 1951, the Examination at Ordinary Level, like the School Certificate Examination, has marked the end of the final stage of the Latin course for the majority of the candidates. It is therefore important to ensure that the Ordinary Level Examination is within the capacity of the average pupil who has done Latin for four or five years for five periods a week. In other words, like our internal examinations, it should be so composed that the average candidate can tackle a large proportion of the questions and be reasonably sure of getting a 50 or 60% mark.

All examining bodies in England and Wales set two papers in Latin at Ordinary Level of about 2 hours each. The first paper usually consists of:

(a) Formal questions on grammar (mainly accidence).
(b) An easy passage of Latin prose for unprepared translation.
(c) English sentences for translation into Latin.
(d) A passage of continuous English for translation into Latin.

Some examining bodies make (c) alternative to (d), others demand both sentences and prose.

Many teachers dislike the inclusion of formal grammar questions in the examination. They teach formal grammar as a necessary part of the means to an end, namely, of enabling their pupils to translate into and out of Latin. It is the business of the examiners to find out whether the end has been attained, not to pry into the means used. The setting of formal grammar questions has been compared by one of its opponents to 'buying filleted fish at the fishmonger's and demanding to see the bones' ('Why Latin?', T. W. Melluish in *Greece and Rome*, June 1944). One examining body has in fact for some years stopped setting formal grammar questions. The chief reason for the inclusion of formal grammar questions in the examination paper is to ensure that the accidence has been taught. From the teacher's point of view, it may also be argued that such questions give a chance to the weaker candidate. For him sentences are a gamble. With fine impartiality he backs in turn the few horses whose names he knows—'*ut* and the subjunctive', 'accusative and infinitive' and 'ablative absolute' —in the hope that occasionally one of them will win. For him Latin unseens are but an inspiration to write nightmare fantasies in which all the laws of natural probability are defied. But he can be made to learn the accidence by rote and be trained to a reasonable degree of mechanical dexterity in dealing with our friends 'the sad old man', 'the longer road' and 'the huge head'. The reader may draw his own conclusions.

Of the unseen passage in the first paper we have little to say except that it should be quite straightforward and simple. It should be a systematic test of the candidate's knowledge of common constructions, idioms and words. For this purpose a completely synthetic piece of Latin is perhaps better than an extract from a Latin author.

Some teachers are against the inclusion of continuous prose in the examination at Ordinary Level. They say that these so-called 'proses' are simply separate sentences each illustrating different points of syntax, strung together to make up a connected narrative. Latin prose composition in the real sense—that is, the recasting of a passage of English prose literature, and its reproduction in a language which differs from English not only in its superficial grammatical structure and idiom but in the underlying processes of its thought—demands an experience and a knowledge of English as well as of Latin and a capacity for abstract thought beyond the powers of the average candidate at Ordinary Level.

There is, however, something between unrelated sentences in English and the prose of Macaulay or Gibbon. There can be simple narrative about concrete events. To say that a Latin rendering of such a narrative cannot be good Latin is to say that Latin prose authors, Caesar for instance or even Cicero, never told a plain story in a straightforward way. At any rate, as has been suggested earlier (p. 36), many teachers will want to do some continuous composition with their pupils, if for no other reason than that it is more interesting sometimes to try and put a story into Latin than to be for ever writing exercises of unrelated sentences. Moreover, a good class will soon pick up the more elementary principles of composition such as connexion and subordination. It would be a pity if such work were not recognized and encouraged by the inclusion of a continuous passage in the examination. Perhaps, however, it should be an alternative and not an addition to the sentences.

Examination sentences in the past were too difficult. The desire of the examiners to test the candidate's knowledge of as many constructions and idioms as possible in the smallest possible space gave rise to trick sentences whose correct rendering in Latin was perhaps more improbable and unnatural as Latin than was the English original as English. Criticisms and suggestions from teachers themselves have led to a considerable simplification. It is fairly widely recognized that each sentence should not test the knowledge of more than one or, at the most, two subordinate clause constructions. In order to ensure that a sufficiently large portion of the basic grammar is covered it might be worth while setting a larger number of sentences than is now usual—say ten—which might be of progressive difficulty.

For the second paper nearly all examining bodies give candidates the choice of unprepared translation or set books. The set books usually consist of about half a book of Caesar's *Gallic Wars* and about 600 lines of Virgil. Discussion on the respective merits of unprepared translation and set books reveals a sharp difference of opinion among teachers, and we think it useful here to state the case on either side.

In favour of set books it is argued that the reading of the literature is the ultimate aim of those who learn Latin and Greek. To take the unseen paper is a temptation to many to spend all the time allocated to translation work on practice in doing short pieces. Thus no portion of the works of any one author will have been read which is of sufficient length to have much value as literature. Furthermore, concentration on the technique of doing unseens will leave little time for the pupil to acquire that knowledge of the historical and literary background which he would gain by a successful preparation of the set books.

A set book, too, is a challenge to long-term effort. It is bracing to tackle something big; a real book by a real author. Not only is it a challenge, but it is also something definite, and this is a strong point in its favour for the average boy. So many lines can be set for each lesson, and each stage is a measurable advance to a clear objective. Knowledge of this fact increases the pupils' confidence.

Successful preparation of set books is a training in concentration and thoroughness, and the boy who has spent his last year of Latin in thus thoroughly preparing, say, part of Livy XXI and Virgil, *Aeneid* II is bound to retain something of permanent value, and he can share his experience with others who have read the same books.

The opponents of set books assert that these arguments rest on a mistaken conception of the real and achievable aims of a Latin course up to Ordinary Level. To teach Latin is to teach a language. Not until our pupils have mastered the mechanics of the language and have acquired the technique of translating from and into Latin with some facility can they be expected to appreciate the literature. In his fourth, or even fifth, year of Latin the average boy has not a sufficient mastery of that technique to be able himself to translate unadapted Caesar, still less unadapted Virgil, fast enough to get through the set books in time. Instead of his doing the translation himself the teacher has to do it for him. Or he buys a crib, sometimes with the open connivance of the teacher. In either case he is not learning Latin but learning someone else's English by heart.

On the other hand the boy who spends all his time on doing unseens is at least learning to translate Latin into English. He cannot do unseens without learning the language. Moreover constructions, idioms and vocabulary met within the single context of a set book tend to be recognized only in that context. To do unseens successfully a boy must have a knowledge that is not only wider but also more precise and more adaptable.

The fear that to take the unseen paper is a temptation to read nothing but unconnected 'snippets' is exaggerated. No teacher worth his salt would tolerate such a policy, if for no other reason than that it would be completely distasteful to anyone with any natural liking for a sustained theme. In the absence, however, of a set-books syllabus the teacher will be able to follow his own taste in the choice of reading material and introduce his pupils to a wider variety of Latin.

We may conclude the discussion of this topic by mentioning a few suggested compromises.

(1) To retain set books but make them shorter.

(2) To allow the combination of a prose set book and a verse unseen, or vice versa.

(3) To retain set books and reduce time spent on composition.

(4) To prescribe for the examination not particular books but particular authors. The object of such a syllabus would be presumably to encourage wide reading of representative authors. In the view of those who argue that preparation of set books encourages thoroughness and concentration this is the worst type of translation paper.

(5) To prescribe, as is done by some examining bodies, books of well-known selections and extracts. Thus, a wider range of authors would be read and some of the advantages of doing set books retained.

(6) To examine knowledge of set books by comprehension tests.

This last method was a distinguishing feature of the set-books paper in a syllabus worked out by a group of teachers in 1939, accepted at that time by the University of London as an alternative in the General School Examination, and since then retained in the Examination for the General Certificate of Education at Ordinary Level.

The originators of the syllabus hoped to retain the advantages of set books as an encouragement to study Latin authors as literature, while eliminating as far as possible the temptation to prepare for the examination by the unintelligent learning by heart of translations. The candidate's knowledge of the Latin *language* was to be tested in the unseens and composition paper, which consisted of two passages of unseen, one prose and one verse (instead of the usual single prose passage), and a choice between sentences or continuous narrative to be put into Latin.

The following question taken from a set-books paper will illustrate the comprehension test method:

CAESAR, *Gallic War* VI, 1–38

1. Read through the following passage carefully. Do not write out the translation, but show that you understand it by answering the questions which follow the passage.

Labienus, hostium cognito consilio, sperans temeritate eorum fore aliquam dimicandi facultatem, praesidio quinque cohortium impedimentis relicto cum xxv cohortibus magnoque equitatu contra hostem proficiscitur et mille passuum intermisso spatio castra communit. Erat inter Labienum atque hostem difficile transitu flumen ripisque praeruptis. Hoc neque ipse transire habebat in animo neque hostis transituros existimabat. Augebatur auxiliorum cotidie spes. Loquitur in consilio palam; quoniam Germani appropinquare dicantur, sese suas exercitusque fortunas in dubium non devocaturum et postero die prima luce castra moturum. Celeriter haec ad hostis deferuntur, ut ex magno Gallorum equitum numero non nullos Gallos Gallicis rebus favere natura cogebat. Labienus noctu tribunis militum primisque ordinibus convocatis quid sui *sit consili proponit.*

(*a*) Why does Labienus think he will have an opportunity to fight?

(*b*) Why did he leave five cohorts behind?

(*c*) At what distance from the enemy did he fortify his camp?

(*d*) Why was the river difficult to cross?

(*e*) Translate *loquitur in consilio palam.*

(*f*) What does Labienus say he is going to do? What reasons does he give?

(g) How is news of this taken to the enemy?
(h) Explain (i) the mood of *sit*; (ii) the case of *consili*.
(i) Give the principal parts of *proponit*.

3. Ordinary Level Papers in Greek

The examination is usually of much the same type as for Latin and consists of two papers of 2 or $2\frac{1}{2}$ hours each:

Paper I (taken by all candidates):
A. One or two pieces of prose unseen.
B. Formal questions on accidence.
C. Sentences (sometimes a piece of narrative is provided as an alternative).

Paper II. EITHER (i) Set books, prose and verse. The prose book is equivalent in length to about four or five chapters of Xenophon's *Anabasis* and the verse book is about 500–600 lines of the dialogue portions of a Greek play. Most examining bodies provide Homer as an alternative to the play. OR (ii) Unseens, prose and verse.

The assumption that only specially selected pupils do Greek may have had the effect of raising the standard of difficulty of the papers. While this may ensure that only the very best win their way through to advanced work, it may also discourage many who would have profited by learning at least some Greek from ever starting the subject at all, especially if a comparison of the percentage of passes in Greek with the percentages of passes in other subjects seems to show that other subjects give better returns in terms of examination results.

Without wishing to water the examination down so that it ceases to test knowledge of the basic elements, we consider that Greek calls for some special consideration. The supreme difficulty of Greek for the beginner is the accidence, and it far outweighs the comparative simplicity of the syntax. A large part of the three years (in many schools it is only two) which is allowed for Greek up to Ordinary Level must be spent on the learning of the accidence. The average candidate at Ordinary Level cannot be expected also to have read enough Greek to have a sure grasp of more than a very limited range of vocabulary, idiom and usage. We would therefore suggest that the examination should be devised to test in a straightforward way the candidate's knowledge of elementary grammar and construction. There should be no trick sentences or little-used grammatical forms. The compulsory unseens in the first paper should be very easy. If selected from Greek authors they should be ruthlessly simplified and the meanings of all but the commonest words should be given. Better in our opinion would be passages specially made up to provide, in conjunction with and complementary to the sentences or composition, a systematic test of elementary grammar in a functional form.

There may be some case for shortening the set books, particularly the verse books. Otherwise the boy in his third or second year of Greek may have to spend the major part of his time in obtaining an examination knowledge of difficult and unadapted Greek literature before he has mastered the elements of the language, or even before he has been introduced to some of them. This is surely an encouragement to use the cramming methods we discussed when dealing with the examination syllabus in Latin.

At the time of writing, examining bodies usually suggest that unseens should be taken as an alternative to set books only by those candidates who have spent a longer time on Greek and therefore have that fuller knowledge of vocabulary and idiom which is obtained by wider reading.

Thus is the official seal of approval set on the policy adopted in most schools—namely, to play for safety and to take set books. The case for and against set books has been discussed in the section on Latin at Ordinary Level, and the same arguments apply. Since, however, a shorter time is given to Greek than to Latin up to Ordinary Level—usually only three (and often only two) years— the preparation and revision of set books will take up a considerably larger proportion of the pre-certificate course in Greek than in Latin. To quote from our chapter on Greek (p. 42)—'the necessity of translating set books *pari passu* with learning all the necessary syntax and revising the accidence is productive of hurried methods and of cramming'. Time spent on laborious revision and re-revision of the set books or, even worse, on learning by heart the English translation, might have been better spent on reading other books and learning more Greek. At any rate we would urge the examining bodies not to weight the scales against unseens; and we would further suggest that the Alternative Unseen paper should be easy, the examination text freely adapted and simplified from the original and plenty of vocabulary help supplied.

4. LITERATURE IN TRANSLATION

Alternatives such as those described in the section on Latin at Ordinary Level (pp. 165–6) are of course examinations in Latin, and, like those of the normal type, are designed for a precise purpose—to test the candidate's knowledge of the language. They must be distinguished from syllabuses in which portions of classical literature are prescribed to be studied partly or wholly in translation. We quote the following syllabuses (which have actually been set in recent years) to illustrate the main gradations of this form of examination:

(a) *Ordinary Level.* All candidates take two papers, as follows:
  Paper I.   Section 1 (1 hour). Translation into English of Latin sentences, and of a short continuous passage.
       Section 2 (1 hour). A classical Latin prose set book;
             OR A classical Latin verse set book;
             OR A medieval Latin set book.
  Paper II. Any TWO of the following sections (each 1 hour):
       (1) A part of the *Odyssey* or *Aeneid* or a selection of Greek plays in translation.
       (2) A selection of Herodotus, Thucydides, or Plato in translation.
       (3) Latin composition (sentences only).

This syllabus was designed to encourage those pupils who learnt Latin up to Ordinary Level to make a wider acquaintance with classical literature than is possible when set books are studied wholly in the original. Section 3 of Paper II is intended for those candidates who wish to satisfy the requirements of Arts faculties where entry to honours courses is conditional on a pass in an examination in which ability to translate into, as well as from, Latin is tested.

(b) *Advanced Level (Greek).* The examination consists of three papers on prescribed authors:

Paper I.   A portion of each author to be studied in the original (3 hours).

Paper II.   The remainder to be studied in translation (3 hours).

Paper III. Unseen translation—of passages chosen from the prescribed authors (2½ hours).

For Papers I and II, candidates select TWO of the following:

(i) Homer, *Odyssey* XXI, XXII and first half of XXIII in Greek and the rest of the *Odyssey* in translation.

(ii) Sophocles, *Philoctetes* (omitting choral odes) in Greek, and Aeschylus, *Agamemnon* and Euripides, *Electra* in translation.

(iii) Plato, *Apology* in Greek, and *Crito* and *Phaedo* (part in translation).

(iv) Herodotus I, 23–119 in Greek, and II and III (to chapter 75) in translation.

The object of this syllabus would appear to be to encourage the study of Greek in Sixth Forms where no provision can be made for it in the main school.

(c) *Ordinary Level.* Greek and Roman literature in translation.

One paper of 2½ hours. Six texts are prescribed each year, three for detailed study and three for more general reading. Context questions are set only on texts prescribed for detailed study.

Specimen syllabus and paper:

I. Prescribed for detailed study:

Sophocles, *Antigone*; Plato, *Apology*; Tacitus, *Agricola.*

II. Prescribed for general reading:

Homer, *Iliad* I–IV; Herodotus I; Virgil, *Aeneid* II–IV.

Specimen Paper

SECTION I. *Answer Question 1 and* TWO *others in this section.*

Each of three parts (a), (b), *and* (c) *of Question 1 must be attempted.*

1. (*a*) Sophocles, *Antigone*.

EITHER (i) 'This time there was no casting of lots; no, this luck has fallen to me.'

Who speaks these words, to whom, and to what do they refer?

OR (ii) 'All this argument of thine is for her.'
'And for thee and me and the gods below.'
'Slave of a woman, do not wheedle me!'

Who are the speakers? Write a clear explanation of this dialogue.

(*b*) Plato, *Apology*.

EITHER 'My son, if thou dost avenge the death of thy companion Patroclus and kill Hector, thou shalt thyself die.'

Whose words are these and to whom are they spoken? In what connexion does Socrates refer to them?

OR 'If then death is like this, I call it a gain.'

Give the context of these words of Socrates.

(*c*) Tacitus, *Agricola*.

EITHER (i) 'He was protected from the snares of vice not only by his own good and healthy disposition but by the fact that from a very early age he had Massilia for the scene and guide of his studies.'

Explain why Massilia was a good centre of education. Give Agricola's confession of his preference in study as a very young man, and Tacitus' comment on it.

OR (ii) 'Yet some tears that should have been shed at your deathbed are not shed, and your dying eyes looked round at the last for something and looked in vain.'

Explain this passage fully as if to someone who had not read the *Agricola*.

2. EITHER (*a*) Summarize the Chorus beginning 'There are many wonders and there is none more wonderful than man', and show how it is connected with the situation which the play has reached.

OR (*b*) How does Creon justify his treatment of Polynices? What keeps him from changing his mind?

3. EITHER (*a*) What sort of people did Socrates test to find out whether the oracle was right in calling him the wisest of men, and what was the result of the test?

OR (b) Describe two occasions on which Socrates displayed moral courage in public affairs.

4. EITHER (a) Summarize from year to year the military progress made by Agricola from the time he entered Britain as governor.

OR (b) In what ways did Domitian actually or possibly show his hostility to Agricola? What reason is given for this hostility?

SECTION II. *Answer all three questions in this section*

5. EITHER (a) How is Helen introduced in the third book of the *Iliad*? Give the main points in Homer's picture.

OR (b) What opinion have you formed of the Homeric gods?

6. EITHER (a) Tell the story of Solon's interview with Croesus, bringing out the difference between Greek and Eastern ideas of life.

OR (b) Describe the career of Cyrus.

7. EITHER (a) What part is played in *Aeneid* II–IV by Creusa, Polydorus and Anna?

OR (b) What is the character of Aeneas as displayed in *Aeneid* II–IV?

We have little, if any, fault to find with the selection of books in such a syllabus, or with the construction of the examination paper. When, however, we ask for what kind of candidates the syllabus and examination is intended, grave doubts arise in our minds. Greek and Roman literature in translation at Ordinary Level would appear at first sight to be just the thing to encourage the sort of studies we have advocated in chapter VII. It is, or should be, taken by the 'B' or 'C' streams in grammar schools and perhaps by 'A' streams in some modern schools, in other words, by those who have not the aptitude to begin Latin or continue with it for four or five years. For we must insist that up to Ordinary Level, and perhaps beyond, the distinctive value of the Classics is to be found in the linguistic training it offers. For those who have learnt Latin or Greek to Ordinary Level an examination on classical literature in translation is irrelevant to their studies and may even be a harmful distraction. On the other hand we consider that very few boys or girls unable to make progress at Latin would be able at the age of fifteen or sixteen to tackle an examination of the kind we have quoted unless they had been crammed for it.

We are inclined to think that this syllabus and examination in a modified form would be more in place as part of an English literature syllabus at Advanced Level. The modification would consist in careful selection, only those books being chosen whose translations were themselves of widely recognized literary merit, or whose structure, thought, or subject-matter had an important bearing on, or connexion with, some branch of English literature. For instance Dr Rieu's translations of Homer or Professor Gilbert Murray's translations of Euripides are worth reading as English; and almost any efficient translations of the *Oresteia* or the Theban plays of Sophocles might be usefully read by the student of dramatic composition.

It seems, however, that the sort of knowledge about Greece and Rome that can be appreciated by younger pupils apart from the knowledge of the Greek and Latin languages is too wide and incidental to be examinable.

5. ADVANCED AND SCHOLARSHIP LEVELS:

We have suggested that the Ordinary Level Examination should be mainly retrospective—epitomizing, as it were, the attainments it is reasonable to expect from the average grammar school pupil of the 'A' or 'B' stream after four or five years of Latin, or three of Greek. For the majority it is the last stage of a course which should be complete in itself, and, provided that the course has been well planned, the teaching effective, and the selection of pupils correct, a reasonable degree of success should be within the reach of the majority of candidates. We have also suggested that the examination should be selective enough to pick out the best candidates, those fitted for Advanced and (in the case of a smaller number) Scholarship work. It follows then, that candidates at Advanced and Scholarship Levels are, to some extent, pre-selected; and for this reason we should expect them to work to fixed and absolute standards of scholarship. In theory our question should be 'Are the candidates good enough to take the examination?' and not, as at Ordinary Level, 'Is the examination suitable for the candidates?' Since the award of State and some other scholarships giving entry to the universities is decided by results obtained at Advanced and Scholarship Level, the universities, which are seats of learning as well as dispensers of vocational training, are justified in insisting on high standards of scholarship from potential honours students.

In practice, however, candidates in Latin[1] at Advanced Level are not a homogeneous group. Their aptitude for the subject and their reasons for taking it vary considerably. First, there are those taking Latin with Greek and Ancient History in a full classical course to University Scholarship Level. For convenience of future reference we will call them Group I. The aim of their studies, discussed in detail in our chapter on Sixth-Form work, is a scholarly mastery of the Greek and Latin languages and a wide understanding of the history, literature, life and thought of the Greco-Roman world. Such a curriculum is complete in itself, and in schools with a strong classical tradition is usually given the generous time allowance it deserves; while a combination of the Advanced and Scholarship Level papers in Latin, Greek and Ancient History, as set by most examining bodies, provides an adequate test of attainment and promise in this many-sided course of studies.

The chief features of the examination are:

(1) Unprepared translation—prose and verse.

(2) Prose composition.

(3) A test on set books—prose and verse.

(4) A history paper or papers.

(5) Questions of a more general nature on antiquities. (Some examining bodies confine these to a separate general paper set at Scholarship Level only.)

(6) Optional papers in Latin and Greek verse composition.

No. (4) is often set separately from the language papers and ranks as a separate subject—Ancient History. Some examining bodies, however, include in the examination on Latin and Greek compulsory papers on Greek and Roman History. Differences

[1] Greek at Advanced Level is almost always taken in a full classical course and does not call for discussion here.

of detail in the make-up of the individual papers and the style of the questions call for some comment, which will, however, be deferred to a later part of this chapter.

Secondly come those whom we may call Group II, candidates taking Latin at Advanced Level with modern subjects, e.g. a modern language, History, English. The difficulties and short-comings which often handicap this group have been discussed in the chapter on Sixth-Form work. Shortage of time and distraction of other subjects with an easier technique tend to make Latin a rather formidable odd man out. The reason for taking Latin to Advanced Level is often utilitarian. There is much how-ever to be said for the combination of Latin with subjects such as English literature and Modern Languages, particularly if the Classics, English and Modern Languages staff can co-operate to point out the linguistic, literary, and historical links between the ancient and modern cultures. This matter has been discussed in our opening chapter. The immediate relevance, however, of the content of the normal Advanced Level syllabus in Latin to some other arts subjects, such as Geography, is not so obvious. In any case candidates offering Latin with modern subjects should not be compelled to take the same syllabus as those in Group I, a principle which appears to be recognized by one examining body. The Oxford and Cambridge Schools Examina-tion Board has two syllabuses in Latin at 'A' Level separate from that for Latin in the Classical Studies Group, viz. 'Latin of Modern Studies' and 'Latin Translation and Roman History'. In the case of 'Latin Translation and Roman History' a second prose unseen takes the place of prose composition, and there is some modification in the set book syllabus.

Thus prose composition, with the single exception mentioned above, is still required of all 'A' Level candidates in Latin; and although there are many who would argue that it should not be compulsory for candidates taking Latin with modern subjects, we would deprecate too ready a surrender of one of the main values of Latin.

There is no Arts subject that does not call for the continuous exercise of English composition, and, paradoxical as it may sound, we insist that Latin prose composition provides an almost indispensable training in the art of writing English. We should in any case never recommend a course that caters for one-way translation only. Unemployed languages are really 'dead'. Nevertheless, since some lightening of the load is necessary, we suggest that an examination for Group II candidates should forgo those grammar questions on syntax, which are really the concern of the specialist, should assume a wider and less intensive study of set books, and should prescribe amounts for reading which make less heavy demands on the time of the candidates. Different set books, however, are likely to prove inconvenient in schools where Groups I and II have to be taught together.

Some examining bodies set a compulsory paper on Roman History for candidates in Latin. The purpose is presumably to broaden the study of the language by linking it with its background. In practice, however, Latin with modern subjects is unlikely to be given more than seven teaching periods a week, of which not more than one can be spared for history. This is quite inadequate for the satisfactory presentation and absorption of what is really a separate examination subject, deserving separate treatment on the time-table. The result is likely to be perfunctory cramming for a bare pass. We would, therefore, strongly urge all examining bodies to give any formal syllabus on Roman or Greek history the status of a separate subject. In the language papers, questions on history should be confined to the subject-matter and background of the set books.

Translation and Prose Composition

The examination in each language, apart from History and verse composition, falls naturally into three sections: unprepared translation, prose composition, set books—each of which should be worked separately. The candidate may then concentrate on one kind of task for the whole of a particular session, undisturbed by the need to change to another technique in the middle, and relieved of the temptation to spend more time than he should on one section. In practice, however, it is difficult to observe this division. To construct an examination time-table which will admit of all the likely combinations of different subjects without clashes, it is necessary to keep the number of papers in any particular subject to a minimum—if the whole examination is not to drag on for an inordinate amount of time. A reasonable compromise in the case of Latin and Greek is to combine unprepared translation with prose composition in the same paper—an arrangement which is at least better than that of one authority, which combines the prose set book with prose composition and the verse set book with unprepared translation.

In spite of warnings, printed on the question paper, not to spend more than $1\frac{1}{4}$ hours of the total 3 hours on the set-book section, and in spite of the fact that 64% of the marks are allotted to unprepared translation and only 36% to set books, the candidate who has not a complete mastery of the set books will be tempted to spend more time than he should in dealing with them.

Of the set books papers we have little to say. If the syllabus is to include set books—in itself a debatable point—the normal type of paper, testing ability to translate, understanding of ordinary syntactical usages and of subject-matter in relation to context, is satisfactory. We would suggest, however, that at least as much weight should be attached to correct answers to the context questions as to correct translation. This will lessen the evil to which set books, even at Advanced Level, are subject, namely the temptation to prepare them by learning a translation by heart.

Passages for unprepared translation should have unity of theme, the parts interlocking in a well-knit whole, so that success depends not on the fortuitous knowledge of the meanings of individual words but on imagination controlled by common sense and a respect for the rules of grammar. Unfortunately for examiners, many of the best 'unseen pieces' have already been claimed by the compilers of unseen books; and the task of choosing suitable passages which are unlikely to have been worked by many of the candidates becomes increasingly hard.

Most authorities set a passage of narrative for prose composition at Advanced Level, to which is added, in the same or in a separate paper, a more difficult passage for Scholarship candidates, often of rhetorical or philosophic content. At neither level should the passage contain much technical phraseology with exact vocabulary equivalents to be found only in particular classical authors. Some passages, about siege warfare or naval operations for instance, might give an undue advantage to the candidate who had been lucky enough to have read the appropriate chapters of Thucydides or Livy. The examiner should look not for an extensive knowledge of specialist vocabulary but for a grasp of the general differences between ancient and modern idiom, and the ancient and modern methods of expressing and describing the non-technical ideas and emotions common to human thoughts and human behaviour in all ages.

Ancient History

Under this title may be included: (1) papers on formal periods of Greek and Roman History; and (2) 'General' questions or papers dealing with wider aspects of the classical civilizations, e.g. literature, life, religion, philosophy, art and architecture. All examining bodies set (1) either as part of the Latin and Greek syllabuses or as a separate subject, or both. Practice varies with regard to (2), some bodies including general questions in the history papers, others setting separate papers, which sometimes are for Scholarship Level candidates only.

As we have already indicated, we consider that for candidates taking Latin with modern subjects, History should be treated as a separate subject and not made a compulsory section of the language examination. The choice between shorter special periods or longer outline periods has already been discussed in the chapter on Ancient History. In view of the small acquaintance with Greek or Roman History that most boys have when they enter the Sixth Form, we are inclined to favour the longer period at Advanced Level, as being likely to encourage a more comprehensive survey of the general field in the early part of the Sixth-Form course. The special period is more suitable for Scholarship Level candidates, a distinction observed by some examining bodies. At Advanced Level, questions should be on the main topics of the period and couched in simple and direct terms. A survey of recent papers suggests that this is usually the case, but occasionally we find an almost studied avoidance of the obvious. For instance a paper set some years ago on Roman History down to A.D. 14 with special reference to the period 290 B.C. to A.D. 14 did not contain a single question on the Gracchi or Marius or Sulla, while in another paper on the period 90 B.C. to A.D. 138 the only chance candidates appeared to have of mentioning Pompey and Cicero was in the following questions:

'What was the *Senatus consultum ultimum*? What use was made of it during the period 70–40 B.C.?'

and 'Discuss the relations between Rome and Parthia from 70 to 20 B.C.'

In a two-year course, starting in most cases from an almost complete ignorance of the subject, boys will have little enough time even to become familiar with the major topics and the outstanding problems and personalities of the prescribed periods. They should not be expected to have explored the side-paths before the main road has been traversed, nor should familiar topics be presented in unfamiliar form. Failing to see through the disguise, a candidate may leave a question unattempted which he could have answered quite well had it been couched in simple terms. It is only fair to say that strong representations from teachers and a change of heart on the part of examiners produced a marked improvement in subsequent papers set by the authority responsible for the questions we have quoted above—a good example of the value of constructive criticism on the part of schools.

General Papers

General papers and general questions are, or should be, of two types, according as they are set for candidates at Advanced Level in the General Certificate of Education after a two-year course or at Scholarship Level either in the General Certificate of Education or in college entrance scholarship examinations. At Advanced Level comparatively few boys can have a wide enough first-hand acquaintance with Greek and Roman originals and sufficient maturity of judgement to be able to write critically on a literary or artistic genre as a whole without being vague or merely reproducing other people's opinions. Questions in the Advanced Level paper should demand not wide-ranging discussion so much as the marshalling of relevant facts in a limited field. Literature questions, in particular, should be related to the set books. Thus it would be wrong at Advanced Level to ask a boy in general terms to compare the moral attitude of Homer with that of Virgil; but if he had taken as set books Virgil, *Aeneid* IV and Homer, *Iliad* XVII and XVIII the question (actually set in recent years), 'Dido and Aeneas could never have appeared in Homer. Discuss.', would suggest, in a suitably definite and restricted field with which he had first-hand acquaintance, important and enlightening differences not only between Homer and Virgil, but between Greek and Roman.

Questions on *realien* from the very nature of their theme will be definite and factual; but a wide choice should be given, since, as we have indicated elsewhere (p. 123), intensive teaching on such matters is not desirable. The teacher should rather encourage individuals to pursue their own differing interests.

A traditional feature of the general paper is a group of short passages from Greek and Latin literature illustrating peculiarities and irregularities of syntax. The candidate is asked to translate, comment on the syntax and, if possible, quote parallel usages. In our opinion syntactical comment should be confined to the set books, at any rate at Advanced Level; and even at Scholarship Level the question on miscellaneous and isolated passages should be optional. Few candidates after two years in the Sixth Form are likely to have read so widely as to be reasonably sure of having met in their actual reading the particular examples chosen and their parallels. It is also unlikely and indeed undesirable that their reading should have been conducted with such intensive devotion to syntax as to ensure their remembering the relevant points in the examination. Lacking the time or the inclination to learn Goodwin's *Moods and Tenses* or Roby's *Latin Grammar* by heart, they will rely on dictated notes or those short books of comparative Greek and Latin syntax which, apart from expository matter, contain lists of the more popular examples. Some of these books are admirable as introductions to the more advanced study of syntax and as works of reference when difficulties or peculiarities arise in the course of reading; but an examination which encourages the learning of examples detached from their context is little better than an incitement to cramming. Trained in this way, the student, on his subsequent first reading of one of the masterpieces of Sophocles, may be reminded of the lady who said she did not think much of *Hamlet* because it was so full of quotations.

6. SCHOLARSHIP EXAMINATIONS

(i) *Examinations set by Colleges at Oxford and Cambridge for the award of Scholarships and Exhibitions*

The following papers are usually set:

(1) Latin Prose Composition.
(2) Latin Unprepared Translation.
(3) Latin Verse Composition (Optional).
(4) English Essay.
(5) A general paper containing questions on a wide range of subjects both classical and modern.

To these sometimes are added:

(6) A paper of passages for translation from modern foreign languages.
(7), (8) and (9) Papers in Greek corresponding to (1), (2) and (3).

(ii) *Scholarship papers and syllabuses in the examination for the G.C.E.*

All examining bodies provide syllabuses in Latin and Greek at Scholarship Level, and some in Ancient History; although only two of the three subjects can be taken at Scholarship Level. The Ancient History Examination at Scholarship Level is usually distinguished from the Advanced Level Examination by an extra general paper.

For Scholarship candidates in Latin and Greek most authorities prescribe the Advanced Level papers (including set books) with additional and more difficult passages for prose composition and unprepared translation.

An interesting exception is provided by the Oxford and Cambridge Schools Examination Board, who also prescribe, for candidates taking both Latin and Greek at Scholarship Level, a Classical General paper. Such Scholarship candidates may take the Advanced Level set books, *but performance in those papers is not taken into account when recommendations are made for the award of State scholarships.*

Freedom from the necessity to prepare set books for the scholarship examination is to be welcomed. More time is left for the extensive reading that is appropriate at this stage; and the examination, with its general paper, is, as it should be, a test of high linguistic ability, and wide and assimilated knowledge, rather than of mere assiduity in preparing within the narrow limits of an examination syllabus.

7. STANDARDIZATION OF MARKS IN THE EXAMINATION FOR THE G.C.E.

To secure equitable treatment for candidates of similar ability and industry, and to maintain parity of examination status between subjects, examining bodies usually modify the marks obtained in the examination for the General Certificate of Education. By this process the highest and lowest marks obtained in all or most subjects at a particular level are respectively equated and the other marks proportionately scaled according to their position in this uniform mark range. Thus a candidate's final mark in a particular subject will depend on the relation of his 'raw' mark to those of the other candidates taking the same subject.

As a general principle we admit the justice of some degree of standardization, at any rate when applied to subjects in which the entry is large and unselective. If, however, subjects taken by small groups of pre-selected candidates are equated to those taken by much larger and much less selected groups it seems inevitable that the narrower range of 'raw' marks in the smaller and more pre-selective groups will be stretched downwards in the process of standardization, with the result that the marks of some good candidates will be unduly depressed. We have reason to believe that examining bodies are aware of the danger, and that, therefore, some of them do not attempt to standardize marks obtained in small subject groups like Greek at Ordinary or Advanced Level and Ancient History at Advanced Level. We trust, moreover, that no examining body will allow standardization to operate to the disadvantage of candidates in small groups, particularly at Advanced and Scholarship Levels, since the award of State (and other) scholarships depends on marks obtained at these levels in the G.C.E.

In the course of this chapter, examining bodies have come in for a certain amount of criticism. We should not, however, like to leave our readers with the impression that these remarks have been made in any spirit of hostility, or with any lack of appreciation of the enlightened and sympathetic common sense displayed by those who undertake the difficult task of setting and marking examinations which are fair to the candidate, and yet exacting enough to encourage and maintain high standards of scholarship. In conclusion we would point out that the success with which this double aim is achieved depends in no small measure on constant exchange of information and comment. If what we have said in this chapter should encourage even more teachers of the Classics to follow our example and contribute to this exchange, we shall be satisfied.

IX

AIDS TO THE TEACHING OF CLASSICS

1. ARCHAEOLOGY

NOWADAYS the study of the Classics is valued not only as a linguistic discipline but as providing also an introduction to the study of the ancient world. Few teachers can be content with the purely grammatical side of the subject without making use of the historical approach. Archaeology can provide a background to history, can supplement its somewhat patchy framework, and even correct its uneven emphasis. Furthermore, the visual and manual study of what is to hand locally provides a fresh and even stimulating progress from the particular to the general. The ancient world ceases to be an arid abstraction.

Archaeology is no mere hobby of the eccentric, but a vital part of the equipment of anyone who wishes to obtain a balanced view of the past. It alone provides us with knowledge of man's progress before written history begins, and in the remaining hundredth part of his duration on this planet it is archaeology which corrects the bias of historical sources, provides fresh fields of evidence, and fills in the *lacunae*.

It is easy to arouse an interest in archaeology among the young. There is an irresistible charm to be found in the contemplation of the monuments of our past, just as there is an almost over-whelming instinct to collect the portable relics of our ancestors. But this contemplation, this collector's instinct, must be directed along the right lines. The two most handy ways by which to arouse this interest are perhaps (*a*) by the display of pictures and by exhibitions or illustrated lectures; (*b*) by practical finds, exploration and visits.

There are many well-illustrated books now on the market (see Bibliography, p. 188). The Ashmolean Museum has for some time been circulating an exhibition of air-photographs. Lectures with slides can usually be obtained locally either through the County Archaeological Society or through the panel of lecturers listed by the Council for British Archaeology. Most areas have ancient monuments worth visiting (see Ministry of Works Guides, Victoria County Histories, Jacquetta Hawkes' *Guide to Prehistoric and Roman Monuments*, etc.). Finds of pottery or flints can usually be made on down or heathlands, or in gravel workings or quarries.

But an uninstructed enthusiasm, aroused but not guided, may result in serious damage. No ancient site should be looted of its finds: unauthorized or unrecorded digging in particular can do irremediable harm to a site and still more to the mind of the looter. What should be a scientific discipline, a synthesis of physical effort and mental alertness, sharpening faculties of observation and deduction, degenerates into a greedy hogging of collector's pieces: what might be vital evidence to a trained intelligence is not only not understood but destroyed. For the evidence consists not merely of the find but of its context. Interest, therefore, once aroused must be guided rightly.

Archaeological Society

This guidance can well be given by means of an archaeological society. Results can then be brought into the light of day and shared, the private treasure-hunt, as it were, being sublimated. The activities of such a society can be grouped under a number of headings:

(1) *Programme of lectures.* These can be by members describing discoveries, by the master-in-charge on some general aspect of fact or policy, or by outside lecturers to be obtained through the local antiquarian society, the Council for British Archaeology, the Roman and Hellenic Societies, etc. Lectures are usually best if illustrated by slides or objects. (Slides together with lecture-notes can be hired by members of the Roman and Hellenic Societies.)

(2) *Arrangement of a small museum.* Surplus flint implements or

pottery sherds can often be obtained from local museums, and would form a valuable comparative series. Such collections ought in the main to be confined to local objects, unless perhaps a classical section can be built up. Unassorted ethnological material is to be deprecated. Maps, plans, photographs and scale models are of great educational value.

(3) *Numismatics.* An elementary collection of Roman coins can be built up with little expense. Coin-collecting is a specialized branch, but for those who get the enthusiasm it can give a fruitful insight into the historical and even political background. Collections of coins can be hired from the Association for the Reform of Latin Teaching.

(4) *Field-work.* It may be possible to arrange visits to local earthworks, excavations, or other sites. It often happens that useful and original work can be done in the observation, tracing, surveying, and mapping of minor earthworks and trackways. The lost course of a Roman road can often be discovered and marked on the 6-inch map, as is described by I. D. Margary (*Roman Ways in the Weald*). Distribution maps of the various types of antiquities or sites can be prepared for suitable surrounding regions, large or small, and thus knowledge can be gained of trade routes and of the effect of geography upon human settlement even in quite small areas with a radius of 10 or 15 miles.

(5) *Surface-collecting.* Surface-collecting of pottery or flints arouses enthusiasm (the collector's instinct) and is a wholly useful occupation provided that the objects themselves are marked or classified by their find-spots, and that the results are published or recorded. In this way a good first-hand knowledge of Roman and prehistoric pottery and other human artifacts can be acquired.

(6) *Digging.* Digging should be discouraged, for reasons explained above, unless it can be directed by a qualified supervisor of experience. Too often irreparable harm can be done to a monument or site by inexperienced digging, and there is not always time during term for this activity to be correctly carried out. There are exceptions to this generalization, but on the whole excavation should be the last, not the first, activity of a purely school society.

(7) *Excavational experience.* Experience of excavation can, however, easily be acquired during the holidays. In most parts of the country there are plenty of excavations during the spring and summer months where volunteers are welcome, and archaeological technique can be acquired from experienced excavators, often with the added attractions of camp life. Lists of forthcoming excavations can be obtained from the Council for British Archaeology.

(8) *Expeditions* by bus, car, or train, to the larger and better-known monuments or museums are a popular combination of pleasure with instruction.

Experience of school archaeological societies shows that quite frequently boys up to the age of fifteen or sixteen are interested, but that after that age the majority pass on to other interests. The growing knowledge of Roman Britain, however, and the increased realization of the educational possibilities of this study, and the larger part it now plays in educational syllabuses, particularly in the Roman Britain special subject in Advanced Level Ancient History, combine to allow a more mature approach. If instead of being always given an academic History period, the students are taken occasionally to visit sites of whose significance they are previously aware: if they are given not merely general works to read, but are allowed to read original reports and research work, and can themselves research fully into the nature of our knowledge of particular towns, villas, or military works such as Hadrian's Wall, many at any rate, if not all, will enjoy the study of Roman Britain in a way in which it is not possible to enjoy the purely text-book history of the classical world. Roman Britain with its fusion of classical and Celtic civilization provides a homely object lesson of the mingling and growth of cultures. Its study thus points the way to the understanding of an important principle of history, and can lead on in its turn to a wider and deeper comprehension of the courses and methods at the disposal of the student of ancient history such as will be valuable at the university.

Bibliography

ATKINSON, R. J. C. *Field Archaeology*. Methuen.

ATLAS OF THE CLASSICAL WORLD. Nelson.

BRITISH MUSEUM. *A Guide to the Antiquities of Roman Britain*.

BRUCE, J. COLLINGWOOD. *Handbook to the Roman Wall*. H. Hill & Sons, Ltd., Gallowgate, Newcastle-on-Tyne.

BURN, A. R. *The Romans in Britain*. Blackwell. (Out of print.)

BUSHE FOX, J. P. *Excavation of the Roman Fort at Richborough*, Vols. I–IV (Society of Antiquaries Research Committee Reports). Oxford.

CHARLESWORTH, M. P. *The Lost Province*. University of Wales Press.

COLLINGWOOD, R. G. *The Archaeology of Roman Britain*. Methuen. (Out of print.)

COLLINGWOOD, R. G. *Roman Britain*. Oxford.

COLLINGWOOD, R. G. and MYRES, J. N. L. *Roman Britain and the English Settlements*. Oxford.

COUNCIL FOR BRITISH ARCHAEOLOGY, 10 Bolton Gardens, London, S.W.5. *Archaeological Bibliography for Gt Britain and Ireland*. (Annually, and Calendar of Excavations.)

THE COUNTY ARCHAEOLOGICAL SERIES. Various authors. Methuen.

CRAWFORD, O. G. S. *Man and his Past*. Oxford. (Out of print.)

HAVERFIELD, F. J. *The Romanization of Roman Britain*. Oxford. (Out of print.)

HAVERFIELD, F. J. and MACDONALD, G. *The Roman Occupation of Britain*. Oxford. (Out of print.)

HAWKES, C. F. C. and HULL, M. R. *Camulodunum*. (Society of Antiquaries Research Committee Report.) Oxford.

HAWKES, JACQUETTA. *Guide to the Prehistoric and Roman Monuments in England and Wales*. Chatto and Windus.

HAWKES, JACQUETTA and CHRISTOPHER. *Prehistoric Britain*. Chatto and Windus.

HOME, GORDON. *Roman London* (A.D. 43–457). Eyre and Spottiswoode.

LONDON MUSEUM CATALOGUE No. 3. *London in Roman Times*.

MARGARY, IVAN D. *Roman Ways in the Weald*. Phoenix House.

MINISTRY OF WORKS. *Illustrated Regional Guides to Ancient Monuments*. Vol. I, *Northern England*. Vol. II, *Southern England*. Vol. III, *East Anglia and Midlands*. Vol. IV, *South Wales*. Vol. V, *North Wales*. Vol. VI, *Scotland*.

MOORE, R. W. *The Romans in Britain*. Methuen.

ORDNANCE SURVEY. *Map of Roman Britain*.

RICHMOND, I. A. *Roman Britain*. Collins. (Out of print.)

SOCIETY FOR THE PROMOTION OF ROMAN STUDIES, 31–34 Gordon Square, W.C. 1. *Journal of Roman Studies; Roman Britain Annual Reports.*

WHEELER, R. E. M. and T. V. *Verulamium, A Belgic and Two Roman Cities.* (Society of Antiquaries Research Committee Report.) Oxford.

ZSCHIETZSCHMANN, W. *Hellas and Rome.* Zwemmer.

2. VISUAL AIDS

'He who doubts from what he sees
Will ne'er believe, do what you please.'   (BLAKE)

Visual aids have been the centre of much controversy among teachers. Some look on them as mere window-dressing and refuse to use them, others are carried away by the novelty and rely too much on them. But, if discrimination is used and a lesson is arranged with a clear end in view, visual aids can be a powerful ally in stimulating interest and in making clear some point not easily explained in words alone. Sometimes it is difficult for a pupil to imagine accurately what the ancient world looked like, and it is not uncommon to find a pupil with erroneous ideas about simple things, ideas perhaps imported from his contemporary surroundings. Modern languages have this difficulty in a very limited degree only. Moreover, teachers of the Classics have a civilization to interpret, not merely languages to teach. It is vital therefore to make use of these aids to some extent. This section surveys the material available and contains a brief list of useful books and of sources of supply. The latter is not exhaustive but will put readers in touch with means of furthering their knowledge, and it supplements what we say here.

There is a wealth of material available, but it is best for a teacher making use of visual aids for the first time to begin on a small scale and to develop his resources gradually. A large notice-board and picture frames whose backs can easily be removed are essential. With them all sorts of visual material can be displayed. At most Roman sites postcards and photographs are available, and those in charge of the sites are very willing to co-operate by sending details of what is for sale. In particular, the British Museum publishes very cheap sets of postcards with brief notes. Some periodicals publish illustrations of classical interest, e.g. the *Illustrated London News, Greece and Rome* and the *National Geographic Magazine.* Good wall charts and maps and well illustrated books are a real help. A teacher, too, should not hesitate to use his own drawings on the blackboard, however rough they may be.

Three points may be made. First, the material should be attractive, should be attractively arranged and should be changed at regular intervals. All one's resources should not be employed at once. What is on display should preferably have reference to the work in hand but it should also be topical; photographs of new finds and excavations should be included, and pupils should be encouraged to bring to school photographs and illustrated articles they find in periodicals and newspapers. This helps to connect class-work with the outside world. Secondly, charts and photographs need little time to arrange and they do our teaching for us in our absence. Even the pupil who does not study Classics will be interested in such displays. Art students in particular will appreciate anything that concerns them. But the attention of pupils should be drawn to new material, and it is advisable to spend some minutes with each class talking about pictures and charts newly put on view. The third point is that a teacher who has not a room of his own will find difficulty in arranging material as he would like. He must either scatter his display or concentrate it and persuade pupils to go and see it.

Pupils may be induced to make their own visual material, and the help of the art teacher can be enlisted. Some examples may be quoted. Effective mosaics can be made by affixing small pieces of coloured paper (*tesserae*) to a large sheet of stiff paper. Triumphal processions and weddings can be the subject of drawings or paintings. Research into costume and the like is thereby stimulated, and the comic element should not be neglected. Charts and maps can be drawn to illustrate campaigns. Models of *tormenta*, houses, ships, etc., can be made from balsa wood. Vases and other suitable objects can be reproduced in papier mâché and afterwards coloured.

Pupils who are keen philatelists will be able to organize a display of stamps that illustrate the Classics. Italy issued series to commemorate the bimillenaries of Virgil, Livy, Horace and Augustus, all with quotations and illustrations. Greece has suitable issues, too.

Realien might well be the next step, and coins form a good beginning. Originals or electrotypes can be obtained quite cheaply. Pupils will be interested if you can say that Romans of Caesar's time must have handled the coins you hold in your hand. It is best to have coins that connect with something the pupils are studying; e.g. a coin with the inscription CAESAR shows Aeneas carrying his father from Troy, another with the inscription FELIX shows Sulla with Bocchus and Jugurtha kneeling before him. Modern Italian coins show grapes, olives, Pegasus, etc. Pupils may like to collect ancient and modern coins, as some collect stamps.

It is difficult to obtain other types of realien for oneself. But it is possible to borrow. Museums usually have loan boxes and, where these are not available, directors may be persuaded to provide them. The Archaeological Aids Committee of the Association for the Reform of Latin Teaching has charge of a collection of antiquities, models, coins, books, pictures and photographs which can be borrowed by members of the Association. Casts can be bought of various objects but they are very dear. It is best to display this type of material in cases with glass fronts or tops. At a pinch, a book-case with movable shelves and glass doors will do.

But to most teachers the words visual aids chiefly mean film-strips, films and their projectors. These have certainly great advantages. The medium is one the pupils know well and a bright picture in a darkened room has a hypnotic effect, especially if it is moving. On the other hand, some preparation of equipment is necessary and, since few schools have more than one projector of either type, arrangements have to be made for it to be available in one's room or the class has to be moved to the room where the projector is set up permanently. Filmstrip projectors are fairly simple to handle and maintain, but to handle film projectors easily requires training and experience. Blacking out a room may present difficulties; some projectors need only a semi-darkness, others need complete darkness, others again work in daylight.

In all cases, with projection from the rear of a classroom, questions of discipline may arise. These may be reduced by using rear projection. Details of this can be found in the books mentioned in the list. Another disadvantage of films and filmstrips is that each sequence or picture tends to efface the memory of those preceding. Moreover, the order is fairly fixed and the pictures are not available when the teacher is not present. The old-fashioned but still useful slide overcomes the difficulty of order: it should not be despised. Some filmstrip projectors can easily be adapted to carry slides of either size, standard or miniature. But slides are usually projected from a lantern or diascope. Another useful machine is the episcope which throws on a screen any picture, illustration or page of a book put under it. These two machines are occasionally built together, the resultant machine being called the epidiascope. It is simple to handle.

Some points require mention. One must be thoroughly conversant with this material and the necessary equipment. It is usual to stress the importance of knowing how to handle equipment, but it is equally important to know thoroughly the content of films and strips so that the utmost value may be gained from their use. It is therefore imperative to study a film or strip in detail before it is used in class and to decide just how relevant it is to the topic under study. This is difficult in many cases. One firm, however, now sells positives of their strips, which are useful for reference and inspection. This practice could well be copied by all producers of strips. Libraries of films and filmstrips are maintained by some educational authorities where they may be viewed in advance, but it may be that the number of classical strips and films in your local library is small. Press for more to be included. The Film Library of the Educational Foundation for Visual Aids sends any filmstrip to any teacher for free preview on a sale or return basis. The Library includes strips made by all the commercial producers. A comprehensive set of filmstrips is held at the Foundation's London Office for immediate inspection by callers. Send for information to The Educational Foundation for Visual Aids, 33 Queen Anne Street, London, W. 1. In using films and filmstrips a teacher must always be on the alert to see that the class is taking an active interest in the pictures. He must guard against mere passive looking. How he will do that depends on himself and on how he follows up his showing of the film or filmstrip. The follow-up may be by oral questioning or by written work, but there must be a follow-up. Above all, there should be no lengthy delay while the projector is being got ready and the room blacked out. Film and filmstrips must be used as an essential feature of the lesson and not as special extras, used only on such occasions as the end of the term. Finally, storage space must be provided for material not in use: the space must be large enough to allow for expansion and to permit any piece to be reached easily. There is no room here to describe how equipment is to be set up and used. That information can be obtained from many sources, some of which are listed below.

It is important to remember that visual aids are only aids. They arouse interest and help pupils to imagine how the ancients lived and what they did. They are no substitute for teaching, though a very pleasant help. Every teacher has to abjure the temptation to lean too heavily on them and he must decide for himself just what part they are to play in his teaching. Their use will vary from form to form: the Sixth Form needs little, the junior forms need most. But care and energy are needed in collecting, preparing and using visual materials and they impose a new responsibility on the teacher. They must be servants, not masters.

Useful Books, etc., and Sources of Supply

Useful Books

I.A.A.M. *The Teaching of Science in Secondary Schools.* Murray.

I.A.A.M. *The Teaching of Modern Languages.* University of London Press.

I.A.A.M. *The Teaching of History.* C.U.P.

KIDD and LONG. *Filmstrip and Slide Projection.* Focal Press. Pamphlet obtainable from the National Committee for Visual Aids in Education, 33 Queen Anne Street, London, W. 1.

SUMNER. *Visual Methods in Education.* Blackwell.

Scottish Film Council, 16/17 Woodside Terrace, Charing Cross, Glasgow, C. 3. Catalogues of Filmstrips.

Visual Education. Monthly journal of articles and reviews. 1s. 6d.; annual subscription 20s. post free. National Committee for Visual Aids in Education, 33 Queen Anne Street, London, W. 1.

This periodical covers most subjects for all types of schools: it follows that classical material forms only a fraction of the total.

The Orbilian Society has completed a catalogue of Visual Aids to the Classics. The Honorary Secretary of the Visual Aids Committee of the Society is Dr R. H. Harte, Belfast High School.

Maps

W. and A. K. Johnston, 30 Museum Street, London, W.C. 1.

John Murray, 50 Albemarle Street, London, W. 1.

George Philip and Son Ltd., 32 Fleet Street, London, E.C. 4.

Ordnance Survey.

See the catalogues of these firms. The Ordnance Survey publishes a map of Roman Britain.

Photographs, postcards, etc.

Alinari (Florence) have an extensive collection of photographs of classical sites and objects. They are obtainable from The Mansell Collection, 42 Linden Gardens, London, W. 2.

George Bell and Sons Ltd. Postcard size drawings with vocabulary.

British Museum. See their list of publications.

Greek Government Department of Information, 34 Hyde Park Square, London, W. 2. Photographs of most Greek sites. Sale and free loan.

Warburg Institute, Woburn Square, London, W.C. 1. Collection of large, mounted photographs of art and architecture. Free loan; carriage both ways is payable.

Wall charts

A. Wheaton and Co. Ltd., Fore Street, Exeter.

Orbilian Society. See above for address.

Realien

Association for the Reform of Latin Teaching (Hon. Sec. Miss M. G. Drury, Prendergast Grammar School, London, S.E. 6). The *realien* in the possession of this Association are available to members only.

Any reputable dealer in coins, e.g. B. A. Seaby Ltd., 65 Great Portland Street, London, W. 1. This firm publishes *Roman Coins and their Values*, by H. A. Seaby. Illustrated with line drawings and plates. They hire three small cases of coins (one Greek and two Roman) at the rate of 10s. per week each. The reduced rate for a school hiring the three at once is 25s. The hirer pays postage in both directions.

Filmstrips (filmstrips are not usually sent for inspection by producers):

A. J. Lockwood Filmstrip Productions, 10 Golden Square, London, W. 1.

Association for the Reform of Latin Teaching. Apply to C. W. E. Peckett, Priory School, Shrewsbury.

Common Ground Ltd., 44 Fulham Road, London, S.W. 3. Distributors, Educational Supply Association, Ltd., Pinnacles, Harlow, Essex.

Educational Productions Ltd., East Ardsley, Wakefield, Yorks.

Hellenic and Roman Societies, 31–34 Gordon Square, London, W.C. 1.

Unicorn Head Visual Aids Ltd., 42 Westminster Palace Gardens, Westminster, London, S.W. 1.

Visual Information Service, 12 Bridge Street, Hungerford, Berks.

Yevonde, The Studio, 16*a* Trevor Street, London, S.W. 7.

Films

Gateway Film Productions, 470 Green Lanes, Palmers Green, London, N. 13.

New Realm Pictures Ltd., Queen's House, Leicester Square, London, W.C. 2.

The National Film Institute of Ireland, 65 Harcourt Street, Dublin.

Slides

Association for the Reform of Latin Teaching.

Hellenic and Roman Societies (a really extensive collection).

(For addresses, *see* under *Filmstrips*.)

3. SCHOOL PERFORMANCES OF CLASSICAL PLAYS

General

It is difficult to over-estimate the value of the presentation by Fifth and Sixth Forms of classical plays—preferably in the original language and before public audiences. The chief advantages to be derived from this practice may be set down very briefly as follows:

(i) Boys who take part in the performances learn a great amount of Latin and Greek outside normal school hours, and without any compulsion. The voluntary nature of the work greatly increases its value—'the labour we delight in physics pain'.

(ii) Both the actors and—to a lesser degree—the audiences make the acquaintance of authors who might otherwise remain unread and unknown.

(iii) Much incidental knowledge is assimilated of classical costume, customs, stage-machinery, colloquial habits of speech—and even music.

(iv) Not only the boys themselves but also members of the general public attending the performances are presented with the idea that Latin and Greek are not the 'dead' languages that they often suppose them to be, and can even be enjoyed. There are no counter-balancing disadvantages.

Few schools are in the happy position of Bradfield, with its delightful open-air theatre, or of Westminster, with its long tradition of productions of Terence—rounded off with witty epilogues rich in punning allusions to present-day affairs. Few schools, on the other hand, are entirely without resources for play-production. A stage is the only vital necessity. Scenery can be constructed without much difficulty (or dispensed with almost entirely by the use of curtains): costumes present a simple enough problem; few garments are easier to make than the *chiton* and the *chlamys*. Even in a small school, the recruiting of the cast should not be a troublesome business: though few cheerful volunteers may be found to construe a passage of Virgil in form, many will usually welcome with alacrity the opportunity of taking the part of Socrates or Sceledrus on the stage. It is most strongly recommended that classical specialists in schools where this has not yet been tried should make the experiment—if only on a small scale at first. The difficulties (if indeed they exist) are far outweighed by the advantages.

Translation or Original Version? Choice of Play

There is a growing—and excellent—practice, especially in girls' schools, of presenting Greek plays in translation—usually in the pleasantly rhythmic (and easily obtainable) versions of Dr Gilbert Murray. One hears, too, of an occasional performance of one or other of the comedies of Aristophanes in Rogers' translation. This method of presenting Greek drama has several advantages; though it should not be hastily assumed that English verses are much more easily learnt than Greek iambics. The chief advantage is perhaps to be found in the fact that the audience is more easily able to follow the plot. The actors, however, lose at least as much as the audience gains by this practice. Although they learn much about the structure of a Greek play, they learn no Greek. On the other hand, it is perhaps too much to expect of an audience largely non-classical to sit for over two hours without hearing as much as one intelligible word![1]

As far as Greek plays are concerned, most schools will probably find that the best method of resolving this dilemma (if they wish to entertain their visitors rather than merely to impress them!) is to present dialogue in English and the choruses in Greek. This

[1] The audiences at the Bradfield plays (happily revived in 1949 with an excellent performance of the *Agamemnon*) must be considered an exception to the general rule.

compromise the spectators will cheerfully accept, as a modern audience does not normally expect to hear the words of any chorus.

Among Greek plays suitable for school presentation, the following may be recommended: Euripides: *Alcestis, Medea, Bacchae, Iphigenia in Tauris*; Sophocles: *Oedipus Rex, Antigone*; Aeschylus: *Prometheus Vinctus*;[1] Aristophanes: *Clouds, Frogs, Knights, Acharnians, Birds*.

By far the most popular authors—to boys at any rate—are Aristophanes and Plautus. The humour of Plautus is robust, sometimes to the point of crudity; his characters are (though 'stock') essentially human; his plots are easy to follow; there is plenty of action, much opportunity for comic gesture and by-play; and his language is usually simple. The more sophisticated Terence, though some will prefer his smoother style, is less suited generally to a schoolboy cast.

Neither Plautus nor Terence should be performed wholly in translation; little is learnt by this method—the position is in no way comparable with that of Greek tragedy. Nor is it really advisable to produce a complete play. By skilful cutting, a shortened version can be made which moves faster and avoids lengthy, static and long-winded soliloquies that add little or nothing to the plot. Alternatively, a few selected scenes may be given. For example, those scenes in *Aulularia* which have their counterparts in Molière's *L'Avare* are lively and straightforward, and by themselves make a satisfactory play lasting about fifty minutes. If this is followed by a shortened version of *L'Avare* in French (with the co-operation, of course, of the Modern Languages department), the result is a most amusing evening's entertainment, with a valuable lesson in it.

If it is feared that the audience may not have sufficient Latin to enable it to follow the patent plots and simple dialogue of Plautus, at least two possible solutions of this problem are available. Both have been tried with success. Stated briefly, they are:

(*a*) The introduction of a 'commentator', a (preferably comic) character who comes to the front of the stage at the beginning

---

[1] If the school's Art and Handicraft departments are able to construct the huge effigy of Prometheus which is essential to the production.

of each scene and tells the audience briefly what is about to happen.

(b) The simple expedient of delivering all soliloquies and 'asides' (i.e. where the actor is addressing the audience, and not his fellow-actors) in English. Where these are insufficient to keep the audience fully apprised of the plot, others can be added without much difficulty.

Suitable comedies of Plautus for school productions are *Aulularia, Menaechmi, Miles Gloriosus, Mostellaria, Curculio, Captivi, Trinummus.*

Texts and Books of Reference

Aeschylus, Euripides and Sophocles: Translations by Gilbert Murray. George Allen and Unwin, Ltd.

Plautus: Oxford Classical Texts, 2 vols.
Loeb Classical Library. Heinemann; 5 vols.
(Editions of separate plays published by C.U.P. and Macmillan and Co., whose current lists should be consulted.)

SAUNDERS. *Costumes in Roman Comedy.* Columbia University Press. (Out of print.)

HOUSTON. *Ancient Greek, Roman and Byzantine Costume.* A. and C. Black.

HAIGH. *The Attic Theatre.* O.U.P. (Out of print).

BEARE. *The Roman Stage.* Methuen.

Herodes: *The Schoolmaster.* Loeb ed.

Texts of simple 'made-up' Latin playlets, suitable for junior forms, are few and far between. A little book containing eight short Latin plays is *Personae Comicae,* by G. M. LYNE (Centaur Books). Those who are anxious to obtain material of this kind might apply to the American Classical League Service Bureau, Miami University, Oxford, Ohio, U.S.A., for a list of the short classroom plays published by it in mimeograph form.

Costume

The toga is a difficult garment to manipulate successfully, and is best avoided; where, however, it is essential to the play, the chapter devoted to it in Miss Houston's book (see above) can profitably be consulted. There is also a useful article on it in Nettleship and Sandys' *Dictionary of Classical Antiquities*, and a brief account in the *Oxford Classical Dictionary*. Fortunately, all extant Latin plays are *palliatae*, and for these the only necessary garments are the *tunica* (*chiton*) and *pallium* (*himation*), both simply constructed and easy to wear. It requires very little ingenuity and

1. *Tunica* (*chiton*) as worn by a slave.   2. *Pallium* (*chlamys*) worn over *tunica*.
3. *Chiton*, as adapted for women's wear.

still less research to ring enough changes on these two simple articles of clothing to cover a diversity of characters. The rich man's *tunica* is long and flowing, and handsomely decorated; the slave's is short and plain, of coarse material, and he wears no *pallium*. The female character has a wider *tunica*, arranged to fall in graceful folds and ribboned over the chest; it is made of finer material, preferably red or yellow in colour: and so on—but, despite all these minor variations, the garment is essentially the same for all the players, and is nothing more or less than a smock.

The accompanying illustrations will serve to give a general idea of a simple form of each of these two garments, inexpensive and easily made. Suitable ornamental design can be added to the borders by means of stencils and poster-paint.

Music

The production of a classical play is greatly enhanced by the occasional use of suitable music. A few plays have been provided with modern scores (e.g. that written by Dr Vaughan Williams for the *Wasps*); but these require an orchestra—which is not always available, and is in any case an anachronism. Preferable is the employment of one or two boys who are skilful performers on the recorder, flute or clarinet. The few remnants of Greek music are just sufficient for the provision of suitable *entr'actes* and choral accompaniments. They are to be found in any good history of music. Probably the most attractive is the *Hymn to the Sun* attributed to Mesomedes (second century A.D.), a transcription of which we append (p. 201).

4. BROADCASTING

The Classics teacher has much for which to be grateful to the B.B.C. The Third Programme in particular has given generously of its time to the broadcasting of Greek plays, to talks on classical subjects of every kind. The Home Service, too, has spared time for Greek plays in translation in its World Theatre series, and for an occasional talk on a classical subject. However, all of this has been aimed at an adult audience, and many teachers feel that the B.B.C. in its programmes for schools could go further and make a valuable contribution to the teaching of Classics in schools.

It would be ungenerous not to acknowledge the value of the Series on the Classics that has in the past been produced by the Schools Department of the B.B.C. The Talks for Sixth Forms on the Legacy of the Classical World and on the Greek Classics in Translation, though it is now some time since they were first produced, were a valuable help. The English and History Series have offered useful background for non-classics specialists, Rex Warner's broadcasts on the 'Iliad' and the 'Odyssey' being particularly successful. It is felt, however, that much more could and should be done specifically for the students of the Classics.

HYMN TO THE SUN

(ATTRIBUTED TO MESOMEDES)

Χι-ο-νο-βλε-φά-ρου πά-τερ Ἀ-οῦς,   ρο-δό-εσ-σαν ὃς ἄν - τυ-γα πώ-λων

πτα-νοῖς ὑπ' ἴχ-νεσ - σι δι-ώ-κεις,   χρυ-σαῖ-σιν ἀ-γαλ - λό-με-νος κό-μαις

περὶ νῶ - τον ἀ-πεί - ρι-τον οὐ-ρά-νου,   ἀκ - τῖ - να πολύ - στρο-φον ἀμ - πλέκ-ων

αἴγ - λας πο-λυ-δέρ - κε-α πα - γὰν   πε-ρὶ γαῖ - αν ἄ - πα - σαν ἑ-λίσ - σων,

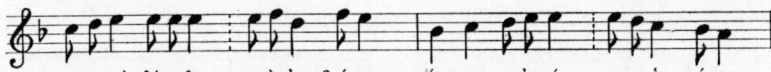

πο-τα-μοὶ δέ σε-θεν   πυ-ρὸς ἀμ - βρό-του   τίκ - του - σιν ἐπ-ή - ρα-τον ἀ - μέ-ραν.

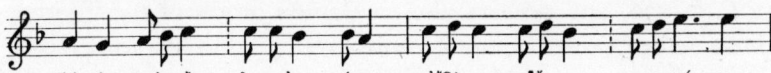

Σοὶ μὲν χο-ρὸς εὔ - δι-ος ἀσ - τέ-ρων   κατ' Ὄ-λυμ-πον ἄν-ακ - τα χο-ρεύ - ει,

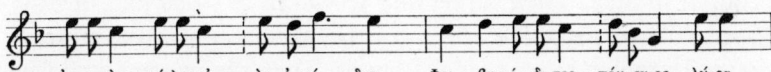

ἀν-ε-τὸν μέ-λος αἰ - ἐν ἀ-εί - δων,   Φοι - βη-ΐ-δι τερ-πόμ-εν-ος λύ-ρᾳ.

Γλαυ-κὰ δὲ πάρ-οι - θε σε-λά - να   χο-ρὸν ὥ - ρι-ον ἀ - γε-μο-νεύ - ει

λευ-κῶν ὑ-πὸ σύρ - μα-σι μόσ - χων   γά-νυ-ται δέ τέ σοι   νό-ος εὐ-με-νὴς

πο-λυ-οί - μο-να κόσ - μον ἑ - λίσ - σων.

The language side, and this is where help is most needed, has not been touched at all. We should like to suggest that experiments be made to produce some first-class lessons on the great writers of Greece and Rome in which, despite differences of pronunciation, seldom the great difficulty it is represented to be, the original language should play a major part. For example, a course of eight lessons could be devised for the Fifth Form, dealing with Lucretius, Catullus, Virgil, Horace, Caesar, Cicero, Livy and Tacitus, each of them on some such lines as the following.

The lesson on Virgil, for instance, might be based on the meeting of Aeneas with Charon (*Aen.* VI, 295–332). It would be expected that the listening audience would have worked through the translation of the passage before the broadcast. First the passage should be read aloud in the original with care for its pronunciation and rhythm. Then two or three translations might be given, e.g. those of Dryden, Mackail and C. Day Lewis, one in full and the others of a few lines, with a short comment on the merits of each. Then the subject-matter would be dealt with, which would call for some explanation of the Greek and Roman view of the after-life, and Virgil's geography of the Underworld could be related to Milton's description of the rivers of Hell (*P.L.* II, 576) and perhaps also to Dante's origin of the infernal rivers in the *Divine Comedy* (I, canto xiv). English literature teems with references to Lethe and Styx, some of which might be brought in here. Then something would need to be said of how Virgil achieves his poetic effects, of the onomatopoeia and alliteration with which this passage abounds. Then the passage could be related to its context and to the *Aeneid* as a whole and some estimate given of Virgil's contribution to European literature and his influence on other writers. Finally, the broadcast should close with a second reading of the original text.

The purpose of this would not be to give an exhaustive treatise on the passage—most of these points would be dealt with in a sentence or two—nor to deliver a profound and learned lecture, but to whet the pupils' appetite for the author and to carry them beyond the routine, slow, and often painful efforts of translation to the realms of appreciation. It may be said that this is what any good teacher could and should do, but the chief object of a series of this kind would be to bring another voice, another viewpoint into the classroom, and to give fresh stimulus to the pupils and perhaps to the teacher himself.

To all this will be objected the fact that the audience will probably be a small one and that the B.B.C.'s Schools Broadcasting time is already fully occupied. But the potential audience is not as small as is often supposed, and the demands on time that such a series would make are comparatively small—perhaps eight lessons of thirty minutes in a session. Surely time could be found for such an experiment.

Again acknowledgment must be made to the B.B.C. for its use of Television to illustrate classical themes. Much has been done for Greek Drama on the television screen, and those who once found the journey to Cambridge or Bradfield impossible may now from time to time have a chance of seeing a Greek tragedy performed in translation at least. But it is in the realm of archaeology that television has a most important part to play, and programmes like Sir Mortimer Wheeler's 'The Glory that was Greece' and 'The Grandeur that was Rome' have stimulated an interest in the ancient world among millions of people who were previously quite unaware of it. So too the programmes on Athens, Crete and Pompeii in the School Television series entitled 'Men of the Past' are all to the good, and a further expansion on these lines would be very welcome.

5. THE SCHOOL LIBRARY

'This books can do; nor this alone, they give
New views to life, and teach us how to live;
They soothe the grieved, the stubborn they chastise,
Fools they admonish, and confirm the wise;
Their aid they yield to all.'   (GEORGE CRABBE)

Just as no school should be without a school library, so no school library should be without a section devoted in some degree to the Classics. Its purpose, and in consequence its contents, will vary with the emphasis laid on Classics in each particular school. It will perhaps be convenient to assume for our purposes here the widest range of possibilities, it being understood that where resources are limited discretion must be exercised. Broadly speaking, the purpose of the classical section of the library may be said to be first, to provide material for those whose main study is the Classics, secondly to cater for non-specialists with little or no familiarity with ancient languages, and thirdly to supply material for illustrating and enriching the teaching of Latin and Greek. Here the school's needs will largely determine the relative strength of each section: texts, technical works and serious works of history being particularly adapted to Sixth-Form Classics students, translations and more general works on the literature, life and history of the ancient world being more appropriate to the second, and a wide range of illustrative material, books, pictures, charts, maps, filmstrips and the like, to the third.

In any case the classical teacher in planning his section of the library must include in his purview material to suit all ages from the youngest boys to the potential undergraduates of the Sixth Form. While books of all grades will necessarily form the main part of his stock, books by no means represent the whole story. The discerning use of periodicals, for instance, will frequently help to dispel the impression that some classical libraries give of being entirely lost in the past. It may be that only a few will find use for the more recondite journals, but *Greece and Rome* affords reading matter well within the capacity of most Sixth Forms, and provides as well valuable material for teachers, while *Acta Diurna* supplies some racy and amusing Latin in the shape of an imaginary Latin newspaper of Roman times. Apart from these more obvious choices, publications like the *Illustrated London News*, and the *National Geographic Magazine* not infrequently provide archaeological illustrations of great interest, to which the alert teacher can refer his class. The library, too, is usually found to be the best repository of collections of maps, pictures, air photos, filmstrips, postcards, lantern slides and all the paraphernalia of visual aids. Nor is it any bad thing if collections of coins, models and other miscellaneous items find a home in the library. There is no classical room—and that is as well;

if they are for all to see, some chance seed may drop on fertile soil.

The selection of books for the library will vary according to the taste and fancy of the librarian, and it is not intended in this section to suggest a list of books so much as to outline the broad principles on which such a selection should be made. The literature of the ancient world must bulk largely in the classical section, whether in the original or in translation. In schools where there is advanced Sixth-Form work it will be found indispensable to build up a series of texts covering the essential part of the corpus of Latin and Greek literature. So much is being published at present in the interests of the beginner, and so little is being done to replace those old scholarly editions that are falling out of print at an alarming rate, that the librarian may be forced to have recourse to second-hand editions. Standard annotated editions of complete works not only are more handsome to look at but are more useful than numbers of smaller text-books of the type commonly used in the classroom. In any case all the standard works must be there, for the need constantly arises to refer a pupil to certain key passages of literature, and it is essential to have the material for wide and rapid reading. Lucky the school which can boast a good collection of Loeb translations for this purpose. It is suggested that other things being equal money is far better spent on translations from Greek literature than from Latin. Yet too narrow an adherence to the classical period is inadvisable. Medieval literature and works like St Augustine's *City of God* should find a place in our library.

In the teaching of Ancient History, of course, the library plays a major role. The careful teacher will get as much of the *Cambridge Ancient History* as he can, and the big standard works, Zimmern, Rostovtzeff, Bury, Mommsen and Grote to supplement the scantier fare afforded by the text-book. Although some teachers may prefer to see Ancient History in the classical section they should bear in mind that, in general, recognized systems of classification do not admit of this, and there may be a positive educational advantage in the distribution of books over various sections of the library. Accordingly, pupils must be carefully taught where to look in the library, or such distribution may lead to neglect. The social life of ancient times has an appeal to others besides classical specialists, and as there are many excellent books in being on this subject, no school, however faint its pretensions to classical studies, should be without some works on the life and society of the Greeks and Romans. Philosophy, religion and political thought have a limited appeal, mostly confined to the scholarship candidates of a Sixth Form. Yet here too there are certain standard works of assured longevity, such as Warde Fowler's *City State of the Greeks and Romans*, that ought to have a place in any library, and to which it may be reasonably expected that other Sixth-Form students, apart from classical specialists, may occasionally wish to refer. Similarly, there should be works on sculpture, architecture and art—among them collections of photographic reproductions of statuary, like those of the Phaidon Press, and good plates illustrative of architecture and architectural detail. This should prove attractive to a wider section of pupils than the pure Classics—and anything is to be welcomed that can break down the former inviolability of the classical shelves.

Dictionaries, Latin and Greek, a library must have, and more than one copy for comfort's sake. A good complete standard grammar in each language is a necessity, as a work of reference for teacher no less than pupil. The English staff, no less than the classical, will require a Lemprière, or its modern equivalent. A dictionary of antiquities is also practically indispensable. On the whole it is better for classical novels to be interspersed among other novels in the fiction section of the library than to be kept with the Classics—many a youngster's interest has been roused by casual reading of this type. Nevertheless, the classical staff should see to it that the fiction section does not lack such novels. An excellent list was prepared by Mr W. B. Thompson, in vol. xxvi, no. 6 (October 1948) of *Latin Teaching*—(A.R.L.T.), with supplement, June 1958—vol. xxx, no. 3, but unfortunately many of the volumes are now out of print. It remains to mention the growing number of books which deal with the debt of the modern world, and in particular of Western culture, to the ancient world. The above are the broad general lines on which

the classical section of the library might be built up, though
it is clear that the requirements of each school will dictate the
emphasis on each division. It need hardly be mentioned that the
satisfactory use of the library is dependent on open access to the
shelves, in spite of the drawbacks such a system entails. A good
school library is one that is well used.

We need not dwell long on the uses to which the library should
be put. Those who would like to study the matter at greater length
will find full information in *A Short Manual of School Libraries*
by C. A. Stott. One of the first duties of the classical master at the
beginning of the year with his new Sixth Form is to take his
charges to the library to show them where and what classical
books are available. This is the occasion to urge pupils each to
adopt in classical studies a line of his own, a means of giving
a pupil a feeling that he has his own special stake in the subject,
and of promoting individual effort. A little harmless flattery in
appealing to the 'expert' at this or that will often repay handsome
dividends. The second use to which the library must be put is for
background reading, free or dictated. It is perhaps no very cynical
asperity to remark that voluntary background reading may often
be an illusion rather than a reality. The erstwhile official exhorta-
tion to 'leave books lying about', on the principle that you can
make horses drink by casually slopping water all over the place,
savours too much of Micawber. Against such optimism may be
set the realism of the librarian to whom such scattered literature
is less an earnest of budding research than evidence of incorrigible
carelessness, or even vestiges of the stricken field. Here and there,
of course, a boy will read unbidden, but he who would assure
himself of this work being done would be better advised to thrust
books into boys' unwilling hands, pestering them for information
thereon, until very shame or fear compels the shiverer to take the
first dip. We need not apologize for such coercion, until the habit
of reading, a slower growth than heretofore in the crowded life
of our schools today, be firmly established. Reference for special
questions, preparation for short essays or lectures, full-scale essays,
are other forms of obligation which will send our pupils scuttling
to the library to piece out their imperfect knowledge with liberal,

if unacknowledged, quotation. The wise teacher will help them with recommendations of where to find what they want. Sometimes an essay may be written on material contributed by a number of boys, sometimes in collaboration with a wholly different group or class. In all these cases the library will be the focus of activity. The use of the library for private study is a virtue born of necessity, but here again it must be owned that some rude shocks await those who would flatter themselves that a monastic silence will always reign in an uninvigilated library, or that seniors not under the eye of authority will always prefer the Peloponnesian War to *Punch*. Last consideration—and often regrettably least—those of the staff whom the time-table allows any leisure for bringing their own knowledge up to date should be able to find in the school library books for this purpose—unless this be the greatest Micawberism of all.

In any event the library should be the school's reading centre. The temptation to imitate the scientific or the geographical specialist, and to insist on a 'classical room', may lead to a 'classical faculty library'. Yet this is a development to be deprecated. The classical books must be in the library, available to the school as a whole. The use of classical books by non-classical students is to be encouraged. Housed in a separate room they could not be easily made available either to other students or other classical forms. Many pupils in History, Art, and the like, will wish to have access to those books. Moreover, it is educationally valuable for classical students to find their books in the general collection, if only to help dispel the all too prevalent notion that classical specialists are somehow a race apart.

So much for the library at present. What are the needs of the libraries in the reconstructed education of the future? Perhaps it is natural that any changes are likely to affect the classical department least of all, although it may be expected that the swing away from the linguistic and philological interests of earlier centuries will be reflected in the choice of books, and that one by one the Dindorfs and the Paleys, and the mustier commentaries of a forgotten generation will go down unhonoured to the school furnace. Yet the filling of the classical shelves must still remain a thorny problem for many an isolated teacher with a meagre grant. Perhaps there is no greater desideratum at the present day than an ample supply of book lists, annotated, and kept up to date. And since the study of Classics is being born again in many parts of the country, prime importance in such lists is being accorded to easy and attractive books for the young, good picture books, and books for the intelligent non-Classic. The provision of these will add further stimulus to a movement towards the humanities, already growing, and likely to be yet further intensified.

APPENDIX I

THE PRONUNCIATION OF LATIN

1. *Introduction*

The 'reformed' or 'restored' pronunciation of Latin unquestionably presents a reasonably close approximation to the actual sounds of the language as spoken by educated Romans in the first century B.C. The support of Roby in his *Latin Grammar* (1871) gained it many adherents both at home and overseas; and before the end of the nineteenth century this method of pronunciation was in increasing use in England, and had become the normal practice in Scotland and the U.S.A. Its general adoption in this country was finally assured when the 1906 Report of the Classical Association's Committee on the Pronunciation of Latin was immediately approved by the Head Masters' Conference, the Incorporated Association of Head Masters, the Incorporated Association of Assistant Masters, and the (then) Board of Education.

The scheme of pronunciation as set out in this Report, and in such books as Arnold and Conway's *Restored Pronunciation of Latin* (1906) and Postgate's *How to Pronounce Latin* (1907), still remains substantially accurate: but improvements in detail have since been introduced by a number of scholars, of whom Westaway in England and Sturtevant in the U.S.A. deserve particular mention. The most up-to-date presentation of the subject is to be found in the second (1940) edition of Sturtevant's *The Pronunciation of Greek and Latin* (published for Yale University by the Linguistic Society of America).

Modern compilers of class-books, in their sections that deal with pronunciation, appear as a rule to be content with reproducing, more or less unchanged, rules that were laid down over forty-nine years ago. The following guide, by incorporating more recent improvements, aims at a closer standard of accuracy. Phonetic equivalents, when given, are enclosed within square brackets.

2. *Vowels*

ā   As *a* in *father* or the second *a* in *aha* [ɑ·].

ă   The same sound shortened, as the first *a* in *aha*. If this proves too difficult for pupils to differentiate from ā, it is better to pronounce *a* as *a* in *fat* than to run any risk of confusion between (e.g.) *puella* (nom.) and *puella* (abl.) or between *bella* (pl. of *bellum*) and *bella* (impv. of *bellare*).

ē   As *ay* in Scottish *day*; less exactly, as *e* in *prey* [eˑ].
ĕ   As *e* in *fret* [ɛ].
ī   As *i* in *machine* [iˑ].
ĭ   As *i* in *fit* [i].
ō   As French *au* in *chaud*; less exactly, as *o* in *note* [oˑ].
ŏ   As *o* in *not* [ɔ].
ū   As *oo* in *fool* or *u* in *brute* (not as *u* in *unit*) [uˑ].
ŭ   As *oo* in *foot* or *u* in *full* (not as *u* in *dull*) [u].
ȳ   As French *u* in *pur* [yˑ].
ў   As French *u* in *du* [y].

3. *Diphthongs*

ae   As *ai* in *aisle*.
au   As German *au* in *Haus*; less exactly, as *ou* in *house*.
oe   As *oi* in *boil*.[1]
ui   As French *oui*.
ei   As *ei* in *rein*.
eu   As Spanish *eu* or Welsh *ew*. '...very nearly like the *ou* in the cockney pronunciation of *house*...never like *eu* in *feud*' (Westaway). '...not like anything in English, French or German;...similar to the diphthong of Spanish *ceuta*, i.e. [eu]' (Sturtevant).[2]

4. *Consonants*

f, k, l, p, qu, z   As in English.[3]
b   Generally as in English; but *bs* and *bt* as *ps* and *pt*.
c   As in *cat* (never as English *s* or *sh*).
ch, ph, th   If possible, these should be pronounced as the *kh*, *ph* and *th* would be in *deck-hand*, *mop-handle* and *hot-house* if the *k*, *p* and *t* were part of the second syllable. If this proves impossible, it is better to drop the *h* altogether, and pronounce simply as *c* (i.e. as *ch* in *chorus*), *p* and *t*.

---

[1] *oi*, occurring in *proinde*, is similarly pronounced.
[2] Note that it can be inferred from pseudo-Virgil, *Ciris* 68 that *neuter* is disyllabic and is therefore one of the words that contain this diphthong.
[3] With *z* this represents the Hellenistic pronunciation of ʒ, which the Romans followed.

APPENDICES

d   Generally similar to French (rather than English) *d*; but final *d* in indeclinable words is pronounced *t* when the next word begins with a vowel.

g   As in *get* (never as English *j*).

gn As *ngn* [ŋn].

h   At the beginning of words, rather less marked than English *h*; elsewhere (e.g. *nihil*) practically silent.

i (consonant)   As *y*.

m   As in English, except when final: in this case it is 'merely a mark of nasalization of the preceding vowel' (Sturtevant). It is suggested that final *m* should be fully pronounced, for convenience, when grammatical forms are being learnt 'in vacuo', but that it should not be pronounced in the reading of continuous prose, and still less in that of verse.

n   As in English, except where otherwise stated below.

nc, nqu   As in English [ŋ].

ng As in *linger* (not as in *singer*).

ns There is much evidence that *n* before *s* was silent in Cicero's day.[1] The preceding vowel is always long:[2] therefore (e.g.) *consul* should be pronounced *cō-sul*, and *insto ī-sto*.

nf Though the preceding vowel is always long, there is no explicit evidence that *n* before *f* was silent. Therefore (e.g.) *infero* should be pronounced *īn-fero*, not *ī-fero*.

r   Always trilled, in the middle and at the end of words as well as at the beginning.

s   As in *gas* (never as in *has*). It is particularly important that this should be observed with final *-ĕs* (e.g. *miles*) and *-ēs* (e.g. *mones, res*).

t   As in French (rather than English) *table* (never as in English or French *nation*).

u (consonant), v   As *w*. The *u* after *q* and in (e.g.) *suadeo, anguis*, is the same letter as that which is commonly written *v*—the consonantal form of the vowel *u*. Many teachers now feel that the time has come to follow the practice of those modern texts (e.g. O.C.T.

[1] Sturtevant says: 'The early inscriptions...show such forms as *cosul* and *cesor*; and that the pronunciation *cosul* was current in classical times is shown by the spelling of Latin words in Greek inscriptions and papyri (e.g. Κλήμης, καστρήσιος), and also by explicit testimony.' He then quotes from Velius Longus—'sequenda est...elegantia eruditorum virorum, qui quasdam litteras lenitatis causa omiserunt, sicut Cicero, qui foresia et Megalesia et hortesia sine n littera dicebat.'

[2] The inference that it was also nasalized is not certain.

212

Livy) that employ a single letter (capital V, small u) both for consonantal *u* and for vowel *u*.

x   As in *extract* (never as in *exact*).

5. Doubled Consonants

cc   As *kc* in *book-case* (not as in *tobacco*).
gg   As in *leg-guard* (not as in *beggar*).
ll   As *lll* in *hall-light* (not as in *holly*).
mm   As in *drum-major* (not as in *summit*).
nn   As in *swan-necked* (not as in *manner*).
pp   As in *hop-pole* (not as in *happy*).
ss   As *sss* in *grass-sown* (not as in *mossy*).
tt   As in *coat-tail* (not as in *butter*).

6. Length of Syllables

In 1913 it was still urgently necessary for Westaway, in his *Quantity and Accent in the Pronunciation of Latin* (C.U.P.), to say 'the length of the syllable and the length of the contained vowel are two totally different things, and must not be confused'. Since then, the warning, has been constantly repeated; and though the fallacious notion of 'vowels long by position' died hard, this confusion has now become quite obsolete.

The quantity of syllables, as distinct from that of vowels, is generally taught in a rough-and-ready way by saying that a short syllable is one that contains a short vowel followed by less than two consonants, while a long syllable is one that contains either a long vowel, or a short vowel followed by two or more consonants (with exceptions such as *qu* and, in verse, mute and liquid). It is more scientific to treat this matter from the point of view of the correct division of Latin words into their component syllables. Rules for doing so, and their application in determining the quantity of syllables, are given fully in books such as Westaway's, mentioned above, and Postgate's *Prosodia Latina*.* The summaries that appear in modern grammars and courses are not always entirely adequate.

For the purpose of verse or rhythmical prose the short syllable was taken as the unit of length. A long syllable was regarded as equivalent to two such units, taking twice as long to pronounce. Since this principle of measurement takes no account of the number of con-

* C. G. Cooper's *An Introduction to the Latin Hexameter*, Macmillan (Melbourne), 1952, may be found useful.

sonants (which may be as many as three, e.g. *scr-*) at the beginning of a syllable, it clearly cannot have reflected accurately the habits of ordinary speech. Hence it is unlikely to have been rigorously observed in reciting prose works or in the practice of oratory, except perhaps in the clausulae. We may be sure, however, that the Romans gave greater precision to the length ratio between short and long syllables when reciting or reading verse aloud. English, of course, has a strong stress accent and our pupils will tend to render Latin rhythms in terms of stresses. To ensure that they read verse as the Romans presumably did, a class might first be taught the elements of musical notation. Latin metre could then be explained on this basis (stressing such obvious points as that an English accentual dactyl = ♩♩♩, whereas a Latin quantitative dactyl = 𝅗𝅥♩♩), and Latin poetry recited by the whole class to the accompaniment of a metronome.

7. *Concealed Quantities*

Most modern grammars and elementary courses are scrupulous in indicating the pronunciation of vowels: the usual practice is to mark all long vowels with the sign ‒, and leave all short vowels unmarked unless there is any special reason at any point for using the sign ᴗ.

There is no doubt that such instruction is now followed with greater care than it used to be when the 'reformed' pronunciation was still something of a novelty to many teachers. Faulty pronunciation may still occur as a result of a teacher's allowing misplacement of stress-accent when declensions and conjugations are being learnt; but the pupil who is not invited to make any distinction between (e.g.) the nominative and genitive singular terminations of the 4th declension, or between the terminations of *regimus* and *audīmus*, is becoming increasingly rare.

In one respect, however, there is still much room for improvement—in the proper pronunciation of long vowels that happen to stand before two or more consonants (or before the double consonant *x*). A pupil who is taught to follow with care the guidance of a typical manual such as Mountford's edition of the *Revised Latin Primer* will pronounce *rēx* as *rakes*, not *recks*; his first syllable of *trīstis* will resemble the French *triste*; he will keep the *u* short in *iungo* and *iungere*, but make it long in *iūnxi* and *iūnctum*.

It is unfortunate that no complete list of words that contain these 'concealed quantities' is readily available to British teachers who desire to aim at accuracy in this respect. But the brief guide that follows covers the words that are likely to be encountered in the first five years of a Latin course.

(i) *General Rules:*

(a) A vowel standing before *nf, ns, nx, nct,* is always long; e.g. *īnferō* (but *intulī*), *ingēns* (but *ingentem,* etc.).

(b) A vowel before *-x, -bs* and *-ps* in the 3rd declension nominatives is long if the vowel is long in the other cases; e.g. *vōx* (*vōcis*) but not *nox* (*noctis*).

(c) In all inceptive verbs, the vowel standing before *-scō* or *-scor* is long. This covers all verbs with this termination except *discō, poscō* and *compescō.*

(d) A vowel standing before *s* in the shortened perfect-stem endings *-āsse, -ēsse, -īsse, -āstī, -ēstī, -īstī,* etc., is always long.

(e) The vowel *a* standing before the noun-suffixes *-brum,*[1] *-crum, -trum,* is always long.

(ii) *List of words not covered by the general rules:*

(Derivatives are not included; e.g. *āctum* implies *āctiō, fōrma* implies *fōrmōsus, mālle* implies *mallem, vāstus* implies *vāstō.*)

āctum	Etrūscus	Īllyria	Mārcus
Āfrica	exīstimō	inlūstris	Mārs
ārdeō		iūrgō	mercēnnārius
ātrium	fāstī	iūstus	mīlle
	favīlla	iūxtā	mūcrō
bēstia	fēstus		
	fīxī	lāpsus	nārrō
cōmpsī	fīxum	Lārs	nefāstus
cōmptum	-flīctum	lēctum	neglēctum
cōntiō	-flīxī	libra	neglēxī
	flūctus	lictor	nīxus
dēlūbrum	flūxī	lūstrum‡	nōlle
dēmpsī	fōrma	lūctus	nōndum
dēmptum	frāctum	lūxī (lūceō)	nōngentī
dīgredior	frūctus	lūxī (lūgeō)	nōnne
dīxī*	frūstrā	lūxuria	nūllus
dūxī†	fūrtim		nūntius
	fūrtum	mālle	nūpsī

[1] This does not include *lăbrum* (lip), where the *b* is not part of the suffix: but it does include *lābrum* (bath-tub).

ēmptum		Mānlius	nūptum
Ēsquiliae	Hellēspontus	Mārcellus	nūtriō

* But *dictum*.   † But *ductum*.

‡ = expiation, etc.; but *lustrum* = lair, etc.

ōrdior	Pūblius	scrīpsī	ūllus
ōrdō	pūrgō	scrīptum	ūndecim
ōrnō		sēgnis	ūsūrpō
ōsculum	quārtus	sēstertius	
ōstium	quīndecim	Sōcratēs	vāllum
	quīnque	sōspes	vāllus
pāctum*	quīntus	strūctum	vāstus
pāstum		strūxī	vēndō
perīclitor	rēctum	sublūstris	vērnus
Phoenīssa	rēgnum	sūmpsī	vēstibulum
Pōlliō	rēxī	sūmptum	vēstīgium
prēndō	rīxa		vēxī ‡
prīnceps	Rōscius	tāctum	vīctum §
prīscus	rōstrum	tēctum	vīlla
prīstinus	rūrsus	tēxī	vīxī
prōmpsī	rūsticus	trāxī †	
prōmptum		trīstis	
pūblicus	scēptrum		

* From *pango*, *pactum* from *pacīscor*.,

† But *tractum*.   ‡ But *vectum*.

§ From *vīvō*; but *victum* from *vincō*.

It will be observed that the above list does not include a number of words in which a vowel standing before *gn*, or before *r* followed by another consonant, is marked long in some books. The authority of Hale and Buck, who deny that such letter-combinations produced automatic lengthening of the preceding vowel, is now generally accepted.

8. *Stress Accent*

There is no doubt that, besides being pronounced quantitatively, most Latin words also bore a stress accent which, though less marked than in English, was nevertheless quite distinct. Apart from the explicit evidence that exists, there are many implicit indications of this. For instance, no one can read hexameter verses for long without coming to realize that their structure is based on harmony between quantity and stress accent in the fifth and sixth feet after conflict in the earlier part of the line.

There are two general rules for Latin stress accent:

(a) Disyllables are accented on the first syllable (e.g. *ménsa*, *cáno*).

(b) Polysyllables are accented on the last syllable but one (the penultimate) if that syllable is long (e.g. *mensárum*, *difficúltas*); and on the last syllable but two (antepenultimate), if the penultimate is short (e.g. *régitis*, *dedítio*, *consulúerant*).

Of many special rules the following are the most important:

(c) Inflected monosyllables are stressed; of uninflected monosyllables, prepositions and conjunctions are unstressed, others are stressed.

(d) All other prepositions are unaccented except when standing after the word that they govern; all other conjunctions are unaccented when standing first in their clause, but accented when they stand later.

(e) Compound words are generally accented in accordance with the general rules (e.g. *ádfero*, *intérea*). But in non-prepositional compounds of *facio* the accent never goes back on the prefix (e.g. *patefácit*, but *intérficit*).

(f) Where an original final syllable that followed a long penultimate has been dropped, the accent is retained on what has now become the final syllable (e.g. *illíc*, *addúc*). This does not apply to neuter nouns in -*ăl* and -*ăr* (originally -*āle*, -*āre*), as the original penultimate has not remained long.

(g) The vocative and genitive singular of nouns in -*ius* preserve the accent of the original forms in -*ie* and -*ii* (e.g. *Vergíli*). The same is true of the genitive singular in -*i* of nouns in -*ium* (e.g. *consíli*).

(h) The enclitic words -*que*, -*ne*, -*ve* drag the accent to the final syllable of any words to which they are attached (e.g. *hominúmque*, *magnáque*).

(i) The inseparable particle -*que* causes the same dislocation when appended to an inflected word (i.e. in *utérque* and *plerúsque*): but other words containing this particle are subject to the general rules (e.g. *utrímque*, but *úndique*). This means that *itaque* is accented on the first syllable when it is a single word, but on the second when it represents *et ita*.

9. Faults in Pronunciation

As Westaway remarks, 'the heavy English accent tends to lengthen the accented syllable of a word and to shorten the other syllables'. Citing the word *societas*, he says that it is rare to hear such a word pronounced correctly, with the last syllable given twice the time of any of the others and its vowel given correct phonetic length, while the vowels in the three short syllables (including the accented -*ci*-) are also given their correct phonetic length. It is therefore important to guard against the lengthening of short vowels in accented syllables.

Whether mispronunciation should be deliberately allowed in the learning of accidence is a debatable question. Some teachers claim that it is vital to stress the changing inflexions of a noun, adjective or verb, and hold that the misplacement of accent that this may involve can easily be corrected if the pupil reproduces it in reading continuous Latin. Others deny that inflexions cannot be properly learnt without being stressed, and insist on accurate pronunciation throughout. What is certainly indefensible is to allow the stressing of an inflexion to pervert the pronunciation of a preceding vowel; e.g. to allow *amābam* to be pronounced with the middle *a* short.

APPENDIX II

THE PRONUNCIATION OF GREEK

1. Introduction

In the preface to his *Greek Grammar* (1879) Goodwin remarks 'it is safe to say that no one could now pronounce a sentence of Greek so that it would have been intelligible to Demosthenes or Plato'. This is still true. Our knowledge of the nature of the Greek pitch accent is imperfect; and even if we knew more about it, we should find it very difficult to reproduce. In addition, we have no direct information, and very little indirect evidence, about Greek stress accent. All that we can aim at is to reproduce with reasonable accuracy the sounds of the vowels, diphthongs and consonants; and the 'reformed' or 'restored' pronunciation of Greek indicates how they sounded in Athens of the fifth and early fourth centuries B.C.

The reformed pronunciation of Greek came into use in English-speaking countries concurrently with that of Latin, and in consequence has long been the normal practice in Scotland and the U.S.A. In England it has become widely adopted since its recommendation by the Classical Association's Committee on the Pronunciation of Greek (1908): but there are still a few schools that have joined the vast majority in employing the reformed pronunciation of Latin, but nevertheless continue to pronounce Greek in the antiquated 'English' way.

The following guide incorporates the results of research by Sturtevant and others subsequent to 1908. It should be recognized that the pronunciations suggested are to some extent approximations for the convenience of English-speaking pupils. Phonetic equivalents, when given, are enclosed within square brackets.

2. Vowels

ᾱ and ᾰ   As Latin *ā* and *ă*.

ε   Not as Latin *ĕ*, but similar to French *é* [e].

η   Not as Latin *ē*, but similar to French *è* [ɛ·].

ῑ and ῐ   Roughly as Latin *ī* and *ĭ*; but as with η ε and ω o, the long vowel in Greek was more 'open' than the short, while in Latin the reverse is the case.

o   Not as Latin *ŏ*, but similar to French *o* in *pot* [o].

ω   Similar to French *o* in *tort*; less exactly, as *oa* in broad [ɔ·]. The change to pronunciation as Latin *ō* did not come until after the middle of the fourth century B.C.

ῡ and ῠ   The original pronunciation was roughly as Latin *ū* and *ŭ*. This continued in use during classical times in many parts of the Greek world; but most authorities agree that in classical Attic the change had already taken place to the pronunciation as Latin *ȳ* and *ў*.

3. *Diphthongs*

αι   This differed slightly from Latin *ae*, but what the exact difference was we do not know. We must therefore be content to pronounce it as Latin *ae*.

αυ   As Latin *au*.

ει   'A long vowel of the same quality as ε' (Sturtevant); like Latin *ē*, resembling *ay* in Scottish *day* [e·]. There is no justification whatever for pronouncing it as English *eye*.

οι   This differed slightly from Latin *oe* or English *oi*, but what the exact difference was we do not know. We must therefore be content to pronounce it as Latin *oe*.

ου   As Latin *ō* [ö]. The change to pronunciation as Latin *ū* did not come until after the middle of the fourth century B.C.

Greek differs from Latin in having diphthongs whose first element is a long vowel. They are the following:

ευ   As Latin *eu*.

υι   As Latin *ui*.

ᾱυ, ηυ   Pronounced by quickly following the sound of the long vowel with the sound of a short non-Attic *ŭ* (i.e. Latin *ŭ*).[1] ᾱυ occurs in ἐμαυτόν, σεαυτόν (and contracted σαυτόν), ἑαυτόν (and contracted αὑτόν), and αὑτός (contracted from ὁ αὑτός).

ᾳ, ῃ, ῳ   Ancient Greek knew nothing of our iota subscript, which 'is not older than the twelfth century A.D.' (Goodwin). In the classical period the diphthongs were written ᾱι, ηι, ωι and were pronounced by quickly following the sound of the long vowel with the sound of a short ι. Later, the iota was neither pronounced nor written.

---

[1] The non-Attic ωυ is similarly pronounced.

4. *Consonants*

β, δ, κ, λ, π, τ As the corresponding Latin letters.

θ, φ, χ As Latin *th, ph, ch*. As with Latin, the fricative pronunciation is incorrect, and the correct pronunciation 'makes much in Greek accidence that is otherwise obscure perfectly comprehensible' [1] (Classical Association Report).

φθ, χθ In these combinations the Greeks were able to give each of the aspirates its usual value. Unless we are using the incorrect fricative pronunciation, the best that we can do is to pronounce them as if written πθ, κθ. [2]

γ As Latin *g*, except when it precedes γ, κ, ξ or χ; it then has the sound of English nasal *n* [ŋ] as in *anger, ankle*, etc.

3 As *zd*, not as *dz*; ancient grammarians make this very plain.

μ As English *m*.

ν Generally as English *n*. But final ν is modified in pronunciation before certain consonants in exactly the same way as (e.g.) the prefix ἐν- is modified in spelling and pronunciation. Therefore final ν is pronounced λ before λ, as μ before β, μ, π, ψ, and as nasal γ before γ, κ, ξ, χ.

ξ As Latin *x*, at the beginning of a word as elsewhere.

ρ As Latin *r*. In ῥ 'the aspiration did not precede or follow the ρ, but accompanied it throughout' (Sturtevant). English speakers who cannot imitate this sound [r̥] must be content with *hr*.

σ As Latin *s*. Pronunciation as *z* before β, γ and μ is incorrect for classical Attic.

ψ As *ps* in *lapse*, at the beginning of a word as elsewhere.

5. *Doubled Consonants*

Apart from γγ, already dealt with, the same principle is generally followed as in Latin, the two consonants being pronounced separately: but two details must be noted:

(*a*) In ρρ the second ρ is aspirated.

(*b*) There is no certainty how -σσ- and -ττ- were pronounced, or whether their pronunciations were identical: it *may* have been either *ts* or [θ] until the Hellenistic period.

[1] E.g. φαίνω (p-haino), πέφηνα (pep-hena).
[2] They were so pronounced and even written in Egypt and Italy during the Hellenistic period.

6. *Breathings*

In classical Attic breathings were not represented; but the words that are now written with a rough breathing over the first letter were pronounced with an initial *h*. Some other Greek dialects possessed the sign ⊢ to denote this sound: and Aristophanes of Byzantium adopted this sign to denote the presence of aspiration, and invented the converse sign ⊣ to denote its absence, simply for the purpose of distinguishing between words like ὅρος and ὄρος. Hence we have developed the signs ' and ' now in use.

Modern practice is misleading in printing the rough breathing over initial letters only. If the initial letter of a word is aspirated at all, it must continue to be aspirated when the word appears as the second member of a compound. This is evident from the spelling of early non-Ionic inscriptions in which the sign for *h* appears (e.g.) before the ε of πάρεδρος, and also from such Latin transliterations as Euhemerus.

7. *Accents*

The Greek accents are diacritical marks that were invented by post-classical grammarians and 'originally used to help inexperienced readers to distinguish between words that might otherwise be confused' (Sturtevant). Subsequently their use was extended to indicate the pronunciation of every word. They are indications of pitch, not of stress: the acute accent means a rise in pitch, the circumflex a rise and fall, the grave a lack of any pitch accent.[1]

It may therefore be reasonably inferred that in ancient Greek 'the rise and fall in pitch was a function of the word rather than, as in English, of the sentence' (Sturtevant). Any attempt to reproduce this change of pitch in ordinary school teaching is not generally advisable; but there is no reason why individual pupils who happen to have a good ear should not be allowed to try it. Apart from such cases, the Greek accents should be disregarded in pronunciation; it is particularly important not to use them as a guide to stress.

[1] There was also a 'middle' accent in polysyllables, about which we know nothing except its existence, as the few ancient authorities who mention it give no illustrations.

8. *Length of Syllables*

What has been said on this subject in dealing with Latin pronunciation applies here also in general; but two particular points must be
noted:

(*a*) Latin has only one double letter, *x*; Greek has three, ζ, ξ and ψ.

(*b*) In choric metres a long syllable that contains a long vowel is
sometimes more than twice the length of a short syllable.

9. *Concealed Quantities*

This problem hardly exists in Greek. The only common word liable
to mispronunciation is πράττω, in which the α is long, as is shown by
the accentuation of πρᾶξαι, πρᾶξις, πρᾶγμα, etc.

10. *Stress Accent*

Beyond the fact that the Greek 'accents' had nothing to do with
stress before the second century A.D., we know practically nothing about
stress accent in ancient Greek. The best that we can do in this respect
is to pronounce Greek words as far as possible with even stress.

APPENDIX III

EXAMINATION REQUIREMENTS FOR ENTRY TO UNIVERSITIES AND PROFESSIONS

This section is intended to serve as a rough guide to the position of Latin or Greek as qualifying subjects for entry to the universities or professions. Since, however, it is likely that in the near future there may be big changes in the whole machinery of selection for entry to the Universities, and in the character of examination requirements prescribed for matriculation, we can only give a picture of the state of affairs at the time of writing. Nor do we claim that the information which follows is exhaustive or accurate and up to date in detail. Such information should be obtained from the appropriate professional or academic bodies.

University Entrance

Oxford and Cambridge

An examination qualification in Latin or Greek is *at present* compulsory, but new regulations will shortly be introduced whereby at *Oxford* entrants who have passed the G.C.E. examination at 'A' level in Mathematics or a Science subject, or who have won a College award in these subjects, *may* substitute a modern foreign language for Latin or Greek, and at *Cambridge* Latin or Greek will no longer be compulsory for any entrant. Both Universities, however, will still require qualifications in two languages other than English from all entrants.

Other Universities

An examination qualification in Latin or Greek is not compulsory but: (i) the 'language other than English' which must be included in a G.C.E. giving matriculation exemption may be Latin or Greek; (ii) a qualification in Latin or Greek is usually necessary for admission to degree courses in Arts subjects or Law. Some particulars of these requirements are given below.

Faculty Requirements

University of Birmingham

Arts. English School; Latin or Greek at least to O.L.—History, French, Italian and Spanish Schools; Latin at least to O.L.

Law. No longer compulsory to qualify in Latin but a knowledge of Latin considered to be advantageous.

University of Bristol

Arts. Pass at 'O' or 'A' level in Latin or Greek.

Law. Pass at 'O' or 'A' level in Latin.

University of Durham

Arts. Pass at 'A' or 'O' level in Latin or Greek for B.A. in General Studies and B.A. with Honours (except in Town and Country Planning, Geography, Geography and Anthropology, Economics and Geography, Economics and Anthropology, Politics and Anthropology, Politics and Economics, and Social Studies).

Law. Pass at 'A' or 'O' level in Latin for the degree of LL.B.

University of Exeter

Arts. Latin at 'O' level is compulsory.

University of Hull

Arts. B.A. Special Degree. Latin at 'O' level is compulsory in the French Language and Literature Course. Latin is desirable in the History Course.

B.A. Joint Degree. Latin is compulsory to 'O' level in the French Course, and is considered very desirable in History and desirable in Law.

University of Leeds

Latin at Ordinary level is required only for special studies in French, or Spanish, or Italian, or in Modern Languages when the combination includes one of these. It is not an essential for Law.

University of Leicester

Arts. Special Degrees. Latin to 'O' or 'A' level compulsory for English, French and German Courses.

University of Liverpool

Arts. Pass at 'A' or 'O' level in Latin or Greek or Mathematics.

N.B. Candidates who have qualified in Mathematics, but not in Greek or Latin, will be required:

(*a*) For the degree of Bachelor of Arts in General Studies: to take not less than five courses of the nine required from the following subjects: Geography, Economics, Economic History, Sociology, Political Theory and Institutions, Psychology, Philosophy.

(*b*) For the degree of Bachelor of Arts in Special Studies: to present themselves in any one of the following six schools: Geography, Economics, Social Science, Political Theory and Institutions, Psychology, Philosophy.

Law. 'The faculty...will not regard with favour any applicant intending to become a Solicitor or a Barrister who, at the date of entry into the Faculty, does not possess the qualification for exemption from the Preliminary Examination of the Law Society or for admission as a student into one of the Inns of Court, as the case may be.'

This in practice would appear to mean that a pass at 'A' or 'O' level in Latin is required.

University of London

Arts. A pass at 'A' or 'O' level in Latin or Greek.

University of Manchester

Arts. A pass at 'A' or 'O' level in Latin for entry to any Honours Course (except Oriental Studies, Architecture, Politics and Modern History, Geography, Modern History with Economics and Politics, Philosophy, Psychology, Town and Country Planning, American Studies, Biblical Studies and Mathematics and Philosophy). *Greek at 'A' or 'O' level will be accepted as an alternative to Latin in the Honours Schools of German and English, and Mathematics as an alternative to Latin in the Honours School of Mathematics.*

Law. A pass at 'A' or 'O' level in Latin for the degree of LL.B. or evidence of such proficiency in Latin as may be satisfactory to the Board of the Faculty of Law.

University of Nottingham

Arts. A pass at 'A' or 'O' level in Latin for entry to Honours Schools of Classics, English, French, German, and Spanish. For entry to the Honours School of History, Latin at 'A' or 'O' level is alternative to French or German.

For entry to the Intermediate course for the degree of LL.B. candidates will normally be required to have a pass at 'O' level in Latin but may be permitted to furnish other evidence of proficiency in Latin satisfactory to the Head of the Department of Law and the Board of the Faculty not later than the beginning of the candidate's second year of study.

University of Reading

Arts. Latin to 'O' level is compulsory in German and Modern History Courses.

University of Sheffield

Arts. All candidates for the degree of B.A. must read for the Intermediate Examination in their first year. They must offer four subjects. Candidates for Special Degrees in certain Honours Schools must include Latin, Greek, or Ancient History in the Intermediate Course, as shown in the following list.

Honours School of:	Compulsory subjects for Intermediate Course:
Classics	Ancient History
Greek	Latin and Ancient History
Latin	Greek★ and Ancient History
English Lang. and Lit.	Greek★ or Latin
French	Latin
German	Greek★ or Latin
Spanish	Latin
Greek and English ...	Latin
Latin and English ...	Greek★
Latin and French ...	Greek★
Latin and Spanish ...	Greek★
Modern Lang. and Lit.	Latin
Philosophy	Greek★ or Latin or French or German
Biblical Hist. and Lit.	Greek★

★ Those who have no knowledge of Greek may be allowed to take the Elementary Greek Course for beginners.

227

For admission to the Special Honours School of History a pass at 'O' level in Latin in the G.C.E. is required.

University of Southampton

Arts. Honours Candidates in English and French must pass Latin or Greek at 'A' level; in German, they must pass preferably Latin or Greek at 'O' level; in History, Latin to 'O' level.
In Law Latin to 'O' Level is considered advisable.

University of Wales

University College of Wales—Aberystwyth. History Honours: a translation knowledge of Latin is necessary.
University College of N. Wales—Bangor. English and French Honours: Greek or Latin to 'O' level is compulsory. History Honours: an adequate reading knowledge of Latin is necessary.
University College of S. Wales—Cardiff. History Honours: a translation knowledge of Latin is usually required.
University College of Swansea. History Honours: a reading knowledge of Latin or French or German or Welsh is required.

Universities of Oxford and Cambridge

Faculty requirements are usually not specified by the College authorities, who sort out the best qualified candidates, relying on the results of Scholarship and College Entrance examinations and reports from Headmasters. *It should, however, be noted that Scholarship examinations in Arts subjects such as History, Modern Languages, or English usually include Translation or General papers in which candidates have to attempt at least one passage of Latin or Greek. The difficulty of these passages is usually above that of those set as Unseens in the Ordinary level papers of the G.C.E.*

Aberdeen University

Roman Law: A pass in Latin in the Scottish Leaving Certificate is necessary.

Edinburgh University

Second ordinary, Intermediate Honours and Honours classes in English: Intermediate Honours and Honours classes in French and Spanish: Latin must be passed in the S.L.C. on the Lower Standard. For English Honours the Higher Standard is necessary.
Faculty of Law. Civil Law: S.L.C. Lower Latin must be passed.

Glasgow University

Higher classes of English, French, German, Italian, Hispanic Studies, Hebrew, History; Honours classes of French, English, German, Italian, Hispanic Studies, History, Scottish History and Literature—S.L.C. Latin (Higher or Lower) is required.

Honours in Hebrew. Greek (Higher or Lower) in the S.L.C. is required.

St Andrews University

Faculty of Arts. Latin or Greek; or Mathematics and a language other than English; or German and another modern foreign language must be passed at the S.L.C. Higher Standard, or G.C.E. 'A' level, or equivalents.

Faculty of Law. S.L.C. Lower Latin or G.C.E. 'O' level must be passed.

Belfast University

Faculty of Arts. Latin or Greek must be passed at 'O' level, or at matriculation.

Faculty of Medicine. Latin must have been passed at a recognized examination.

Entrance to Professions

An examination qualification in Latin or Greek is not compulsory *except for admission to the Law Society (Latin to 'A' or 'O' level) and to the Inns of Court.*

Many professional bodies, however, demand from entrants a G.C.E. showing passes in certain compulsory subjects (usually English and Mathematics) and varying numbers of optional or 'other subjects'. Latin or Greek might normally count as one of these optional or 'other subjects'. This appears to be true of the following professional bodies:

> Certified and Corporate Accountants
> Accountants and Auditors (Incorporated)
> Accountants (Chartered)
> Architects—R.I.B.A.
> Advertising Association
> Advertising (Institute of Incorporated Practitioners)
> Society of Apothecaries

Auctioneers and Estate Agents (Chartered)
Building Societies Institute
Certified Secretaries (Corporation of)
Chemistry (Royal Institute)
Association of Secretaries in Commerce
Cost and Works Accountants, Institute of
Library Association
Municipal Treasurers and Accountants
Naval Architects, Institution of
Physiotherapy, Chartered Society of
Secretaries, Chartered Institute of
Chartered Surveyors, Royal Institute of
Training and Supply of Teachers
Transport, Institute of
Town Planning Institute.

Alternative Syllabuses in Latin at 'O' level

Some examining bodies have included in their schedules 'Alternative' examinations at Ordinary level in the G.C.E. These usually consist of *one* paper of $2\frac{1}{2}$ hours instead of the normal *two* papers of 2 or $2\frac{1}{2}$ hours each and usually test translation from Latin to English only, instead of Latin to English and English to Latin.

Inquiry has shown that some universities will accept a pass in an alternative syllabus as a Faculty requirement in Latin. Others, however, are not prepared to recognize an examination which does not test ability to translate from English into Latin. This applies particularly to admission to Honours Degree courses in Modern Languages.

APPENDIX IV

SHORT BIBLIOGRAPHY ON THE TEACHING OF CLASSICS

The Teaching of Classics

Spens Report (pp. 176–7, 228–35, Appendix V). H.M.S.O.

Norwood Report (Curriculum and Examinations in Secondary Schools). H.M.S.O. (Chapter 10.)

The Classics in Education (1923). H.M.S.O. (Out of print.)

Suggestions for the Teaching of Classics, 1959 (M. of E. Pamphlet). H.M.S.O.

Secondary Education in Scotland (Report of Advisory Council, 1958) (pp. 79–86). H.M.S.O.

Classics in Secondary Schools (Scottish Education Department). H.M.S.O.

Organization and Curriculum of Sixth Forms (Chapter 7), 1938. H.M.S.O.

Report on the Standards of Marking Latin (Educational Institute of Scotland).

The Teaching of Classics in Secondary Schools in Germany. H.M.S.O. (Out of print.)

Classics in Girls' Schools—Memo II. Incorporated Association of Assistant Mistresses. U.L.P.

The Teaching of Latin and Greek. The Classical Association (1912). Murray. (Out of print.)

HUNT, H. K. *Training through Latin*. Melbourne U.P. (Out of print.)

A Special Course for Beginners in Greek. 'Greece and Rome', Vol. xv, No. 45, pp. 81–91.

LEWIS, L. W. P. *Practical Hints on the Teaching of Latin*. Macmillan. (Out of print.)

BENNETT, C. E. and BRISTOL, G. P. *The Teaching of Latin and Greek in the Secondary School*. (American Teachers.) Longmans.

PYM, DORA. *Outlines for Greek Teaching*. Murray. New edition in preparation.

SWEET, W. E. *Latin, a Structural Approach*. Michigan U.P.

WILDING, L. A. *The Teaching of Latin*. I.A.P.S.

General Works on Classical Education

FARRAR, F. W. *Essays on a Liberal Education* (vid. *The Theory of a Classical Education*, by H. Sidgwick). Macmillan (1867). (Out of print.)

LIVINGSTONE, R. W. *Rainbow Bridge.* Pall Mall Press.

MACKAIL, J. W. *Classical Studies* (some chapters) *and Pamphlets.* Murray.

Presidential Addresses to the Classical Association (from R. G. Tetstall, University Coll., Cardiff).

BALDRY, H. C. *The Classics in the Modern World.* O.U.P.

CLARKE, M. L. *Classical Education in Britain, 1500–1900.* C.U.P.

CLASSICAL ASSOCIATION. *Greek in the Twentieth Century.*

FERGUSON, J. *Roma Aeterna, The Value of Classical Studies.* Ibadan.

VALENTINE, C. W. *Latin: its Place and Value in Education.* U.L.P.

WHITEHEAD, A. N. *The Aims of Education* (Chapter V). Benn.

The Direct Method and Special Methods

APPLETON, R. B. *Teacher's Companion to 'Initium'.* C.U.P. (Out of print.)

GRAY. *The Teaching of Latin.* Appleton. (Out of print.)

JONES, W. H. S. *Via Nova.* C.U.P. (Out of print.)

MUNDAY, A. R. *Classroom Phraseology.* Wilding (Shrewsbury).

PECKETT and MUNDAY. *Principia.* Teacher's Edition. Wilding (Shrewsbury).

ROUSE and APPLETON. *Latin on the Direct Method.* U.L.P. (Out of print.)

Useful Books

BAYNES. *A List of Books in the English Language on Ancient History for the Use of School Teachers.* (The Historical Association.) Routledge.

The Claim of Antiquity (Books on the Classics). O.U.P.

DALE. *A Guide to Pronunciation of Latin and Greek.* Wilding (Shrewsbury).

DOVER, K. J. *Greek Word Order.* C.U.P.

NAIRN. *Handlist of Books relating to the Classics and Classical Antiquity.* Blackwell.

On the Terminology of Grammar. Murray.

Periodicals

Classical Quarterly. O.U.P.

Classical Review. O.U.P.

The Classical Outlook. American Classical League, Miami University, Oxford, Ohio, U.S.A.

Vita Latina. Musée Théodore-Aubanel, 7 Place Saint-Pierre, Avignon, France.

Greece and Rome. O.U.P.

Latin Teaching. Wilding (Shrewsbury).

Proceedings of the Classical Association. Murray.

The Classical Journal. 1232 Central Avenue, Wilmette, Ill., U.S.A.

Acta Diurna. The Orbilian Society. Centaur Books, Slough, Bucks.

Note. While many of the publications listed above are out of print, they have been included, as second-hand copies are sometimes obtainable.

Gramophone Records

The Sounds of Ancient Greek (with accents and quantity).

The Alphabet (with specimen words and sentences).

Passages from the Greek Classics. Recorded by Dr W. H. D. Rouse.

Latin Readings. Well-known passages in verse and prose in the 'restored' pronunciation. Recorded by H. A. B. White.

Full details from Linguaphone Institute, 207–209 Regent Street, London, W. 1.

APPENDIX V

CLASSICAL SOCIETIES AND COURSES

1. *The Society for the Promotion of Hellenic Studies*

Its object is to advance the study of the Greek language, literature, history and art. It maintains conjointly with the Society for the Promotion of Roman Studies: a library of some 30,000 volumes, some 20,000 lantern slides, some in sets with lecture notes, and some film-strips. Books and slides can be sent to members by post.

MEETINGS. In the rooms of the Society of Antiquaries, Burlington House, Piccadilly, W. 1.

PUBLICATION. *The Journal of Hellenic Studies.*

Applications for membership and inquiries to the Secretary, 31–34 Gordon Square, London, W.C. 1.

2. *The Society for the Promotion of Roman Studies*

Its object is to effect for Rome what the Society for the Promotion of Hellenic Studies does for Greece. The library, slides and filmstrips are shared with the Hellenic Society, and there is the same arrangement for loans.

MEETINGS. In the rooms of the Society.

PUBLICATION. *The Journal of Roman Studies.*

Applications for membership and inquiries to the Secretary, 31–34 Gordon Square, London, W.C. 1.

3. *The Classical Association*

Its objects are to promote the development and maintain the well-being of classical studies, and in particular (*a*) to impress upon public opinion the claim of such studies to an eminent place in the national scheme of education; (*b*) to improve the practice of classical teaching; (*c*) to encourage investigation and call attention to new discoveries; (*d*) to create opportunities for intercourse among lovers of classical learning.

MEETINGS. Easter: 3–4 days at a university. March: Week-End Course for Teachers—in London. In addition numerous local activities consisting of lectures, school lectures, short courses, reading competitions, etc., are organized by twenty-eight District Branches in England and Wales.

PUBLICATIONS. *Proceedings* (free to members); *The Classical Review, The Classical Quarterly, Greece and Rome.*

Applications for membership to the Hon. Treasurer, Mrs Edna M. Hooker, Birmingham University; inquiries to either of the Hon. Joint Secretaries, Professor L. J. D. Richardson, University College, Cardiff, and Mr T. W. Melluish, Bec School, S.W. 17.

4. *Triennial Meetings of the Joint Societies*

In addition to the separate activities of the above three Societies, a triennial meeting is arranged by a Joint Committee of all three, open to their members, for a week in August at Oxford and Cambridge alternately. Lectures are given by distinguished scholars from this country and abroad.

5. *University of London, Institute of Classical Studies*

The objects of the Institute are to promote the advancement of the study of Classics; to provide opportunities for contacts between scholars in the Classical field, both within the University and from other centres of learning at home and abroad; and to arrange facilities for advanced study and research and for the training of postgraduate students in Classics and cognate subjects. The library of the Institute and the library of the Hellenic and Roman Societies are housed in the same building and are complementary to each other.

Further particulars may be obtained from the Secretary, 31–34 Gordon Square, London, W.C. 1.

6. *The Association for the Reform of Latin Teaching*

This body exists for the furtherance of improved methods in Latin (and Greek) teaching. It has been specially though not exclusively concerned with the 'Direct Method' as used at the Perse School, Cambridge, by the late Dr W. H. D. Rouse, and elsewhere.

MEETINGS. The Association holds an annual summer school for teachers of Latin and Greek; in addition, in conjunction with the Classical Association, the A.R.L.T. holds a week-end course for teachers in London during March.

PUBLICATION. *Latin Teaching* (twice yearly; free to members). A collection of archaeological and visual aids, *realien*, etc., is loaned to members.

Hon. Secretary: Miss M. G. Drury, Prendergast Grammar School, London, S.E. 6.

7. The Virgil Society

The purpose of the Virgil Society is to unite all those who cherish the central educational tradition of Western Europe. Of that tradition Virgil is the symbol.

MEETINGS. Five meetings a year on Saturdays at 3 p.m. in London.
PUBLICATIONS. Summaries of lectures, often complete versions, and printed copies of presidential addresses are published and sent free to members.

Applications for membership to Dr A. J. Gossage, King's College, Strand, London, W.C. 2.

8. The Horatian Society

The aim of the Horatian Society is to cherish the memory of Horace and to foster the reading of his verse. An annual dinner is held, at which speeches are made in honour of the poet. Membership is by invitation.

The Virgil and Horatian Societies jointly offer a prize for the reading of the works of these poets, organized in connexion with the Classical Association's Reading Competitions for Schools, and in addition the Gilbert Murray Trust Fund offers prizes for the reading of Greek.

9. The Orbilian Society

The main function of the Orbilian Society is to publish three times a year *Acta Diurna* (price 10d.), a newspaper in Latin dealing with the events of 2000 years ago, and including many other items of interest. In addition the Orbilian Society has published wall-charts, maps, a word list, and is engaged on bibliographies, etc. Membership of the Society is by invitation. Inquiries concerning *Acta Diurna* or other productions to D. W. Blandford, Esq., Trinity School, Croydon, Surrey.

10. The Warburg Institute

The Warburg Institute promotes research on the survival and revival of classical antiquity in European civilization. It has a large library on a wide range of subjects including Classical Religion, Language, Literature, Folk-lore, Scholarship, Archaeology, Fine Arts, and Social and Political Life. It has a fine collection of photographs for exhibition. It issues a *Journal* and various other publications. Permission to use the

Library and inquiries to the Director, The Warburg Institute, Woburn Square, London, W.C. 1.

11. *University and other Libraries*

University libraries are usually open to graduates of their own universities and to other students if special application is made to the Librarian, backed by a recommendation from some responsible person; sometimes a small charge is made. Admission to the Reading Room of the British Museum is given on formal application to the Director with a recommendation from a London householder.

12. *The British School at Athens*

Founded to promote the study of Greek archaeology in all its departments. Archaeological excavations are conducted in Greece under the auspices of the school. Studentships are offered to researchers, and accommodation is available at the School.

PUBLICATION. *Annual of the British School at Athens.*

For particulars apply to The Secretary, 31–34 Gordon Square, London, W.C. 1.

13. *The British School at Rome*

The School is a centre for advanced study of monuments and records preserved on Italian soil. Various studentships are offered to researchers.

PUBLICATION. *Papers of the British School at Rome.* Annually.

For particulars apply to The Secretary, British School at Rome, 1 Lowther Gardens, London, S.W. 7.

14. *Ministry of Education Courses*

Short courses for teachers of Classics are organized by H.M. Inspectorate for a week in the summer vacation at Oxford or elsewhere. A programme of short courses is issued by the Ministry and is displayed on Staff notice-boards. Local Education authorities frequently grant assistance to teachers attending these courses. Application should be made in accordance with the directions given.

GENERAL INDEX

239

GENERAL INDEX

Obligation constructions, 68–9
Olympic Games, 132, 145
Oral work, 30, 34, 73, 76, 83, 102–5, 192
Orbilian Society, 236
Ordinary Level (G.C.E.), *see* Examinations *and* General Certificate
Oxford and Cambridge Schools Examination Board, 174, 181

Participles, 27, 35, 65–6
Pastoral poetry, 126
Phaidon Press, 206
Precepts for first two years of Latin, 29–31
Principal parts of Latin verbs, 34
Principate, the, 120
Principles and aims in teaching Classics, 14–22
Private study, use of, 112–14
Project Method, for Sixth Forms, 109–10, 122; for Secondary Modern Schools, 145, 147–8
Pronunciation of Greek, 48, 76, 219–23; of Latin, 30–1, 54, 76, 210–18
Prospective time clauses, 69–70
Purpose clauses, 27, 35, 74

Reading aloud, 21
Reading matter in early stages of Latin, 28; in middle-school Latin, 36–8; in first three years of Greek, 46–7
Reading programme for Sixth Forms, 91–3, 96–7
Reading, rapid, 111–12
Relative clauses, 27, 35, 63–4, 74
Report on the Classics in Education, 44
Report on the Value of Classics, 4
Result clauses, 27, 35, 74
Retranslation, 61
Roman Britain, 109–10, 186
Roman Society, *see* Society
Romance languages, 10

Scholarship (University) examinations, 180
Scholarship Level (G.C.E.), *see* Examinations *and* General Certificate
School Certificate Examination, 158, 160
Secondary Modern School, general curriculum of, 128–9, 136, 138; scope of Classics in, 130–5; equipment of teacher, 134, 135–8; material for lessons in Classics at, 131–3, 139–52; report on project at, 147–8

Selection of pupils for Greek, 40–2; for Latin, 25
Sense of style and logic, 21–2
Sequence of tenses, 35
Set books, 92, 95, 162–9, 173–6
Simple sentences (Greek), 47; (Latin), 26–7, 52, 55, 73, 74, 84
Simplified Latin authors, 37, 52, 80
Simultaneous start of Latin and French, 24
Single-period talks to Sixth-Formers, 123–4
Sixth-Form work, 8, 85–115; reading programme for, 91–3, 96–7
Sixth-Form course, full classical, 87–93; Classics with Modern subjects, 93–7; Classics to Ordinary Level, 98–9; Greek for beginners, 48–9; Latin for beginners, 98–9; time allowance, 86–7, 91, 96, 117
Society for the Promotion of Hellenic Studies, 234
Society for the Promotion of Roman Studies, 234
Specimen papers, 156–7, 165–6, 169–71
Speeches in ancient historians, 126
Stamps illustrating the Classics, 190
Standardization of marks (G.C.E.), 181–2
Stress accent (Greek), 223; (Latin), 216–17
Subordinate clauses, 27, 35, 55–6, 63–4, 69–71, 74
Supines, 35, 62
Surface collecting, 185
Synthetic Greek, 75
Synthetic Latin, 37, 52, 80

Television, 203
Tests (oral), 34, 73, 83; (written), 29, 34, 84
Time allowance, 31–2, 39, 48, 86–7, 91, 96, 117
Time clauses, 27, 69–70, 74
Town-planning, ancient, 13
Traditional method of teaching Classics, 51–71; its principles, 51–4; claims on its behalf, 62; defects of, 62–3
Training colleges, 136–7, 138
Translation (into English), 3–4, 15, 20, 57–9, 72–3, 87–9, 100, 104, 111–12; (into Greek), 46–7, 166; (into Latin), 26–7, 52, 55–6, 61, 63–70, 73, 74, 84, 105–7, 157, 160, 168–9. *See also* Unseen Translation
Translation, Ancient Literature in (as an examination subject), 168–72

INDEX OF ANCIENT AUTHORS
AND THEIR WORKS

INDEX OF MODERN AUTHORS
AND PUBLICATIONS

245

PRINTED IN GREAT BRITAIN
AT THE UNIVERSITY PRESS, OXFORD
BY VIVIAN RIDLER
PRINTER TO THE UNIVERSITY